Desert Survival Skills

For my father,

DALE ALLOWAY,

who taught me to be at home in the wilderness;

and for my sons,

IAN AND SEAN,

who will inherit this legacy.

And always for my mother,

SHIRLEY ALLOWAY,

who not only gave me life, but the love to live it.

Remember the days of old,
Consider the years of many generations,
Ask your father, and he will show you:
Your elders, and they will tell you.

—Deuteronomy 32:7

When you teach your son,
you teach your son's son.

—Talmud

CONTENTS

Desert Survival Skills

by David Alloway

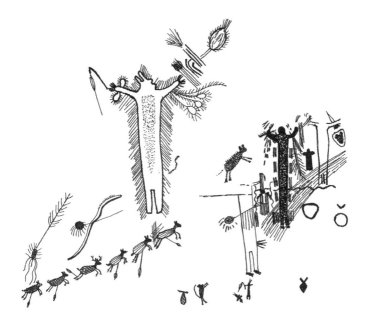

University of Texas Press, Austin

Requests for permission to reproduce
material from this work should be sent to:
Permissions
University of Texas Press
P.O. Box 7819
Austin, TX 78713-7819.

♾ The paper used in this publication meets the minimum requirements
of American National Standard for Information Sciences—Permanence
of Paper for Printed Library Materials, ANSI Z39.48-1984.

LIBRARY OF CONGRESS CATALOGING-IN-PUBLICATION DATA

Alloway, David, 1957-
    Desert survival skills / by David Alloway.—1st ed.
        p.   cm.
    Includes bibliographical references (p.   ) and index.
    ISBN 0-292-70491-7 (alk. paper) — ISBN 0-292-70492-5 (pbk. : alk. paper)
    1. Desert survival.   2. Desert survival—Chihuahuan Desert.   I. Title.

GV200.5 .A45   2000
613.6'9—dc21

                                                                                99-053302

Cover photo by David Alloway, © 1999.
Cover design by Allen Griffith/EYE4DESIGN.

A Philosophy of Survival in the Desert

PLEASE READ THIS SECTION FIRST

To survive in desert conditions, we must strip away preconceived notions of what the desert is. The true question for the human race is not if we will survive the desert, but if the desert will survive us. The motto of my desert survival courses is "Down with eremophobia!"

Eremophobia is the fear of the desert. Throughout this book are real-life examples of tragedies that happened in desert surroundings. These are not meant as scare stories to frighten people away, but as examples of incidents that could have been avoided with preparation and practical knowledge. When we exchange fear for respect, we are ninety percent on our way to not only surviving the desert, but helping it survive as an ecosystem. We can do this in several ways.

The blueprint for desert survival is found in the plants and animals that live there. If we can imitate their survival strategies, we can become a part of the desert's ecosystem instead of an antagonist. Learning to sit out the heat of the day, equating water with life, and becoming nocturnal are not only easy steps, but basic desert living skills. Learning to travel, work, and rest with the rhythm of the desert, we do not waste time and energy struggling against things we cannot change.

When we learn to respect the desert and its resources, we are no longer in a fight for survival, but in a partnership. Although I strongly advocate that the reader practice certain survival skills found throughout this book, I would be very saddened if it caused wanton destruction of desert resources. Many of my students have been sent by the military and law enforcement agencies and have a strong need to learn long-term survival strategies. This is why I have included a lot of specific information in this book. Ninety-nine percent of people entering the desert will never need these advanced strategies. But I have also elected to write for the one percent who may need this knowledge. Please use it wisely.

It is important to remember that some of the procedures in this text, such as harvesting certain plants, and some hunting, trapping, and fishing techniques, are very illegal—and with good reason. They are to be used as a last resort, a condition that will seldom arise. The average person will be pretty well off with a water source and fire. This again is the rhythm of the desert. Take what you need and leave the rest.

We can also defend the desert when we are away from it, at the polls, in the legislatures, in the courts, and through education. I earnestly ask that you use this book as a maintenance manual for our desert environments, and not an excuse for exploitation. No plant or animal that lives in the desert destroys the resources it depends on. The key to our own survival is to follow this example.

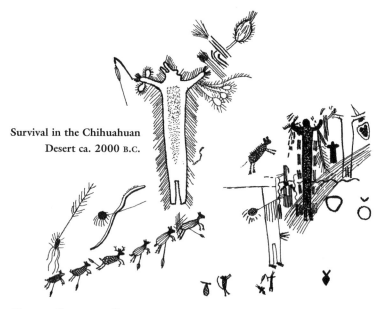

Survival in the Chihuahuan
Desert ca. 2000 B.C.

Acknowledgments

Special thanks are due to many people who helped make this book possible: To Bill Wright and Bryce Jordan of the University of Texas Press advisory board for promoting the idea. To Shannon Davies, Sheryl Englund, Sharon Casteel, and Leslie Tingle for being patient editors. To Bob Cooper, Bob Hunter, and Keith Smith for insightful views of survival strategies from Australia's deserts. To my fellow trekkers in Australia's Pilbara—The Southern Cross Survivors. They are Tracey Riley, Terry Gadean, Cameron Proctor, Alison Phipps, John Rippon, Eric Pyatt, Craig Leat-Hayter, and Paul Paterson. They are now my Australian family. To Roger Amis for advice on aircraft survival kits, air rescue operations, and forward-looking infrared (FLIR) systems. To Jeanne Amis for advice on medications and wilderness medicine. To both of them for being wonderful in-laws. To Dr. Frank Yancey and Dr. Clyde Jones for information on zoology, for friendship, and for quite a few beers at the Badlands Saloon. To Jeffrey Huebner for sharing his research on the diets of archaic Chihuahuan Desert hunter-gatherers. To Tom and Betty Alex for insights into the Chihuahuan Desert archeological record. To Dr. David Sissom and Dr. Richard Hensen for information on venomous arthropods. To Dr. Dean Watt for sharing his extensive research on scorpion venom. To Cathy Fulton for hours of hard work during the Big Bend Ranch State Park desert survival workshops. To Seth Burgess for helping me survive computers, and to Reverend Judy Burgess who made sure I survived the times my spirit was tried. To dozens of Mexican cowboys and ranch women who kept the knowledge alive and passed it on to me. To Texas Parks & Wildlife Department and especially Luis Armendariz, Superintendent of Big Bend Ranch State Park, for support, guidance, and generally keeping me out of trouble. To David Long for help with the cover. To the staff at Big Bend National Park. To the multitude of past students whose enthusiasm motivated this book. And to the members at large of the Chihuahuan Desert Liberation Organization (CDLO). You guys know who you are.

INTRODUCTION
People and the Desert

Also, of course, the people: though rare as radium you find,
if you can find them, a superior breed in the deserts—consider
the Bedouin, the Kazaks and Kurds, the Mongols, the Apaches,
the Kalahari, the Aborigines of Australia.

—Edward Abbey, *Desert Solitaire*

YOU ARE MADE FOR THE DESERT

To most urbanized people the desert is a forbidding place, inhospitable to life in general and openly hostile to humans. This is a cultural misconception, created in recent times by novels and films. Whether you believe the cradle of humankind to be in an African gorge 3 million years ago or at the confluence of two rivers in Iraq a short six millennia past, humans have lived in arid lands for longer than the reach of our collective memories. People have inhabited regions in North America for longer than the current deserts have existed. Despite the fact that people have moved on to many other areas of the globe, the human race is well adapted to the desert.

Walking upright in sunny areas has a great advantage over walking on four legs. Bipedal creatures receive sixty percent less solar radiation than quadrupeds. Because air currents move slower close to the ground, bipedalism exposes more of the body to cooling breezes. The sparse body hair of humans allows for greater air cooling, but thick hair is needed on animals going about on all fours to protect the skin from large areas exposed to the sun's rays. A large brain must be kept cool, so the human head is usually well covered with hair to ward off the sun. Because humans in a natural state forage instead of graze, bipedalism is a convenient form of locomotion to free the hands for carrying and work.

Anthropologists once believed that human bipedalism evolved to facilitate the making of tools, but current findings now place this form of locomotion 2 million years prior to tool manufacture. In other words, bipedalism is an environmental advantage—you are made for the desert.

Dark-skinned people have the further advantage of pigments that protect them from harmful ultraviolet rays. People like myself, whose ancestors lived in northern Europe, developed light-colored skin to help assimilate vitamin D in a region with cloudy skies and short winter days. A little knowledge can help even us fair-skinned Celts who have settled in the desert. Walking on two legs means a wide-brimmed hat can shade most of your body. Wearing long pants and a long-sleeved shirt further protects us from the sun, while a loose fit still allows air to cool our unhairy bodies. The hat also helps cool our large brain, which is by far the best survival tool we have.

The desert will not support thousands of people for very long. Old-world archeological sites and contemporary North American suits over water rights bear this out. But for you and me, quietly making our own way and taking only what we need, the desert is a provider. Everything we need to survive is here if we adapt our behavior to desert realities. We have a precedence to survive in deserts that goes back to the dawn of our species. To survive, we must not fear the desert; we must learn how to live with it once again.

WHAT IS SURVIVAL?

The word "survival" has been devalued in recent years to a point that it no longer necessarily refers to matters of life and death. Vapid talk shows host people who claim to be survivors of everything from bad divorces to tax audits. Manufacturers append the word to all sorts of junk to sell to unwary persons. Many people believe I teach American Indian survival techniques, but I disagree. The original American desert people were no more practicing survival skills than I am as I watch a football game with a cold beer. They were living.

No doubt they often encountered life-threatening situations, but were these situations more dangerous than what we experience in rush-hour traffic?

In our context, survival is when a person from an industrialized society is suddenly put back into the ecosystem without material support or the knowledge of what to do. This book is not about fleeing into the wilderness to avoid doomsday, about guerilla warfare, or about how to start a back-to-nature lifestyle. This book is about when, for reasons beyond our control, we are thrust back into the natural environment and cannot leave of our own free will. The ecosystem covered is the desert—specifically the Chihuahuan Desert.

WHY THE CHIHUAHUAN DESERT?

Of the North American deserts, the Mojave, Sonoran, Great Basin, and Chihuahuan, the Chihuahuan Desert is the least studied and contains some of the most remote locations of the four. There are several ways to define a desert, the simplest being as a region that receives an average of less than ten inches of rainfall a year. By this definition, the Chihuahuan Desert is the largest on the continent. Chihuahua is a Tarahumara Indian word that means "hot, sandy place." In other words, it is such a magnificent desert that we must say it twice in two languages!

The Chihuahuan Desert extends through the Mexican states of Zacatecas, Durango, Coahuila, and Chihuahua, into Texas, southern New Mexico, and southeast Arizona. It is a high desert, ranging from 1,000 to 6,000 feet above sea level. The altitude range combined with diverse geology makes for a great variety of life. It does not have many tall cacti, so often associated with deserts in fiction, but its plant life has provided food, beverages, fiber, dye, medicine, construction materials, and fuel for thousands of years of human occupation.

Most books on desert survival are written with the Mojave and Sonoran Deserts in mind. These are the most "popular" deserts: the Sonoran with its giant saguaro cacti, and the Mojave with its famous Death Valley. Many of the survival strategies found in those books will work in the Chihuahuan Desert, and much of

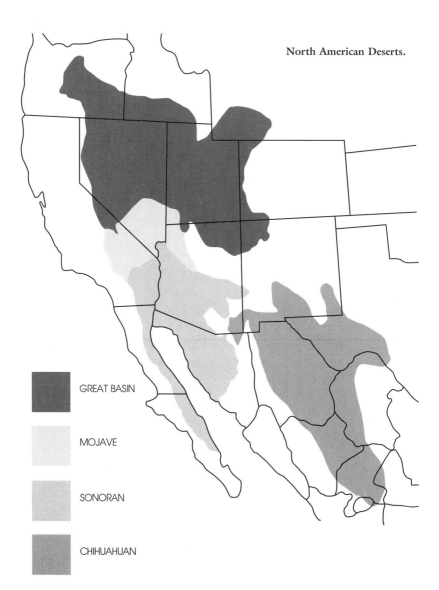

North American Deserts.

GREAT BASIN

MOJAVE

SONORAN

CHIHUAHUAN

the information in this book can be used elsewhere. The more specific your knowledge in any given area, however, the better your chances of surviving emergency situations.

Within the U.S. portions of the Chihuahuan Desert are national parks and state parks. Mexico has a few parks within its limits, with very large ones planned across from the Texas border in Chihuahua and Coahuila. Mexico is becoming more interested in tourism from outdoors people—hikers, campers, rafters, and equestrians out

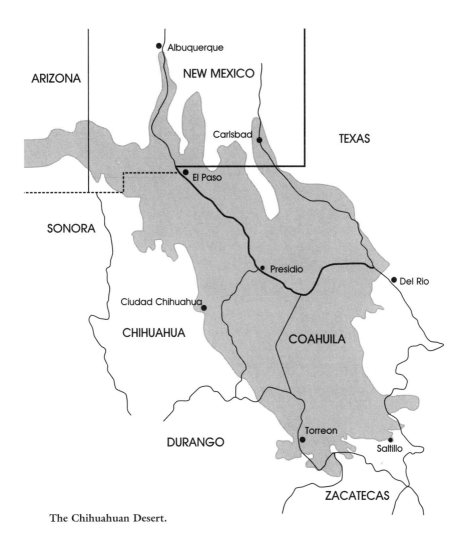

The Chihuahuan Desert.

to see the rugged beauty of this great desert. There has been little development so far, a fact that will attract many adventurers. Persons entering this area will need to be prepared to help themselves in emergencies. Even in Big Bend National Park, Texas, with a staff of over one hundred people, there are occasional deaths due to dehydration, injury, hyperthermia, and hypothermia. There is a need for public education on preserving this desert, and how to survive it.

At Work and at Play in the Desert

I focus on the Chihuahuan Desert because it is my area of special knowledge. I grew up in this desert and explored it with my family. My experiences range from college biology courses to working on area ranches and learning from Mexican cowboys. I have been a guide in the Big Bend of Texas and northern Mexico (both Chihuahuan and Sonoran Deserts). I am currently an interpretive naturalist for the Texas Parks & Wildlife Department on the 287,000-acre Big Bend Ranch State Park, where part of my duties is to teach classes in desert survival, archeology, plant uses, and to help in search and rescues. The Chihuahuan Desert is my life and livelihood. I have no choice but to write about it.

The Ultimate Survival Tool

The brave man is not he who feels no fear, but rather is the man who subdues fear and bravely encounters the danger.

Lorenzo de Zavala, *Texan patriot*

What separates humans from other animals is intellect. Humans can communicate, plan ahead, use logic and reason, recognize problems, develop solutions, and manipulate a situation to alter future events. What kills many people in emergency situations is not making use of the intelligence that makes them human. They give up control of the situation and become like animals, except they lack the instinct that keeps our fellow life forms alive. All of the best equipment in the world will not keep someone alive who will not rationalize their problem and develop a strategy for survival. The brain is the best survival tool. Keep it alert, in the shade, in control, and hydrated. Learn everything you can about an area, and be prepared to adapt and improvise.

PREPARATION

It is common sense that persons entering any wilderness area would want to make preparations to ensure their safety. Although it is obvious that prevention is the best way to avoid emergencies, deaths due to people traveling in remote areas without ample provisions or training are all too common.

A Good Example of Bad Planning

The following incident illustrates just about everything that can go wrong in lack of planning and preparation. On September 5, 1994, a U.S. Deputy Marshal from Del Rio, Texas, and a female companion were traveling in a remote area of Big Bend National Park, Texas, when their pickup truck overheated. The couple had not carried a sufficient supply of water for either themselves or the vehicle. The only water available to them was meltwater in the ice chest, which they used entirely for the truck's radiator in an attempt to start it again. When the truck failed to start, they were stranded with no water on a poorly traveled backroad. The couple stayed with their vehicle during the cool of the night—while sipping on a bottle of liquor—and started walking when the sun came up.

The man was dressed in shorts and a T-shirt, with much skin exposed to the sun. With no water, and the previous night's alcohol acting as a diuretic, they walked past two springs, one of which was marked as such with a sign. The man began to succumb to hyperthermia and dehydration. His friend took his handgun and attempted to signal for help, but no one heard. Realizing her friend was in mortal danger, she continued until she reached a paved road and flagged down a passing car. By the time park rangers arrived, the man was dead. He had attempted to remove the few clothes he wore and had been badly sunburned.

Local citizens were shocked by the death. The man was a federal law officer stationed in the Chihuahuan Desert, but apparently had no training for such emergencies. No preparation was made for sufficient water or protective clothing. Instead of walking in the cool of the night on a well-defined road, the stranded couple stayed with the vehicle and accelerated dehydration and hindered proper decisions by drinking alcohol. The couple failed to recognize water sources. One paid the ultimate price for venturing into the desert unprepared.

Preparation includes selecting and packing proper gear, taking enough provisions, and training. Firsthand experience and practice are some of the best assets anyone can have going into the desert. Mental preparation is the best thing you can take along, and education is a keystone. One way to get education is to enroll in a survival course. Make sure you are getting a course that deals with environmental emergencies and not some paramilitary exercise (unless that is what you want). Get references for instructors. Make sure they teach realistic techniques and center their course around the psychology of survival. A list of well-respected courses is in Appendix A.

ATTITUDE

The sheer will to live is necessary in any emergency. It would seem this is instinctive, but I see more and more people each year who seem unable to adjust to discomforts, let alone true life-threatening situations. We are a protected society whose members are becoming less and less responsible for their own safety and well-being. We believe we have put ourselves above the ecosystem and are surprised when nature sneaks up on us. In any wilderness emergency we must recognize that we are truly a part of the environment and have the ability and right to participate as such. To be blunt, you will be part of the food chain. Whether you participate as predator, forager, or carrion will be up to you. The lack of will to live will negate any training or equipment.

THE PANIC FACTOR

In the onset of crisis, control of panic is all-important. Panic can cause lost hikers to push on or walk faster instead of staying in one spot or getting their bearings. Panic can make familiar surroundings seem strange or hostile. Panic can induce a feeling of hopelessness and keep one from developing a plan for survival. Recognizing panic and taking control of it is a major step in staying alive. Panic is blind fear. Fear is not an altogether negative emotion. It gives us concern for our safety and encourages us to take steps to survive. Panic, however, is fear without resolution. Try to keep a philosophy used by pilots—"Be afraid to panic." Advice given by Siberians for

Someone who gave up the will to live is a U.S. Air Force pilot who crash-landed in the Arctic. Air Force flight crews have some of the best survival training in the world but this person lacked the essential will to live. Looking at the bleak horizon, he climbed out of the cockpit, smoked a cigarette, unholstered his pistol, and blew his brains out. A short time later a Russian fighter flew by and reported his position. He would have been rescued within a couple of hours. The pilot was going through some personal problems, and probably used the situation as an excuse not to live.

lost people is to sit down and remember the last person with whom you shook hands. This helps organize your thoughts and prepares you for rational decisions.

Australian survival instructor Bob Cooper uses the following mnemonic called the ABC of Survival:

A. ACCEPT the situation. Do not waste time and energy chastising yourself and blaming others.

B. BREW up a drink. A cup of tea or coffee will help keep you calm and focus your attention and start up the thought process. The real objective is to start a fire.

C. CONSIDER your options while drinking your tea or coffee.

D. DECIDE. After you have considered all your options, make a decision and a plan.

E. EXECUTE your decision and stick to it!

I tell my students to decide they are going to be there one week. If you think help is forthcoming, you may not take the necessary steps for a survival plan. On the other hand, thinking in terms of over a week can cause a hopeless attitude that may make you think the plan is not worth the effort.

Group survival will test all manner of attitudes, especially if the members are strangers to each other. Pessimists can bring down the entire group's morale—"We are going to die!" Those who try to assume leadership may know the least about the subject of survival—"Once I saw a movie. . . ." If you have done your homework,

The following three stories give good examples of people who found reasons to live. Some motives were noble and others were not. Alvar Núñez Cabeza de Vaca and three companions became castaways on the Texas Gulf Coast in 1528 and began an eight-year ordeal that is probably the greatest survival epic in North America. They were enslaved by Indians, escaped, and walked across mountains and deserts toward the west coast where they knew there were Spanish colonies. They learned American Indian ways on their journey and how to survive in diverse environments. While wandering naked through south Texas, de Vaca was the victim of the tangled thorny vegetation, tearing and ripping his bare skin. At these times de Vaca would remind himself, "In these labors my only solace and relief were in thinking of the sufferings of our Redeemer, Jesus Christ, and in the blood He shed for me, in considering how much greater must have been the torment He sustained from the thorns, than that I there received." De Vaca's narrative is full of times his faith carried him through.

Mountain man Hugh Glass had a less noble reason to survive. In 1823, Glass was a member of a trapping brigade in North Dakota when he was mauled by a grizzly bear. Lying unconscious, his friends dug a grave and waited for him to die. Glass held on to life and, even in a coma, could hear what was going on. The brigade moved on, leaving John Fitzgerald and a teenaged Jim Bridger to bury him when he died. Glass continued to hang on, and Fitzgerald eventually persuaded Bridger to abandon him, sure he would die anyway. Leaving, they took his rifle, knife, and other "possibles," convinced that a dead man would not need them. Glass awoke next to a grave as empty as his hands. He began a six-week journey to cover over two hundred fifty miles to the safety of Fort Kiowa, crawling much of the way. On the way, with maggots swarming his wounds, he ate rattlesnake, grubs, and rotting buffalo carcass. His extraordinary survival was fueled by vengeance—to kill Fitzgerald and Bridger. Glass did not fulfill his goal, but he did live to confront the two, who accepted his presence almost as a ghost.

An unnamed pilot, flying from Arizona to California, is famous in survival lore not because of his preparation or knowledge, but for his sheer will to survive. The man filed an inaccurate flight plan and wandered off course. When his plane went down in the desert, a search was initiated two hundred miles away. He carried no survival gear, signal devices, or extra water. Trying to keep cool, he cut the sleeves off his shirt and the legs off his pants, exposing large amounts of skin to blistering UV rays. He started walking, but failed to identify water sources along the way. His sheer will led him to safety, although severely dehydrated and badly sunburned. His motivation for pushing on was that he was going through a divorce, and he had not changed his power of attorney. If he died, his wife would get everything! The point is: find a reason to live and stick with it.

it is best to go about making a personal plan and implementing it. Others will notice, and leadership by example can overcome the more forceful or pessimistic personalities. One instructor I studied under suggested, "The problems of morale and food in group survival can be overcome in one step by killing the pessimists and eating them." I would suspect, however, some legal entanglements from implementing such a plan.

Our intelligence is what gives us the edge in survival situations. The person who surrenders to panic discards an important survival tool—the ability to anticipate and alter future events. The person who considers the situation hopeless and gives up will wind up as a statistic unless help arrives very soon. The following are some nonsurvival attitudes I have come across while working in deserts:

"My idea of roughing it is a Holiday Inn without a live band in the lounge." — Tourist trying to make a joke.

"I don't need no water." —Man walking twelve miles in 100°F heat to see a friend about an auto part, refusing my offer of water. Use of double negative is also inappropriate.

"It's gorgeous up here! I bet a lot of kids come here on prom night." — A college woman in a desert ecology class who had driven 105 miles past the nearest high school and then ridden four hours on horseback to reach the South Rim of the Chisos Mountains.

"I'm cold! Why is it so cold?" —Woman, on horseback at 7,400 feet on a misty January day, who had worn tennis shoes and a light windbreaker despite everyone's advice.

"It's in a national park. It can't be that bad." —Man deciding with wife to take a Cadillac down a fourteen-mile dirt road in Big Bend National Park against advice of a volunteer at an information center. The car had a dealer "doughnut" spare tire. Cost for towing and tire repair—$160. Transmission shot. It was, of course, the fault of the National Park Service.

"I don't need that much water. I never wear a hat. It's not that far. I have enough gas. I don't think it (1) will rain, (2) get that hot, (3) get that cold. I'm going to get my water from cactus. I'm going to get my water from a solar still." Ad nauseam—A cross section of people who took their own welfare too lightly. Some were lucky and came out okay. Some are compost.

PRACTICE

Would you submit to surgery from someone who had once read about it? It's the same concept for people who read a survival book, including this one, but do not try out the methods for themselves. This book will not give you the physical coordination to signal a passing aircraft with a hand mirror. When a high wind kicks up is the wrong time to try to start a fire with a hand drill for the first time. To complicate matters, the information in some survival books is by authors who obviously have not tested these ideas for themselves. Here are some myths I have read in some books about desert survival. They could be fatal if taken for gospel: "Solar stills can supply all of your water needs. All cacti fruit are edible. All cacti flesh is edible. Barrel cacti are virtual kegs of water."

Survival books have their place. They can be used as reference, inspire someone to practice skills, and give fresh ideas. They can also be torn apart and used to start a fire or for latrine sanitation. Please do not read this book and think you can walk into the desert and make it. Please do not read this book and think I know everything

Temper, Temper

Some emergencies come about because people let their emotions override good sense. Twice I have been involved in searches where a couple started arguing and separated, with one becoming lost. In both cases the reporting party did not want to tell searchers how they became separated. One of these occurred in the summer of 1996 when I was called by the owner of a rafting company as it was getting dark. Earlier in the day a couple had rented a small paddle raft to float a canyon on the Rio Grande. Due to a drought the river was sluggish and running only two feet deep. After paddling (and dragging) the raft less than a mile, the couple quit rowing, and the man walked back to the highway to hitchhike back to the raft rentals. The man was reluctant to tell me where his girlfriend was. After a lot of questioning he told me they had an argument and she had thrown her shoes at the bank, but they fell short and floated off. She then told him good-bye and waded off downstream.

I asked if she had her life jacket on when she left, as she might encounter deep pools.

"Yes, she did."

"Would she keep it on or throw it away if she thought she would not need it?"

He thought she would keep it on.

"Did she know how to float through fast water on her back with feet pointed downstream?"

He had never heard of that and had not received any safety instructions when renting the raft. Further questioning revealed that neither of them had much outdoor experience.

Because of his hesitance in giving me information about what happened, I feared a possibility of domestic violence, with the female injured. I received permission from my

about the subject. I learn new lessons every day. Please *do* take this knowledge and experiment with it to find out what works in your area and within your abilities.

Practice can be an enjoyable experience. Take a weekend and make an expedient shelter with the kids. They will enjoy playing in it later. Dangle a toy plane or helicopter from a pole and practice illuminating it with a signal mirror. Practice firemaking until you superintendent, Luis Armendariz, to start an active nighttime search, which is usually against our policy. Fellow ranger David Long, who is a skilled boatman, and I put out on the river a little before midnight. We put Cayalume sticks, which glow from a chemical reaction, on the raft for her to see us and proceeded into the canyon, blowing a whistle and calling her name. The deeper we got into the canyon the more we worried that she may have decided to walk out one of the two side canyons or try to climb out—barefoot through rock and cacti with only the light of a half moon.

We found her much further down river than we expected —only half a mile from the takeout area where her boyfriend was waiting. Barefoot, with her life jacket still on, she had waded, walked, and floated almost nine miles. She was about thirty feet up the side of a cliff on a ledge waiting for dawn.

Most people, especially women, are very excited and grateful when found. This woman gave us a curt thank-you, similar to the type you say when someone hands you some type of unwanted pamphlet at the airport. Her whole attitude was "I guess I showed him!"

This person could have met a real tragedy instead of just a soggy hike. Especially discouraging was the fact that she did not even know how lucky she was, and did not learn anything from it. The man compounded the problem because he would not level with us and caused suspicion, since violent crimes have been made to look like wilderness accidents. Keeping control of your emotions will go a long way toward avoiding trouble for yourself, those with you, and the search people who need to be available for real emergencies. To this day I think the woman threw her shoes at the man, and missed. We call this case *Row v. Wade*.

can start a fire under the most adverse conditions and with the most primitive means. Make hikes and camping trips experiences you can later fall back on. Get to know your survival kit and how to use it. There are some things that should be practiced with care or not at all. If your experiments in signaling are so effective that an unnecessary search is launched, you could pay for it.

If you cut the top off a barrel cactus out of curiosity to see how much moisture it really does contain, you may have killed something older than the United States. I have no qualms about trapping animals in a survival situation, but it does not justify an animal suffering needlessly. Also bear in mind that some of the techniques I describe later, such as quail traps and fish poisons, will attract negative attention from game wardens in most states.

When collecting plants for different projects, be selective and collect thoughtfully. For my courses I collect only a few leaves from each yucca, one or two sotol hearts, and just enough lechuguilla. I do not collect in the same place each time. I am not saying that in a life-threatening situation you should walk over a large area, but please practice conservation for experiments. While its appearance is rough and rugged, the desert is actually a fragile ecosystem. Because of the infrequent rains, the plants are slow growing and the animals are on constant rationing. Any damage done is a long time healing.

Wilderness survival schools are a great place to get practice and experience. It doesn't necessarily need to be a desert survival setting. I was making some Inuit-style snow goggles out of a sotol *quillote* once when one of my students from the Air Force said, "But that's for the Arctic!" It doesn't matter—extreme sunlight can blind you whatever the setting. I have also taken examples (not artifacts) from archeological sites and modified them to fit my needs. I have been criticized for not being accurate. That is not the point. I am building on and modifying past knowledge to fit the current goal of staying alive. You should borrow, steal, or twist any idea or method that can help you survive.

Studying the art of survival has many benefits. It teaches us to be once again locked into the ecosystem we ultimately depend on. It takes us out of the specialized mold our industrialized occupations set us in and shows us that diversity as hunters, gatherers, fire and weapons makers, and builders is still within our means of existence. It takes us out of the grocery store and makes us aware we are still a part of the food chain. It gives us confidence and independence. It teaches us how to live in nature in a nonexploitative way. It helps us conquer our fears of the unknown and makes us emotionally stronger. In the long run, it may save our lives.

The Priorities of Desert Survival

The life of the desert lives only by virtue of adapting itself to the conditions of the desert. Nature does not bend the elements to favor the plants and animals; she makes the plants and animals do the bending.

—John C. Van Dyke, *The Desert*, 1901

When developing a survival strategy or plan, it will be necessary to set priorities. Different environments and circumstances will cause a shuffling of priorities. It stands to reason that Arctic survival and jungle survival call for different sequences of priorities. The order of priorities in desert survival is water, fire, shelter, aiding search and rescue (*SAR*) personnel, deciding to stay or leave, food, making expedient tools and weapons, and debriefing SAR teams. Do remember, circumstances may require changing the order. Adaptation and flexibility are assets in a survival scenario.

WATER

Deserts are defined as such by their low amount of precipitation and high rate of evaporation. Despite its mantle of ice, some define Antarctica as a desert because it averages less than ten inches precipitation a year. The low precipitation in hot deserts leads to a scarcity of water. The "Rules of Three" illustrate how important water is: Three minutes without air, three hours without warmth, three days without water, three weeks without food. In many desert climates you can cut the three days without water to one and a half days, making water the first priority. Carrying ample water is the best safeguard. This includes for yourself, others with you, any animals, and your vehicle. On search and rescue operations I carry six quarts, which is a heavy load, but I realize I may need to share with a victim who tried to lighten their load by not carrying enough. It is important to recognize water sources and signs that will lead you to them. It is also important to have a way to purify water once it is obtained. An understanding of the physiology of dehydration will also be necessary to best use water.

FIRE

Why, in a hot desert, would I place fire so high on the list? People have died of hypothermia in hot deserts, but warmth is not the only benefit of fire. It may be needed for signaling, purifying water, or cooking. What many people fail to think about is the psychological value of fire. You are never quite as lonely if you have a fire. Fire needs nurturing, grows, moves, and must be fed. It is almost like having a companion. Fire gives warmth and chases back the darkness when the night makes the area stranger and amplifies your worries. Firemaking is the foremost of the survival skills in any environment. It must be practiced, and you should be proficient in several methods that utilize modern and primitive resources.

SHELTER

Because shelter includes clothing, preparation in this subject should begin before entering remote areas. Shelter type will depend on many variables. Shelter may be needed from sun, wind and dust, cold, or rain. The location and available construction materials will also play a large role in the choice of shelter. Some survival writers, with good reasoning, place shelter before fire, because in some conditions it may be necessary to build a shelter from inclement weather before it is possible to start a fire. Once again, clear thinking and flexibility may reorganize priorities.

AIDING RESCUERS

Once physical safety and immediate needs are secured, the survivor should start planning ways to attract the attention of search and rescue (SAR) teams. This is one reason firemaking is second on the list. In an emergency, some measures in aiding rescuers should be taken immediately. If you are gathering firewood and your signal mirror is still encased in your survival kit, you may not be able to retrieve it quickly enough if a fast aircraft approaches unexpectedly. Hang it around your neck. Aircraft not involved in SAR functions will not be looking for lost persons, and you will have only a short time to get their attention. It may take time to set up signals such as smoke or ground-to-air markers, and these should be done as soon as you have your water, fire, and shelter. Having a well thought out signaling plan may make the difference in whether you are merely inconvenienced or stay for a good length of time.

DECIDING TO STAY OR LEAVE

At some point you will need to make a very important decision—whether to stay or leave. If you have adequate water, have told others of your plans (and have stuck with them), and are not in immediate physical danger, the best option is to stay. It is easier to locate a stationary person than one who is moving. This is especially true of one who is lost and moving in an erratic manner. It is much easier to see a stranded auto or downed plane from the air than an individual, so it makes sense to stay nearby if this is the situation. Some situations justify relocation. This could be if your water supplies are dwindling and a new source must be discovered. You may find yourself in an area that poses a direct danger to you and your party. In the worst case, relocation is necessary because you were not prepared, nobody knows you are missing, and there will be no search. Unfortunately, this is often the case in SAR. I hope after reading this book or going through one of my courses you will not be among this group.

FOOD

This subject is given too much status in many survival books and certainly in novels and films. When people start pursuing survival studies, they often fall into a "living off the land" fantasy. Such a lifestyle is possible, but most people are walking around with a sufficient supply of rations under their belts. In cold-weather

In September of 1996 I was invited to attend the toughest survival trek in Australia open to civilians and became the first non-Australian to finish. We carried only two one-liter canteens and cups, an emergency medical blanket, a shirt pocket survival kit, and a sheath knife. We walked two hundred kilometers, navigating from water source to water source, in nine days. For environmental reasons, we were not allowed to kill wildlife except for fish and feral cats (which we did not see). All the food I had was one six-inch spangled perch, a handful of wattle seeds and small fruits, and a half a dozen bulrush stalks. I lost twenty pounds before we reached the Indian Ocean, but I did not have any real hunger pangs the whole time. We were much more concerned with finding water. I can attest that in warm to hot weather, food is not as necessary as some people worry about.

situations, food is necessary to keep up metabolism and maintain body temperature. Many desert scenarios, however, will be better handled by fasting.

There are some important considerations in the subject of food, especially in desert survival scenarios. If water is in short supply, you should not eat anything, as water is needed for digestion. Something also to consider—what if eating something strange under duress causes vomiting or diarrhea? Such ailments can cause rapid dehydration. What is a discomfort elsewhere can be life threatening in the wilds. Still, there are some ways to get food with relative safety and little effort. In such cases food should not be passed up. If you are a healthy individual who has been getting three square meals a day, there are many other things to worry about before considering food.

MAKING EXPEDIENT TOOLS AND WEAPONS

Making tools and weapons has about the same priority as obtaining food, because it may be necessary to make tools to gather plants or to make traps and weapons to take animals. Toolmaking and weapons use are some of my more popular demonstrations, but are very low on the list of priorities. These are skills that absolutely must be acquired by previous practice, as they do not come easy. This is especially true of weaponry. You can make a deadly sling in less than five minutes from the tongue and laces of your boots, but unless you have lots of practice, you may wrap it, along with a hen egg-sized rock, around your head. Some skills, such as cordage-making and trapping are very good to have, but still require some prior familiarization. Making stone tools takes much time to become proficient in, but with a little practice, usable cutting flakes can be produced with little modification. This is another area that causes much fantasy in film, novels, and among beginning survival students. It is one of my favorite areas of study, but in short-term survival scenarios it takes a low priority. Remember also to spring or remove any traps you have set before you leave an area.

DEBRIEFING RESCUERS

After you have been discovered and rescued by a SAR team, please take the time to debrief those who found you. SAR is no longer a group of conscripts who walk abreast beating the bushes. The search is a highly organized function that takes into account weather, terrain, and the victim's age, sex, experience, preparations, physical condition, and psychological profile. From interviews with past victims, data is compiled for future rescues. Do not be embarrassed. Tell them where you made mistakes. Also tell them mistakes they may have made.

While you may not be excited about hanging out any longer after your ordeal, you owe it to these people and future victims to debrief. Be sure to also tell them things you did right, improvisations that helped, and how you controlled your emotions. Survival is an ongoing study, and you will have something to contribute.

Feedback

A valuable debriefing involved a man who was missing overnight on a nineteen-mile trail in Big Bend Ranch State Park. He was thankful but also had some valuable criticism. He had become disoriented and missed the trail. Part of the reason was that the person who gave him his permit was not familiar with the trail and gave him bad information on direction of travel and reasonable time required for the strenuous hike.

He was dressed in shorts and a T-shirt, and had two extra T-shirts with him. He had planned to do the entire hike in one day, and in fact was quite experienced in twenty-mile-a-day hikes, though in different terrain. Because of his ill-informed direction of travel, he missed the trail markers and wound up in the wrong canyon. Not having matches and not knowing how to start a fire by primitive means, he spent a chilly night, cutting the extra T-shirts down the back and wrapping them around his legs.

When his wife reported him missing after sundown, we started a passive search that night with lights and car horns, and persisted until 3:00 A.M. At dawn we started an active search on foot, horseback, and using U.S. Border Patrol air operations. At that time, he started out the way he came, knowing he could retrace his route. When he was found, his legs were badly sunburned, bleeding, and criss-crossed with scratches from the vegetation. We had found the man because our SAR team had been well trained, but we failed in training our people at the basic level of education and information.

Survival Kits 3

Raw nature is seldom mild to the unprepared.

—Donald C. Cooper, Patrick "Rick" LaValla,
and Robert "Skip" Stofell, *Search and Rescue Fundamentals*

Outside of your brain, a good survival kit is one of your best assets in an emergency. Survival kits will vary with many factors. A kit designed for the desert will be different from one for the Northern Rockies. The size and contents of a kit will vary with its mode of transport. The basic component is a kit that can be carried in a shirt pocket. Kits expand upward for those worn in a belt pouch, on a mountain bike, in a saddlebag, and on to those carried in four-wheel drives and aircraft. All survival kits have common elements. They should carry essential items of good quality. Ideally, many of the items should have more than one application. Finally, the kit should be compact and light weight to ensure that it gets taken along.

There are two approaches to obtaining survival kits: buying them or building your own. Buying the kit has the advantage of being cheaper, as the manufacturer has the volume to buy the contents wholesale. The problem is, to keep the retail price low and attractive, they may fudge on the quality of some of the kit's items. There are some notable exceptions, and these are found in the Equipment Sources list at the end of the book. Buying a kit also gives little control over the area you intend to use it, such as desert environs. Since the Gulf War, many belt pouch and backpack kits are being sold with four-ounce disposable retort pouches of water, averaging nine pouches per pack. In most desert conditions you will need a minimum of one gallon of water per day. A much better plan would be to buy sufficient reusable water containers with some purification tablets. Anyone who grabs a pack and heads for the desert with only thirty-six ounces of water is asking for trouble.

Building your own kit may be more expensive, but with your life at stake, it may be worth it to invest in the best. On search and rescues, I carry a twenty-four-hour pack laden with water, first-aid supplies, and a personal survival kit that is larger than most, but still fits into the thigh pocket on my military-style trousers. If I need to leave my pack while investigating a side canyon or scaling a bluff, my survival kit leaves the pack and always goes with me. The kit cost me about $150 to put together, but I would not settle for less. One strategy is to buy a good quality commercial kit and customize it to your personal needs.

Be selective not only in quality, but in quantity. It is easy to get carried away and add too much. Beware also of companies that sell ordinary camping gear under the term "survival." You can buy everything from shovels to lanterns under the "survival" label these days. On the subject of survival, Geoffrey Norman once wrote in *Outside* magazine, "At some point, I decided, you become well enough equipped so that you're no longer in a survival situation—you're mounting an expedition."

Survival kits. *Left to right:* personal survival kit used by author, author's search and rescue kit, car kit.

A good personal kit should be small enough to fit in a shirt pocket, so it can be carried at all times. There are situations in the outdoors where you may not be able to get to your kit in time, or lose the presence of mind to bring it along. An example of this is a geologist who was driving off-road in the Australian outback. Dead grass balled up underneath his vehicle and ignited from the exhaust system. In his haste the man pulled out the two-way radio from under the dash and left the vehicle. Standing there with the radio in his hands, he watched his survival kit, water, food, and the car battery—which powered the radio—burn. He was missed and later rescued, but if his personal kit had been in his shirt pocket, he would have been better off.

Once again, become familiar with your kit and practice with it, replacing the contents as you use them. One of the reasons so many of the dubious survival tools sell so well is because of the psychological magnetism of tools. Tools tend to draw you in, especially ones that seem to project power. We can be seduced into thinking that tools can solve our problems for us. I see people all the time carrying wicked-looking "Rambo" knives that could get them arrested if worn in public, but are not what is needed to survive. Pick your kit and tools for the right reasons, not to stroke your ego or impress others.

All survival kits should start with a personal kit that can be carried in a pocket. From there you can expand upward, adding things for your mountain bike, horse, raft, or four-wheel drive. The personal kit, however, should be self-contained and kept in a pocket when in the wilds.

PERSONAL KIT

The materials listed below should be the core of any larger kit. The personal kit is the last option other than using natural resources. At first glance, some of the contents will seem odd, but they have their uses. One way to get a start on the kit is to go to an Army/Navy surplus store and buy a parachute pack survival kit. This small kit is far from comprehensive, but has some ingredients to add to your personal kit, such as a button compass, tinder cubes, snare wire, large needles, and small knife. Ask for "Survival Kit," Parachute Pack SRU-16/P, 4240-00-741-9713LS. If you are making your own kit, look for items that are flat, or with squared corners for a good fit. The items listed below are suggested items for an arid land personal kit.

GENERAL ITEMS

CONTAINER: This can be metal or plastic, a soap dish being the most common type. If a soap dish is used, the type with a lid that slides down over the bottom will hold more than the type with a hinged lid. Also, get one without drain holes for better waterproofing and so the container can be used as a cup.

DUCT TAPE: This is put around the joint between the top and bottom to help waterproof the kit. It is also wrapped around the kit two or three times to hold the kit together. The tape can be used for mending, construction, and first aid.

MATCHES: Get the wooden strike-anywhere type. Select ones with the biggest tips. Cut off about a third of the stick and use one drop of wood glue per match to attach to a thin piece of cardboard with the heads alternating. Cut a piece of the striker from the box or some fine sandpaper and glue to the back of the card. Put the card in a small reclosable plastic bag (like jewelers use for small items) to waterproof. Do not rely on matchbook matches.

LIGHTER: You may want to substitute the matches with a small butane lighter, which has up to 300 lights in it. Get the childproof kind, as these help prevent the button from being depressed, causing the loss of all of the butane in the kit. If you have room (or for an expanded kit), the piezo-electric type of lighter works best. Be careful where you store your kit. I left my kit in a hot car and the lighter exploded inside. **MAGNESIUM BAR AND FLINT:** For starting fires. Striker flint can also be used to signal at night.

TINDER CUBES: For quick fires. Two or three small ones will do. Save the foil wrapping to bait fish or bird hooks.

COMPASS: For direction finding. A small button compass works well.

KNIFE: A small, compact, and flat knife. Bob Cooper's MK III Survival Knife is specially designed for personal kits.

SIGNAL MIRROR: High priority for daytime signaling. The unbreakable two-by-three-inch signal mirror by Gerber fits in most personal kits. You can also take any cheap acrylic mirror and cut it to fit.

WHISTLE: To signal with and scare away animals (real or perceived). Buy a small flat one for your kit.

MAGNIFYING STRIP: To start fires and help see small spines.

PLASTIC BAG: For carrying water, as transpiration bag, and keeping tinder and other articles dry. Should be clear plastic and sturdy. Turkey-sized oven bags work well.

FISHHOOKS, LINE WEIGHTS, BRASS SWIVELS: Fishing in the desert? In many places it is not only possible, but the easiest food source. Fish hooks can also be baited to catch birds. Pack small fishhooks, as big ones catch only big fish. Properly used, small hooks will catch all sizes of fish and many birds. Use split shot weights for sinkers and swivels to keep line from tangling.

SNARE WIRE: For trapping, fishing leaders, mending, and construction. Small-gauge brass wire works well.

DENTAL FLOSS: Compact and strong, the floss serves as fishing and bird line, for snares, tying, used with needle for sewing, etc. Take the spool out of the dispenser and tape off the loose end. Some small button compasses will fit in center of spool.

CONDOM(S): Huh? Condoms are often touted as water bladders if they are carried in a sock or shirt sleeve, but in reality they break without much abuse. They can be used for waterproofing items such as tinder or matches. Be sure to use the nonlubricated type.

TWEEZERS: For removing spines and doing delicate work. Get some with needle points. The Sliver GRIPPER is compact and the best made for the job.

POCKET COMB: Cut a small pocket comb in half and put one half in the kit. Some cacti stick to you in detachable joints that can be hard to get off without getting your fingers full of thorns. Slide the comb under the joint and flip away from you to remove.

NEEDLES: For repairs and minor surgery. Get big straight ones and put two or three in the kit.

BOUILLON CUBES: For a comforting and nutritional salt-replacing beverage. Save the foil wrapper to bait hooks.

TEA BAGS: Used as a stimulant, hot beverage, and for comfort. If black tea is used, it can also be used topically to ease sunburn.

PENCIL STUB AND PAPER: For taking notes and leaving messages. Paper can be placed over mirror to help protect it.

SUGAR: For flavoring, energy boost, and mixing with potassium permanganate for combustion. May be granulated and carried in small reclosable plastic pouch or as glucose tablets.

POTASSIUM PERMANGANATE: In some places referred to as Condy's crystals. For starting fires when mixed with sugar. Depending on amount used, also for purifying water, as an antiseptic, and fungicide. Put in reclosable plastic pouch. DO NOT PRE-MIX WITH SUGAR!

COTTON BALLS: Any small spaces in the kit can have cotton balls (or pieces) inserted to stop rattling. The cotton is also easily ignited for tinder.

BINOCULAR: While it will not fit in the kit, a binocular is a good adjunct to the kit. These greatly increase your ability to gather information, such as spotting water location. Arizona survival instructor Dave Ganci considers binoculars to be the third most important survival item after water and matches.

MEDICAL ITEMS

SCALPEL BLADE: Comes sterile in foil. Save foil for hook bait. For minor surgery and delicate cutting jobs.

ADHESIVE BANDAGES: For minor cuts, scrapes, and blisters.

WATER PURIFICATION TABLETS: Keep in date and make sure the type used will kill *Giardia* protozoa.*

ALCOHOL SWABS: For disinfecting wounds and firestarting tinder. Save the foil packet for hook bait.

SALT: Ordinary table salt can be used to replace salt lost to perspiration, *if* there is plenty of water available. It can also be used to make a saline solution to clean wounds and the eyes at a rate of one-half teaspoon per pint of warm water. Salt tablets can also be carried and ground up for seasoning.*

PAIN RELIEF TABLETS: If you can take it, aspirin is the best all-around choice because it reduces pain, fever, and inflammation. Aspirin with an enteric coating lasts longer in the kit. Tylenol is good for pain and fever, but not inflammation. Ibuprofen is good for pain and is anti-inflammatory, but does not reduce fever. It is also hard on an empty stomach, which is very likely in survival situations. If you can get a prescription for Tylenol No.3, it is good for major pain.*

ANTINAUSEA/VOMITING TABLETS: Meclizine is available by prescription, but it is psychotropic and can cause irrational thinking. Dramamine is available over the counter, and while it can cause drowsiness, it does not affect judgement.*

ANTIDIARRHEAL TABLETS: Lomotil is often prescribed for travelers, but it can severely complicate dehydration and electrolyte imbalances, both likely in desert environs. Consult your physician even if you have a prescription. Immodium A-D caplets are a good nonprescription alternative.*

ANTIHISTAMINE CAPSULES: Benadryl capsules are a good nonprescription choice for several reasons. The capsules are taken internally for allergic reactions. The capsules can be broken open and with a moist finger the powder applied directly to the soft palate of the mouth for swelling of the throat from allergic reactions. The contents of the capsule can also be moistened and made into a paste to apply directly to insect stings and dermatitis caused by plants. Benadryl also helps you sleep and relax in stressful situations.*

Be sure to include any special medications you need, such as drugs to use if you have severe allergic reactions to insect stings. It should be remembered that women on birth control pills may go into menses shortly after regular medication is suspended. Extra medication may be included in the personal kit and tampons or sanitary napkins should be considered in larger kits.

* Note: Store tablets in small reclosable plastic pouches with slips of paper plainly identifying the contents and the expiration date.

EXPANDED KIT

You may go into areas where you want more than what is in the personal kit. With an expanded kit you can make improvements over a soap dish kit by substituting a bigger knife, bigger signal mirror, a better compass, louder whistle, and so on. The expanded kit I carry is in a two-by-three-by-six-inch metal container with a rubber gasket in the lid that holds a few extras, such as a water-proof matchbox, an aerial flare, and a smoke bomb. Expanded kits can be custom made for special activities. A mountain bike kit can contain an expanded kit similar to mine, with the addition of small tools and parts for the bicycle. Despite making room for more items, do not stuff it full of junk. It must still be a well thought out kit. The Storm Kit from Tacoma Mountain Rescue Unit is a good addition for an expanded kit. The expanded kit is also easier to adapt to your personal and environmental needs. The following are some suggested items:

> **CONTAINER:** A metal container like mine can be carried in a vest, jacket, or large thigh pocket. Other ideas are belt pouches or fanny packs. If these are used, put the contents in a freezer-size Ziploc bag to keep the kit dry.
> **CANTEEN CUP:** The rest of the expanded kit can fit in the cup. The cup is metal and can be used for drinking, boiling water, and cooking.
> **SPACE BLANKET:** These are metallic disposable sheets designed to reflect your body heat back to you. They can also be used for fire reflectors, rain covers, or ground markers for aircraft, although they are somewhat easy to tear. If you think one of these will keep you toasty warm without proper clothing, you should take one out for a test some

chilly night! Buy two—one to play with and one to put in the kit, because once taken out of the package it is never going to fit back again.

WHISTLE: You may want to add a better whistle than what you can carry in a soap dish. The Fox 40 is the loudest I know of.

FOOD RATIONS: These can be energy bars, powdered rations, and so on.

POCKET STONE: A small pocket stone or knife sharpener will keep an edge on your blade, making it easier and safer to use. The stone can also be used to sharpen fishhooks.

PARACHUTE CORD: For bigger lashing and tying jobs. Make sure you purchase real parachute cord and not just any nylon cord. Parachute cord has a nylon sleeve with several very strong filaments inside that can be used for fish line, netting, bowstring, and smaller tying jobs. Make your boot laces out of parachute cord as well.

TUBE TENT: This is a plastic tube that can be made into an emergency shelter.

PLASTIC SHEET: A clear plastic drop cloth can be used to keep water off gear, collect rainwater, and used in some condensation techniques to get water. It can also be used for emergency shelter. Try to get a heavy thickness for durability.

AERIAL FLARES: Skyblazer makes a good compact flare that is great for night signaling and of lesser visibility in the day. Red is the best in emergencies.

SMOKE BOMBS: For daytime signaling. Again, Skyblazer makes a good forty-five-second smoke bomb small enough for the kit. Blaze orange is the best color for desert terrain.

LARGE GARBAGE BAGS: You can keep dry even in downpours with two large garbage bags. Stand in one and tuck it under your belt. Cut a hole for your face in the other, pull it over your head, and sit down. This also gives some protection from wind.

FLASHLIGHT: The small flashlights available today do not take much room, and neither do the batteries. I like the Solitaire from Maglite. Turn the bottom battery around backward; in case it is accidentally switched to the on position, nothing will happen and your batteries will not run down. Turn it around when you are ready to use it. If you have the space, there is another option called Firefly Plus. It is a four-ounce flashlight/strobe combination that runs on two AA batteries and can be used for signaling or regular flashlight duty.

WIRE SAW: These are twisted wires with rings or T-handles on each end that can be used as a saw. I like the SAS (Special Air Services) type with teeth. Some of the smoother wire saws have one small ring that can pass through the other so that the saw doubles as a snare.

CANDLE: Candles are handy to save matches (light the candle, then the fire), but in hot areas they tend to melt and run all over your kit. If you carry one, put it in plastic cling wrap.

SNAKEBITE KIT: There is some doubt as to whether suction kits actually can extract appreciable amounts of venom, and many people do not include them. Thoughts on this vary from region to region. I have found suction kits useful for insect stings and bringing small spines and slivers up to the skin surface. I recommend The Extractor for reasons described later.

EXTRA FIRST-AID SUPPLIES: With an expanded kit you have the advantage of having more medical supplies, such as triangular bandages, butterfly closures, antiseptic and burn ointment, and eye ointment.

AREA MAPS: Carry a map—what a concept! The trouble is, a lost person is often found with maps, but without the ability to read them. Carry some map and compass knowledge, too.

SADDLEBAG KITS

Not too much has been written about survival kits for equestrians, but they need to plan for emergencies like everyone else. When planning a kit to carry with you, make considerations for the horse also. Just because the horse is carrying the kit, don't think you can load it up, especially if the bags are carried behind the cantle. Too much weight on the back of the saddle will bruise a horse's kidneys. Specially fit bags, called *cantinas* in Mexico, can be hung on each side of the fork (that's pommel to you English riders), which places the weight over the animal's center of gravity. Still, resist the urge

Some people are going to poke fun at you for having a survival kit on your steed, like the time I was following my boss out of the Tom Miner Basin in Montana with a string of pack mules leaving our hunting camp. (I was taking a working vacation from the desert.) A lodgepole pine had fallen across the trail, and we had left our axe in camp. We tried to budge and push, but it was immobile four feet above the trail with a drop-off to the side. I suggested we use the wire saw from the kit. "Ha, ha, ha." We pushed some more. Now it was "Cuss, cuss, cuss." Finally, he said, "Okay. Get out your toy." In ten minutes we had the six-inch diameter trunk cut in two places and the trail cleared. We left with him muttering something about "gettin' one of those."

to carry more than necessary. I still subscribe to the cowboy belief that God will judge you by how you treat your horse more than most other things. Don't just make up a kit and hang it off one side; balance the load. Too much weight on one side can cause the saddle to lean off center, soring the horse's back. Divide the kit into two bags of equal weight.

For the saddlebag kit, take an expanded kit and add the following:

FENCING PLIERS: The uses of this tool are legion. They can be used as pliers, horseshoe nail pullers, hammer for setting shoes, wire cutters, and the staple puller on the end makes a good hoof pick. The tool can be used to pull out porcupine quills from a horse, reset or tighten a shoe, and fix tack. They can also be used to fix fence! Fencing pliers do not even need to go into a saddlebag; you can buy or make special holsters to hang them from the flank cinch.

KNIFE: Horse people have some different knife requirements. A folding knife with a leather awl is good. Some have marlin spikes for splicing rope. Some, such as Buck Knives' PRCA Horseman folding knife, have a special blade to act as a hoof pick.

HORSESHOES: You may need to replace a shoe, especially on rocky ground. This, of course, will take some specialized knowledge and skill. Long ago they made "carriage shoes," which had a hinge at the toe set flush. The branches of the shoe could be moved in and out to fit the hoof until a better fitting shoe could be set. I don't know of anyone who stocks these, but there are still some anachronistic blacksmiths around who would do it at the right price. You can also carry prefit shoes. On most horses and mules you would need one size for the front and another for the back. Another option is the Easyboot, which is rubber and slips over the hoof and is tightened with small cables and latches. These are bulky, but do not weigh more than two iron shoes. An additional advantage of the Easyboot is that it does not require a knowledge of shoeing.

HORSESHOE NAILS: If you plan to pack a carriage shoe or prefits, you will need a couple dozen nails of the proper size for the shoes.

HOOF RASP: It may be necessary to level the hoof before a shoe can be set. The common shoeing rasps today are too long for a saddlebag kit, and the tang is sharp and dangerous unless fitted with a handle, making it even longer. A good answer is a split rasp, which is made to cut in both directions. It is shorter and has rounded ends, although it is harder to learn to use. The rasp doubles as a clinch block when setting the nails and is also used to smooth the clinched nails.

LEATHER STRINGS: A small bundle of leather strings or lacing will facilitate tack repairs.

VETERINARY GRADE IODINE: A small unbreakable bottle of 7% iodine (human grade is 2.5%) and some cotton swabs can be used to disinfect wounds on the mount. Do not put it directly in the wound, as that will cause further injury. Swab the edges of the wound, working outward, to help keep further infection away. The wound can be safely cleaned with a saline solution of one-half teaspoon of salt per pint of warm water. The iodine can also be used to purify water. To be safe, a quart of clear water needs two drops of 7% iodine or five drops of 2.5%, added and shaken, then allowed to stand for twenty minutes. Cold and/or cloudy water needs three to four drops of 7% and up to ten drops of 2.5% for safety. Also let stand at least twenty minutes.

OFF-ROAD VEHICLE SURVIVAL KIT

By necessity, the off-road vehicle kit is going to be much bigger than those previously discussed. So many things can go wrong with a four-wheeler, plus conditions caused by bad weather or poor judgment, that an off-road adventure can be stopped dead in the worst places. A few simple multipurpose tools and some neat little survival tricks are not going to fix a major mechanical problem or extract a vehicle that is incredibly stuck. In these times those "survival" shovels I was deriding earlier have some very real applications.

The vehicle kit will need to have proper tools, some replacement parts, and various stocks of liquids in order for you to keep out of trouble. In the case of a vehicle kit, you do not need to be so self-limiting in what you pack and can indulge in moderate urges to take more. For instance, the ability to haul adequate water is greatly increased. Be sure to have enough not only for passengers, but also for the vehicle. A real blanket or sleeping bag is going to be better than a thin space blanket.

There are some good multiperson survival kits on the market. Many are seventy-two-hour kits designed for families in disaster situations such as earthquakes. These are compact and come packaged in sturdy boxes, bags, or backpacks. Unfortunately, almost all of these come with retort pouches of water, which I believe take up room and add weight to the kit. Even in autos, I believe water should be carried separately in large sturdy containers for adequate supply. My own off-road kit is stored in a tool box and a military surplus ammo can that is sturdy, but does not take too much room.

Having an auto means you can also have a comprehensive first-aid kit. First-aid kits are much cheaper to buy than building your own. As a matter of fact, many contain items you probably would not be able to get in small quantities. Unlike some survival kits, most advanced first-aid kits are sold to be used by professionals who are hard to hoodwink, and the majority are designed for specific skill levels and for practicality. Most are also self-contained in fold-out bags, fanny packs, jump kits, or day packs. A quality first-aid kit is a good investment, and so are some classes to go with it. Do not make a comprehensive survival kit and stow it behind the seat. Make sure the basic items are handy.

TOOLS

JUMPER CABLES

FLASHLIGHT: Perhaps two—one large lantern for lots of light, and one small enough to put in your mouth to direct a beam while using both hands.

ADJUSTABLE CRESCENT WRENCH

WRENCH SET (WITH OPEN AND BOX ENDS)

SOCKET SET WITH RATCHET DRIVER

SPARK PLUG SOCKET

REGULAR AND PHILLIPS SCREWDRIVERS

PLIERS WITH WIRE CUTTERS/NEEDLE-NOSED PLIERS

EMERY PAPER: For cleaning contacts, wires, battery posts, etc.

PLUG-TYPE TIRE REPAIR KIT

FOXHOLE SHOVEL

CHAIN WINCH OR COME-ALONG

FOUR-FOOT METAL STAKE: For anchoring winch to.

THREE-POUND HAMMER: To pound in stake.

STRIPS OF CARPET (One-by-six-foot): To put under tires for traction.

HIGHLIFT JACK

FIRE EXTINGUISHER

SUPPLIES

ENGINE OIL: Three quarts

ENGINE COOLANT

STARTING FLUID

BRAKE FLUID

AUTOMATIC TRANSMISSION FLUID: Two quarts, if needed.

WD-40: Not only good for lubricating locked parts, but for displacing water from electrical connections.

TIRE INFLATOR/SEALER: Two cans.

DUCT TAPE

ASSORTED HOSE CLAMPS

EPOXY GLUE OR PUTTY: To seal holes in radiator or oil pan.

EXTRA FAN BELTS: Emergency belts that adjust to size can be bought to replace fan, alternator, and other engine belts.

EXTRA LENGTH OF FUEL LINE

EXTRA CAN OF GASOLINE

WATER: At least five gallons, more is better. Carry enough for both car and passengers.

SPARES

Consult your mechanic for a list of your particular needs.

TIRE(S)

WATER PUMP

DISTRIBUTOR KIT

SPARK PLUGS

STARTER RELAY AND SOLENOID

VOLTAGE REGULATOR

RADIATOR HOSES

EXTRA FUSES AND BULBS

SURVIVAL ITEMS

PERSONAL KIT: One per person.

EXPANDED KIT

COMPREHENSIVE FIRST-AID KIT

FOOD

BLANKETS OR SLEEPING BAGS

SMALL TENT

RESCUE BLANKETS: These have a metallic side like a space blanket to reflect body heat, and a red or blaze orange side for visibility. Can also be used for shelter construction. These are bulkier than space blankets, but reusable.

ROAD FLARES

BOOK(S): With extra room you may want to take some books on survival and first aid, and mechanical guides for the vehicle.

THE AIRCRAFT SURVIVAL KIT

The first time I saw the parachute pack survival kit issued to U.S. Air Force pilots, I was disturbed. It comes in a box in a cloth sleeve that wouldn't accommodate a decent-sized candy bar! However, it has to be the ultimate definition of traveling light, because the pilots wear their parachutes in flight, and in certain maneuvers too much weight creates excessive G's (a measurement of inertial force that seems to increase gravity). The kit is attached to the parachute harness.

Crew-served aircraft have bigger kits in jump bags that contain a lot of what was outlined in the expanded kit, plus some extras such as larger strobes and an Air Force survival knife with a sheath and stone. When some of my students showed me the kit, I still felt we were shorting our men and women in the service. The food rations consisted of Charms candy.

The U.S. Army crew-served aircraft have survival gear that include survival vests, .38-caliber revolvers and ammunition, sleeping bags, a comprehensive fishing kit, insect headsets, frying pan, and so on. Depending on the areas they fly over, Arctic and over-water items are included. The food they carry is not great, but it beats what I've seen in the Air Force kits. I feel that by using the expanded kit and selecting items for weight, the average private pilot would have as good, or possibly better, an aircraft kit than is issued to the people who risk their lives for us in military aircraft.

A two-person survival pack built specifically for light aircraft is available from Sporty's Pilot Shop. It carries items for first aid, food, water, signaling, tools, shelter, and fire. It weighs only six pounds (minus water) and is a compact 11-by-10-by-4 inches. I would add extra water containers and snare wire.

Survival kits for aircraft need to be well thought out. In small aircraft, weight is critical, so what is carried must be important and useful. A broad purpose survival kit is desirable for aircraft that may be flying over quite different terrain than desert. The pilot and passengers will need an adaptable kit and must understand the need to change priorities to cover various situations. Water is heavy, but a good supply should be carried just in case. Once again, the essentials, such as a personal kit, should be with you. If your aircraft kit is stowed somewhere like a baggage compartment, you may not be able to retrieve it in a fire.

There are several things you can do to dress and outfit kids, including toddlers, to increase their chances for surviving being lost. Small children can slip away easily and have no sense of direction to get back. One way to help this is to lace small bells on their shoes. Also, any child can learn how to use a whistle—getting them not to blow it needlessly is the problem. A child with a whistle can signal rescuers and can use it at night to scare away animals (real or imaginary). At four years old my son Ian could use a signal mirror, and has his own made from unbreakable plastic. Because of a child's limitations in skills and experience, the kit is obviously for short-term emergencies. The child's survival kit can be made extremely cheaply, and as such, kids should be encouraged to play and experiment to learn how to use it. The contents can be replaced for pocket change.

CHILDREN'S SURVIVAL KITS

Let's step back to the basics now. I firmly believe that even children need survival kits and training. No matter how good parents are, children and parents can get distracted and separated. The Hug-A-Tree program conducted nationwide is one of the best investments of time for parents and children. Children's survival kits are covered in the course, with some practice in using things such as whistles and signal mirrors. What is included in your child's kit will depend on their age and level of responsibility. Obviously, some children will not be ready to use knives and matches.

You can make this kit largely from items around the house. The Storm Kit mentioned previously from Tacoma Mountain Rescue Unit is ideal for children. If you make one including garbage bags, the kit will be too big to fit in a child's pocket. A small fanny pack will work well if the child is not wearing a jacket with big pockets. Items for a child's kit are the following:

CONTAINER: May be a can with plastic lid, unbreakable plastic jar with screw on lid, or can with friction lid. It is hard to find flat cans, but they are less bulky to carry. The Storm Kit comes in such a can.

DUCT TAPE: To seal the lid on tight and help waterproof the contents. Make sure your child knows the tape is reusable for repairs and not to throw it away.

MATCHES: Fix the same way for the personal kit. Parents will need to consider if the child is ready for this item or not.

SMALL KNIFE: Once again, the parents will need to make a responsible decision and provide proper training.

CANDLE: Necessary only if matches are included. Remember, these can make a mess of a kit in hot climates if not wrapped in plastic cling wrap.

CANDY OR SUGAR CUBES: This gives an energy boost, aids in heat production, and can be of some comfort to a frightened child.

WHISTLE: The can will be large enough to accept a big loud one.

SIGNAL MIRROR

GARBAGE BAGS: To be used as described in the section on expanded kits. Some parents go berserk when I suggest their child put a plastic bag over their head, but most suffocation deaths from plastic bags are infants or toddlers. That is why we must teach children how to use the kit. Bags are cheap, so let the children learn how to tear or cut a hole for their face on several of them. Get the brightest color possible.

ADHESIVE BANDAGES: Children know almost instinctively how to use these. (If you took all the Band-Aids off my sons, they would fall apart.) Three or four are enough.

ALCOHOL SWABS: One or two for disinfecting wounds —if you can get the child to do it.

TELEPHONE CHANGE: Add a couple of quarters for a telephone call.

There may be other things to add to fit your child's needs and skill levels. The kit should change as the child grows. While some programs will help, you are ultimately responsible for the safety of children you take into the wilds. Giving them a good kit and the knowledge to use it puts them way ahead of the dozens of lost children SAR teams look for each year.

KNIVES

A good knife is one of the most incredibly useful survival tools in any situation. Unfortunately, the term "survival" is abused to sell knives more than any other tool. A large number of so-called survival knives sold are actually combat blades, or blades designed to have a menacing look. These are mostly sold to armchair commandos who fantasize about being put into survival situations that require them to chop their way through platoons of communist mercenaries. Every time a Rambo-type movie comes out, knife sales go up. Most people, myself included, know nothing about knife fighting; nor will they ever be put in situations where it is needed.

The U.S. Army knows this. At their SERE (Survival, Evasion, Resistance, Escape) school at Fort Bragg, the preferred survival knife is a short-blade locking folder—a large pocketknife. The knife has to meet small chores, such as skinning small animals, processing plants, shaving wood, and so on. It has a softer steel than other blades so it can be easily sharpened in the field with natural stone. It has no menacing attributes but it is the knife used to train our men and women in the Army on how to avoid being prisoners of war.

Knives recommended for survival use. *Left to right:* Cold Steel® SRK, Aitor® Skinner JK II, Leatherman® Pocket Tool, Australian MK III.

In a survival situation any knife is better than none at all; but since you must make your knife selection beforehand, you have the advantage of making a practical decision. You can spend hundreds of dollars on a custom knife, or you can buy a stock knife at an affordable price and make some modifications to fit your needs. We will discuss knives in four categories: heavy duty, middle sized, combination tools, and kit sized.

HEAVY-DUTY KNIVES

The heavy-duty knife is used primarily for chopping, splitting, and perhaps digging. The blade should be durable enough to withstand prying and the edge must be able to stay reasonably sharp with heavy use. Heavy-duty knives are fixed blade and carried in a sheath. Many survival knives are constructed with a hollow handle to store small items like matches and fishhooks. The cheaper of these have the blade and handle forged separately, often not even from the same type of metal, and then the two are welded together. This weld is a weak link that can break, causing you to suddenly own a spear point and a heavy matchbox. There are some hollow-handled survival knives, such as those made by Chris Reeve, that are milled from a single piece, with no weak weld to break.

First consider the blade. Eschew blades that have blood grooves, holes, or cut out areas in them. These weaken the blade and have other drawbacks. If you find it necessary to butcher large game, when splitting the sternum you may find your knife hopelessly stuck in a joint between the breastbone and ribs because of a depression or opening in the blade. The blade should be thick enough to handle abuse. The length is largely a matter of your preference, but blades six inches long and up (within reason) are better for chopping, prying, and digging.

Next consider the tang, the part of the knife that the handle attaches to. Full-tang knives are the strongest for jobs such as prying, digging, or chopping. A full tang means that the tang is almost as wide as the blade and continues to the butt of the knife. This usually means you can see the tang along the top and bottom of the knife because the handles are slabs attached to the sides. The exceptions are some knives with Kraton or rubberized handles that will conceal the tang. Other tang styles, such as half tangs or tapered tangs, either do not go all the way to the butt or are much thinner than the blade and are concealed by the handle material. These are weaker and not as reliable as a full-tang knife. Some knives have interchangeable blades, such as skinning, serrated, and saw blades. While the adaptability of these is attractive, their tang length, and therefore their strength, is severely compromised.

A handy option for knives is a solid metal surface on the butt (called a pommel) for pounding or hammering. Beware of knives that call themselves "the ultimate survival knife." There is no such thing. There are just too many variables in survival situations for any one knife to be able to handle every need with one hundred percent effectiveness. Instead, consider your needs and activities, and shop for a knife that comes closest to your specifications. For search and rescue operations I carry a Cold Steel SRK (Survival Rescue Knife). It has a thick six-inch blade with a clip point and Kraton handles for a sure grip. This is the blade I chose to carry on my trek in Australia, and it worked admirably. If I were to order a custom knife for SAR operations, it would be basically the same as the SRK, with a shiny blade, blaze orange Kraton handles to locate it easier, and a solid pommel for crushing or pounding. Heavy-duty production knives I recommend for desert survival include the following: Cold Steel SRK, Master Hunter, or Bush Ranger; Gerber LMF (Light Multi-Functional) Tactical or BMF (Basic Multi-Functional) Survival System; SOG Government, NW Ranger, and SEAL Knife-2000; Camillus Navy MK III Combat; Ontario Knife Company Spec Plus series SP5 Bowie Survival, SP4 Navy, Navy Mark I, or U.S.M.C. Parachutist; EK Warrior Bowie; Beck Knife and Tool Company Outdoor Companion or Magnum Camp; Buck Knives Skinner or Frontiersman; and the Busse Steel Heart II.

Knives and the Law

Check into local laws before carrying large knives in public. Some laws identify very useful survival knives as "fighters" by blade length, double edges, or guards. I see visitors to my area casually strolling into places that sell alcoholic beverages with knives on their belts that could land them in prison for ten years by Texas law. Most law officers in rural areas have an appreciation for the value of a good sheath knife, but are leery about someone who wears one when not actually camping or wears one in an intimidating manner. Please use good sense.

MIDDLE-SIZED KNIVES

For reasons of weight, space, or legalities, it may not be practical to pack a heavy-duty blade. In addition, some chores, such as cleaning small animals, birds, or fish, and preparing plant fibers are too delicate for large knives to do easily. A good compromise is a middle-sized knife, which can be either fixed blade or a folder. Fixed-blade knives should be evaluated in essentially the same way as heavy-duty knives in regard to blade and tang styles, but on a smaller scale. Folding knives are the most convenient, as they may be carried in a pocket or on a belt sheath for easier access. Folding knives are so popular that the choices are seemingly endless. One drawback of folding knives compared to fixed blades is that they are weaker because they essentially have no tang, but are pinned to the handle to rotate. Some are extremely strong, but should not be depended on for heavy prying, stabbing, or chopping despite any manufacturer's claim. If a folding knife is chosen, try to get one with a mechanism that locks the blade when in use. Some chores, such as using the point to make a hole can cause nonlocking knives to close on your fingers, inflicting nasty cuts. Unfortunately, some states and municipalities are considering lockback folders to be fighting knives and are making them illegal. To me this is the same as banning safety goggles. Once again, check the law before you buy or carry.

An option you will have with many folders is a straight or serrated edge. Both have advantages and disadvantages. Serrated edges cut more aggressively and stay sharper longer than a straight edge. A serrated edge is good for slicing fibrous plants such as yucca leaves, cutting rope and seat belts in emergencies, various steps in butchering, and some skinning. However, serrated edges are impossible to sharpen without specific tools. Straight edges are favored for more delicate tasks that require precision, but will also handle larger jobs with a little more effort. Carving and whittling is much easier with a straight edge. Straight edges can be sharpened in the field with natural stone if the blade is not made of an extremely hard steel. For all-around survival use, I recommend a straight edge over a serrated edge, but you can also have both. Several fixed and folding models offer blades with both straight and serrated edges. The Camillus Mini Promaster Expedition is a lockback folder that has two blades, one with a straight edge and the other serrated.

Some folders are designed to open one-handed, which is certainly an advantage in tight spots. A rubberized or Kraton handle is a good choice for a firm grip. It would not be feasible to list all the excellent middle-sized folders available, but the following are some of my favorite for survival use: the Schrade Outback series; Gerber LST series; Case "Caliber" lockbacks; Spec Plus lockbacks by Ontario Knife Company; Cold Steel Voyager clip points; Remington "Grizzly" lockbacks; and the Buck Knives Bucklite series.

COMBINATION TOOLS

For good reasons, some of the best-selling items today are combination tools. These are folding kits with one or more knife blades and with additional tools such as small pliers, files, screwdrivers, leather awls, and so on. I have used my Leatherman for everything from fixing my Jeep to making yucca fiber sandals. I find I use it more than any other tool in the field. Combination tools are not, however, a panacea. At best they are a compromise between a knife and a tool kit, and they do have their limitations.

Perhaps the best known are the Swiss Army knives and their spin-offs. You can buy these with almost thirty tools crowded into one handle. The question is, "Are they all necessary?" Once W.C. Fields said, "It reminds me of my journey to the wilds of Afghanistan. We lost our corkscrew and had to survive on nothing but food and water for several days!" In most modern survival situations a corkscrew is unnecessary, but it is often found on such knives. These combination knives can be included in an expanded survival kit, and are a good asset. I would opt for the simpler ones with fewer, but helpful tools. Victorinox, the maker of Swiss Army knives, offers the small SOS Survival Kit, which includes a "Swisschamp" knife and additional survival items in a belt pouch. A combination tool with a highly portable survival kit in a small belt pouch is an excellent idea. I have found that the scissors on Swiss Army knives are excellent for trimming toenails, which is very important for foot care. For that reason a friend of mine, ex-Green Beret Ron "Tex" Houston, gave me one to carry on my Pilbara trek in Australia. It served well.

A newer and more useful combination tool is a type of folding pliers with an array of blades and tools hidden in the handles. The front-runners for these are the Leatherman models—the Gerber MultiPlier and Military Provisional Tools—and the SOG Paratool and Power Plier. Each has its advantages and disadvantages. All can be conveniently carried in the pocket, belt pouch, or expanded kit. The Leatherman Mini Tool is small enough to be included in some personal kits.

Camillus makes the standard Military Multi-Purpose G.I. pocketknife. While it does not have a locking blade, it is durable, with a spear-point blade, leather awl, bottle opener, slot screwdriver, can opener, and lanyard bail.

KIT SIZE

I like to include a small knife in my personal kit as a last-resort tool. My oversized personal kit has a five-inch overall Aitor Skinner JK II fixed-blade knife. It has a gut hook for skinning, a bottle and can opener, and a skeletonized handle. I modified it by putting a few small fishhooks into the opening in the handle, wrapping the handle with twenty feet of small-gauge snare wire, and wrapping that with blaze orange nylon cord, leaving a loop to attach a lanyard if needed. I can unravel the handle to use the cord, wire, or hooks. I made a special thin leather sheath to replace the bigger canvas one included with the knife. The knife with modifications cost about nine dollars.

Small folding knives can be fit into a personal kit, and there are many lockback versions that are compact enough to consider. Some good ones are the Gerber Microlight L.S.T.; the Case Mini Camper; and the Buck Knives Minibuck. While they do not have locking blades, many of the smaller Swiss Army knives will fit into the personal kit. Most of the small folding knives mentioned come in red or blaze orange colors, making them harder to lose.

While it will increase the cost of a personal kit, the Tool Logic Credit Card Companion will fit easily into a personal kit and save lots of room. It is about the same dimensions as a credit card, and only five-sixteenths of an inch thick, and has a serrated-edge knife, small compass, magnifying lens, slot screwdriver, awl, can/bottle opener, tweezers, toothpick, and ruler. It fits easily in a wallet, also. It would be even better if they had made the back shiny for a signal mirror.

Knife Myths

There are some survival myths to bash concerning knives for survival use. Some knives are made with holes the manufacturers recommend to use to lash onto poles to make spears. At a glance, the Australian MK III would look ideal for this, with its spear-point shape and holes in the handle. Bob Cooper is adamant about not using it as such. He says if you have a pole, you can use the knife to make a sharp point for a spear. The MK III's handle holes are designed to attach a more comfortable handle. Knives can be lashed to poles for other purposes, such as gathering fruit from out of reach places. Throwing knives is also a bozo no-no. Your knife is one of the most important survival tools you have. Treat it like your life depends on it—it does!

One of the more unusual survival knives that was specifically designed for personal kits is the MK III Survival Knife from Australia. The knife was designed after a small stone knife made by Australian Aborigines and worn in their headbands. The knife and sheath are very flat and fit well in the kit. The short, broad handle has a hole for good thumb grip, with smaller holes for lashing to a handle. Both sides of the blade are sharpened with a chisel edge, meaning only one surface is beveled. This makes it very easy to sharpen in the field and good for scraping.

FIREARMS

The use of firearms in desert survival situations is limited to food procurement, signaling, and, to a small degree, self-protection. Some argue it would be better to take an equal weight of water into desert environs and leave the gun and ammo at home. Many places, such as national and state parks and the entire country of Mexico, have rather strict regulations on carrying firearms, which further limits their practicality. Yet there are still times when a handgun, rifle, or shotgun can be a handy item.

The first thing to decide is whether to carry a firearm at all. If you decide to do so, you must make a firm commitment to get the proper training, use discretion, and always act in a safe manner.

Every time a death, injury, or property damage occurs from the thoughtless use of a firearm, we come closer to having our right to own them reversed.

As for self-protection, there are few natural predators in the Chihuahuan Desert that will need the attention of a firearm. I would be more concerned with what might have crawled into your boot at night. Mountain lions are reclusive and rarely attack people, black bears are generally not aggressive, and the Mexican wolf survives only by human care. Coyotes sing for you. In fact, most of the desert lives under a laissez-faire policy. This pretty well nullifies the need for a large-caliber gun, unless you need protection from other people.

There are times when a firearm will be a great asset, but it should not be considered an answer to all problems. The calibers, types, actions, and capabilities of different guns have filled volumes, so I will be rather basic here. If a firearm is carried in a vehicle, the shooter will have a wide range of options. If a sidearm is to be carried, the selection is more critical.

As a rule, shotguns are ill suited for our criteria. For hunting purposes they are generally used for taking small game and birds with bulky ammunition. They can be useful as combination guns, usually with a rifle barrel on top and a shotgun on the bottom. For self-defense purposes, some shotgun models are about the most effective weapon an ordinary person can own, but they are rather limited in wilderness applications.

Most people think about shooting large game in survival situations. In desert terrain this usually necessitates a large caliber for long shots at animals such as mule deer, unless you conceal yourself downwind of a waterhole. Most game will be mid to small sized. For this reason I believe the .22 long-rifle cartridge to be a good choice. I am not saying, as some have, that the .22 is the ultimate survival weapon. Just as with knives, there is no ultimate survival firearm. I believe the .22 is a good desert choice for the following reasons:

The cartridges are cheap and can afford the shooter a lot of practice for good accuracy. Their low recoil makes it possible for almost anyone to shoot one accurately. The shells are small, and many can be carried as opposed to an equal volume of high-powered rifle cartridges and especially shotgun shells. In the absence of large animal threats, the .22 will handle most of the food-gathering needs (if needed at all). Some models are very lightweight, and one will not use up as many calories and expend as much sweat carrying one compared to a large-caliber rifle.

The .22 also has some distinct disadvantages. It is woefully inadequate for large game except at close range and very well placed shots. It is a poor choice for self-defense against people. It is not as good for audible signals as a high-powered rifle. The rimfire cartridges are not as well made as centerfire cartridges and are more susceptible to moisture or oils, which can render them useless. The lighter models are more fragile than weapons of a larger size.

There are several excellent choices in the .22 long-rifle category. The first is the AR-7 Explorer Survival Rifle. This is a unique .22 semiautomatic rifle that looks like something off of *Mission Impossible*. The weapon breaks down and fits into the stock, which is then covered by the butt cap, making it waterproof. The gun will float either assembled or stowed. The clip holds eight rounds, and because of its compactness and light weight, it is a favorite survival gun for many private pilots. It is also relatively inexpensive and is a good addition to a vehicle kit.

For a sidearm I like the semiautomatic Ruger Mark II series, which comes in a wide selection of barrel lengths and designs. I like the five-inch bull barrel for accuracy. It is heavy for a .22 pistol, but very durable and accurate. I have also shot the Browning Buck Mark, another .22 semiautomatic, and found it quite effective.

For revolver fans, the Smith & Wesson Model 63 Kit Gun is an outstanding choice in .22 caliber. It comes in barrel lengths from two to four inches and is also available in .22 magnum. The late survival gun writer Mel Tappen recommended the Magnum Kit for signaling because it was so loud. I have yet to shoot the new Smith & Wesson Model 17, a ten-shot .22 LR revolver, but it looks promising.

Combination guns are well worth a look if you have room. The one I carry in my vehicle is the M6 Survival model from Springfield Armory, which has a .22 long rifle barrel on top and a .410 shotgun barrel on the bottom. The M6 was designed as a survival gun for the U.S. Air Force and can be broken down into two pieces and stored in a 24-by-5-by-2-inch space. It has storage in the buttstock for fifteen .22 long-rifle cartridges and four .410 shells. The gun has an unusual trigger that is squeezed with all the fingers, so it can be used with mittens in extremely cold environments. It takes a while to get used to the trigger, but .22 ammo is cheap. Older ones do not have a trigger guard, so one should not disengage the safety until ready to fire. I have carried one in bouncing four-wheel drives for ten years and find it very durable and accurate. The gun is also made in a .22 Hornet/.410 combination.

Most .410 shells come in No.4 shot or smaller, making them useful only for rabbit-sized game at short ranges. You can buy rifled slugs, which can be used on larger game at close distance. In addition, .410 flares are made to be fired from shotgun barrels such as the M6 Scout. These would increase the firearms' versatility in emergency situations. They are available from All Purpose Ammo listed in Appendix B.

Savage Arms makes an excellent line of combination guns in their Model 24 series. The rifle barrel can be had in .22 LR, .22 Hornet, .223, or .30-30 calibers. The shotgun barrel comes in 20 and 12 gauges. The older Model 24C Camper in .22 LR/20 gauge has a storage space in the butt for extra ammo. These guns take up more space than the previously mentioned long guns, but the selection of caliber is better for more diverse use. The 20 gauge far outperforms the .410 shotgun, and the 12 gauge is better yet. If space and weight permit, these are good for long-distance pilots who fly over changing terrain. The new Model 24F-12T in .223/12 gauge would be my selection for an all-around combination gun.

Recommended firearms for desert areas. *Upper left:* Ruger Mark II; *upper right:* Smith & Wesson® Model 63 Kit Gun; *middle:* Springfield Armory® M6 Survival model; *bottom:* Explorer AR-7 Survival Rifle.

Throughout this chapter I have advised discretion and minimization in the selection of survival gear, but then given long lists of useful items. If I were asked to select three items other than water, and dump the rest, here would be my selection: a heavy-duty knife, a signal mirror, and a magnesium bar. With these I could gain shelter, fire, food, signals, tools, and weapons in most desert areas. As for water—that will be covered in the next chapter.

4 Water

*"This is Abu Tabara," Jibrin said, smiling. We climbed a hump
of sand, and he showed me a single well, covered in flat stones.
"They have all gone," he said. "They must have left only days ago."
It was disappointing to find the place uninhabited, but the survival
instinct was stronger: I was overjoyed to find water.*

—Michael Asher, *A Desert Dies*

Water will be the primary concern in most desert emergencies. Besides the obvious need of water for personal consumption, locating water is important for other reasons. There will be a greater diversity of vegetation to use near water sources, especially natural ones. Water will also attract animals, whose taking may be a part of your survival strategy. And too, water locations will be among the first areas SAR personnel will look for a lost person.

Here are some rules to remember when it comes to water in the desert:

- Carry enough for yourself, for others with you, and for your vehicle.
- Select your water containers for durability from shock and make sure they are leakproof. Twice I have had guests sign up for hikes who brought untried water flasks with belt clips that leaked around the rivets.
- Do not rely on condensation techniques, plants, or any thing else you may have read about as a primary water source or a reason to pack less water.
- Ration sweat, not water. If water supplies are low, do not eat anything or drink alcoholic or caffeinated beverages.

HUMAN PHYSIOLOGY AND DEHYDRATION

To help conserve water in emergencies, you should know beforehand about the process of dehydration and how it affects you. In areas with low humidity, water loss can happen without being noticed. After a lecture on water consumption I was once told by a person from east Texas, "I sweat more driving to work than you do all day here." What people do not understand is that in hot climates with low humidity, sweat does not stay on the skin and cool like it is intended, but rapidly evaporates. We desert folk may wind up smelling better, but we lose water with little cooling effect. In addition, water is lost by respiration.

People who have physically adapted to desert environs obviously have the advantage over the newcomer. Acclimatizing to new environments, such as heat, cold, or altitude, can take from days to weeks. As a matter of fact, a Japanese study done in the tropics during World War II stated that the number of sweat glands operational in adulthood was determined by the amount of hot weather a person had been exposed to as an infant. People visiting deserts in the spring often make statements to locals about how hot it is, when the acclimated people are enjoying a sunny day.

Psychology also plays into this. If you are not used to the heat (or cold or altitude), you are going to be uncomfortable. In turn, the discomfort creates depression or moods that can have a further effect on a person's physical being. This is further aggravated when people do not take steps to minimize their discomfort by wearing hats, staying in the shade, or taking the good old siesta. We desert rats face high temperatures with a little philosophy and humor. Swamp coolers also help.

One of the best studies done on arid land water needs is *Physiology of Man in the Desert*, by E. F. Adolph and Associates. The book illustrates how increases in temperature and physical exertion speed up dehydration. For instance, Adolph's research showed that a person at complete rest with daily temperatures of 100°F in the shade and ten U.S. quarts of water would have an expected survival time of 9.5 days. A person with ten quarts who walks at night until exhausted and rests in the same 100°F temperature in the shade during the day cuts their expected survival time to 5.5 days! See why rationing labor is so important?

Many desert safety instructors, myself included, recommend at *least* one gallon per person per day at temperatures under 100°F during moderate hikes. This is for drinking only, and does not include needs such as cooking freeze-dried food. The problem is compounded by the fact that water weighs about eight pounds per gallon, and the more you carry the more you sweat. The one gallon rule is only a guideline. Individuals will vary in their needs. This is a good reason to start desert excursions at moderate temperatures and exertion levels, until you find your personal needs.

As temperature rises, or if work is performed, water needs go upward at alarming rates. As the body loses water, the ability for rational thinking is greatly diminished. I could relate several accounts of people doing very strange things when dehydrated.

Most people are aware that the normal body core temperature is 98.6°F, but many do not know that the average skin temperature is 92°F. Once the skin exceeds this temperature, it will start producing sweat to cool the body. There are ways to keep skin temperature below 92°F and decrease water loss. Try to sit in the shade and exposed to any breezes if possible. It is important not to sit on the hot ground or rocks, as these will often be hotter than the ambient air temperature. If possible, sit in the shade on something that allows air circulation under you.

Save safe water sources for internal use. If you have a suspect source of water, it can be used to wet the skin or clothes. While it sounds disgusting, urine has been used for this purpose. It may smell offensive, but urine from healthy people is usually fairly sterile. I carry a biodegradable disposable diaper in my twenty-four-hour rescue pack, after hearing about a trick used during the Gulf War. These diapers will hold water without spilling it, and can be used to sponge down the body both for cooling and sanitation.

Limiting physical exercise will also conserve body fluids both from perspiration and respiration. Always try to gauge the amount of water to be expended for each chore. I have armchair experts tell me all the time that you should dig down to damp soil and bury yourself to stay cool. How much sweat would you lose in the effort? What if you didn't reach damp soil? In my area you would be covering yourself with hot rocks! The same goes for ideas like solar stills. Will you regain the amount of water you sacrificed in the effort? You should think of these things now, because one of the results of dehydration is an addled mental state. Eating will

Dehydration Dementia

Both poor planning and the psychological effects of dehydration are illustrated with the story of a young man who attempted a day hike to a prominent mountain ten miles away with only a can of soda. As with many persons not used to the desert, he had greatly underestimated the distance. With his measly twelve-ounce can of caffeine and sugar—which cost him more water to process than his body absorbed—he became dehydrated far short of his goal. After his mother reported him missing, his car was spotted along the shoulder of the highway. Before he was found, completely addled, his adventure included taking off all of his clothes, eating ants, and being chased around a pasture by a bull. A rule of thumb among SAR personnel in the urgency of search is, "Down in twelve hours and dead in twenty-four." In hot desert climates, this is optimistic if the victim does not understand the problems of dehydration.

be another consideration. Digestion uses water, and so does the expulsion of its waste products. Eating now could cause you to use more water than you really needed, which could cause a shortage later. If I were near a good water supply and had a means of purification, I would consider eating. Most of us, however, would benefit from a reasonable fast. Some books counsel that it is okay to eat high carbohydrate foods, as water is produced during its digestion. This water is not metabolized, however, so do not eat carbos, either. There is a lot of difference between a human and a kangaroo rat who metabolizes all of its water from food!

Beware of diuretics such as alcohol and caffeinated drinks. A cold beer will take more water to flush it out than it puts in. The same goes for coffee, caffeinated sodas, and, to a lesser extent, tea. Beverages can be put in your car radiator or on yourself for cooling down. Be careful not to apply strong alcoholic drinks to dehydrated skin, as you will absorb it. Also know that dousing yourself with a soft drink will not only make you a sticky mess, but a magnet for swarms of insects. Remember, no matter how enticing that beer in the ice chest is, it will do nothing for clear decisions. Save it to share with your friendly SAR team back at their base camp.

Sports drinks also have their perils. These are excellent to replace salts and electrolytes, but they also tend to numb the sensation for thirst. Many people do not drink enough water as it is, and will drink less with these beverages. I like Gatorade at about half-strength solution. This helps replace electrolytes, but will not completely kill thirst sensations. Powdered electrolyte drinks store well and help flavor unpalatable water.

It is very important to drink enough in hot climates. Sometimes you must force yourself to drink. Rationing water has led to numerous deaths from bad decisions, and people have often been found dead with water in their canteens. It must be inside you to do any good. An archeologist friend of mine was trying to save water to stay longer at a remote desert site when he doubled over with a severe pain across the lower abdomen. His water rationing plan had caused kidney stones!

There are some simple ways to monitor your physical water and salt needs. You should be able to urinate clearly twice a day with little odor. With heat-related victims, our local medics will try to catch urine from a patient on a bandana and smell it to determine the extent of dehydration. If sweat gets into your eyes, and does not sting, you may need salt, which also has problems. A friend of mine monitors her salt loss by occasionally tasting the skin on her arms for salt residue.

Many people are concerned about too much salt in their diet, and take this attitude to the desert. We often eat the same foods as our grandparents who labored outside, while we do brain work in air-conditioned offices, leading to excessive sodium in the diet. When we get put out in the desert and get physically stressed, we need salt or we will suffer muscle cramps and metabolic disorders. The way we take salt is important. First, we must have adequate water for salt to be effective. I have worked places where they hand out salt tablets to take. This is dangerous because some people will take them with just a sip of water. Salt intake demands a good amount of water, or it will actually speed dehydration. Be well hydrated before taking salt.

Two major enemies to a person in risk of dehydration are vomiting and diarrhea. Diarrhea can be caused by ingesting poisons, unaccustomed foods, or microbes. If there is plenty of water to keep rehydrated, diarrhea is not so critical, since the water passes through the body and some of it does get to vital organs. Vomiting is another concern, no matter the reason. Even if you have an unlimited supply of water, vomiting prohibits it from being ingested, and dehydration will result quickly. Medicines from the first-aid kit or eating charcoal can help in both these situations. A lump of coal from the fire, preferably hardwood, can be powdered and mixed with water to drink to stop diarrhea or vomiting caused by ingesting toxins. It is important to use black charcoal, as the white campfire ashes can be caustic.

There are some myths to shoot down about water intake: (1) "Cold water is metabolized faster." Wrong—and neither is hot water. Water must be within a few degrees of body temperature before it leaves the stomach. (2) "Sip water or you'll get stomach cramps." If you drink a large amount at first, it can cause problems, even vomiting, but sipping will not help. Sipping water does not get it to your brain and other vital organs. Instead, cells of lesser importance pirate it away. Drink enough at first so that it gets to your core organs and brain and drink more after the stomach can accommodate it. (3) "Putting a smooth pebble under your tongue decreases thirst." Even if it did, would it be a good idea? Why not drink the water your body needs? Perhaps if you had no water it would be okay, but not as a means to ration.

Medication and Dehydration

Of additional concern are the effects of some drugs and medications on water loss. Some drugs, such as for high blood pressure or dieting, are diuretics, and greatly increase urine output. Other drugs, called diaphoretics, increase sweating or other secretions. These can all promote dehydration. Some drugs, such as tetracycline, can cause the skin and eyes to become extremely sensitive to sunlight. In May of 1997 a group of illegal aliens in the Big Bend were returning to Mexico on foot, hiking cross-country. Although the men were well acclimated and used to the temperature and terrain, one of them collapsed and died. Law enforcement officials found some pills on him that were not identified. His partners said they were for "energy." It is believed that whatever the pills were, they accelerated dehydration and killed the man.

PURIFICATION

There are three ways to make biologically contaminated water safe to drink: boiling, chemicals, and filters. These will not make chemically contaminated water safe. If you have a way to purify water, use it.

Chemical means are the most convenient and can be included in small survival kits. These usually are in the form of tablets or crystals that are dissolved in water that is allowed to set for a specified period of time. When selecting the type, make sure it will kill the protozoa *Giardia lamblia*, which can cause fatal diarrhea. Be sure to carefully follow the instructions provided with the brand you select. Also make sure the chemicals are kept in date. Chemicals, in date or not, will alter the taste of the water, and not for the better. Drink it anyway.

Potassium permanganate from the survival kit can be used to purify water. Only two or three crystals per quart are needed. The water should be tinted a light pink. Be sure to let it sit for at least twenty minutes. If you fill a canteen or water bottle by dipping it in a water source, after chemicals are added and the water has set, place the cap on loosely and shake the container to allow some of the treated water to get on the threads and where your mouth is going to touch. If you don't do this, untreated water on the lip of the container will be ingested, and all of your purification procedure will have been wasted.

Boiling is the most effective way to make water biologically safe. Water boiled for ten minutes at low altitudes and twenty minutes at higher altitudes will kill harmful microbes. This will leave the water flat tasting, but this can be remedied by pouring from one container to another several times.

There are many mechanical filters on the market with a wide range of prices. None are really compact enough to be carried in a belt kit, but they are very handy for vehicles and are the preferred purification system of many backpackers and do not negatively change the taste of the water. Once again, buy one that guarantees to be effective against *Giardia*. Some even have activated charcoal filters for certain types of chemical contamination.

It is a good idea to strain or filter the water before using any of these methods, to remove dirt and debris. Using a clean cloth will help, but there are also improvised methods that work. Using a sock or plastic bag with a small hole on one corner, fill with a layer of sand, and a layer of charcoal from the fire on top and let the water trickle through it into a container. This helps remove particles that may shield microbes from sterilization and makes it more appetizing to drink.

Chemical contamination is another problem altogether. I feel this is the only time that the solar still has a truly valuable application, as it can be used to distill some forms of chemically contaminated water. I had a woman argue with me about using a common biological filter to purify water from the Rio Grande. The Rio Grande has been called the most polluted river in North America, with everything from sewage and pesticides to heavy metals found in it. This person's filter would have made it biologically safe, but would have left the chemical pollutants intact. In addition, some of our creeks near local silver mines have been contaminated with cyanide that was used to process the ore years ago.

In some parts of the Southwest, natural chemical contamination, such as arsenic springs, occur. We don't have such serious problems on my turf, but some creeks have a high level of epsomite, a naturally occurring form of Epsom salts. Needless to say, it's great to soak your feet in, but will be a laxative if taken internally. Some people turn up their nose at pools with algae and aquatic insects. Remember, water is life, especially in the desert. I fear pools with no life.

What if you have no means of purification? If you are in dire straits with no water reserves, you will need to take the risk. In order to be treated for contaminated water, you must survive to get to the hospital. My coworkers once helped three men who, though sitting at a beautiful spring, were afraid to drink the water and were approaching dehydration. They were six miles from their car. They could easily have drank the water, been to their car in three hours, and seen a doctor for prophylactic treatment. Instead, they were going to risk death by dehydration before drinking the water. I would not have given much thought to drinking from that particular spring.

If you can, it is still a good idea to filter the water even if you have no means of sterilizing. This will get out the bigger organic pieces. If you find it necessary to drink unpurified water, take comfort in the fact that there is a good chance you will have no ill effects, and even if there is a biological problem, it will take up to two to three days to incubate.

LOCATING AND ACQUIRING WATER

The ability to spot water sources in the desert is worth more than all the neat little survival tricks ever written about. First, you should be aware of unintentional traps to catch you dry. Maps of arid land are often crossed with washes identified as creeks and dotted with springs, tanks, troughs, and windmills. These do not necessarily have water. The creeks and springs are often intermittent and run only after rain. Many windmills, tanks, and troughs are included as *landmarks*, not water sources. We have a saying here, "If you fall in the creek, get up, dust yourself off, and go on." Conversely, people have walked past springs marked as such with a sign, and died of dehydration.

Hold Your Water

It is important to keep whatever water you drink in your stomach. While in Australia, we were forced to collect water at billabongs (waterholes) with a brackish flavor. One had a dead kangaroo at its edge and another had a dead sheep on a rock isolated out in the pool. Although we purified the water, it was not often palatable, and twice I had to fight off nausea after leaving the water source to keep what I had inside me.

Don't go psychosomatic and start vomiting. I met one of my customers on a train in Mexico enjoying a drink in the dining car. He told me he was safe, drinking straight scotch on the rocks. I reminded him the ice was suspect, and within an hour he was complaining of cramps, nausea, and sure he was coming down with tourista. I explained it was too early for Montezuma's revenge, and that his discomfort was his imagination or from not drinking scotch neat, as it should be.

ARTIFICIAL SOURCES

Because of ranching, even in deserts, it is very possible to come across windmills, pumps, pipelines, tanks, and troughs. All of these may be sources of large amounts of water. Because wells are usually isolated from people and animals, most are biologically safe. Small animals do sometimes fall down the well casing and die, so you should purify this water if possible. Always try to collect artificial water at the source. Artificial water sources will generally be chemically safe, though not necessarily palatable. Even as we go into the twenty-first century, the nineteenth-century windmill still provides a reliable water source.

WINDMILLS

Windmills are easy to spot, but they can be deceiving. They can be seen in the distance, spinning away, and upon your arrival, be pumping dust. There are, however, a few quick methods to fix a windmill. First, find out if the windmill is on a well or is a booster mill. Booster mills are set on pipelines to boost water along, usually up a steep incline. If there is no nearby storage tank with a pipe or hose going to it from the mill, and the bottom of the mill is covered with boards, sheet metal, or has a trap door, take a look. There may be a small reservoir under the cover from which the mill sucks the water and compresses it into the pipe to "boost" it along. If the reservoir is dry, look for a float valve, which will look like one in a toilet tank, only larger. This may be wired up to shut it off. If so, free it and let it drop. You may hear air rushing at first and then see some cruddy, rusty water, followed by better water. If nothing comes out in a few minutes, the line is inoperable and there is nothing you can do.

If a windmill is located over a well pumping into a storage tank, your options are increased. Windmills require a lot of service, and active ones can often be identified by fresh grease on the polish rod (see diagrams for windmill anatomy), discarded oil cans and grease cartridges, and perhaps tools left on site for maintenance. The first thing to determine is if the brake is off. If the brake is on, the tail will be folded next to the fan, to turn it out of the wind. The brake will be a lever or windlass at the base of the tower. Releasing the brake will let the tail extend perpendicular to the fan, and turn it

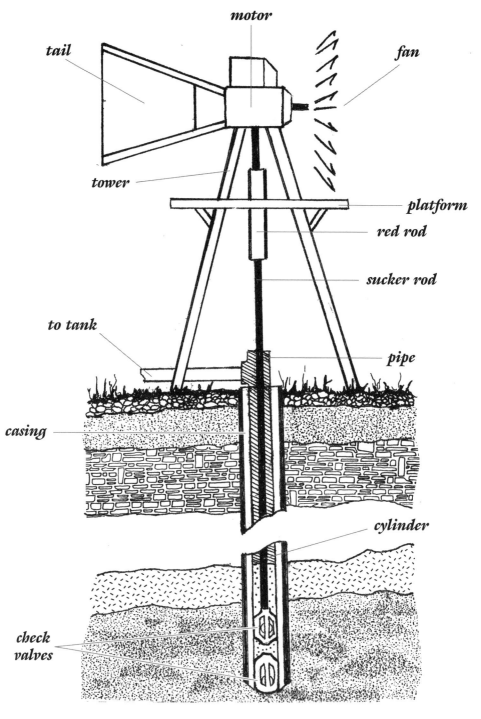

motor

tail

fan

tower

platform

red rod

sucker rod

to tank

pipe

casing

cylinder

check
valves

Windmill anatomy.

into the wind. If there is a strong enough wind, the fan will start turning, and if the mill is operational, water should surface within a few minutes. Be advised, however, that the word "if" was invented specifically for windmills.

If the brake is released, but there is not enough wind to turn the fan, it may be possible to turn it by hand. If it is a very large fan, the well is probably very deep, and you may not have the strength to turn the fan to haul a long column of water to the surface. Smaller fans can often be operated manually. You will first need to put a container on or under the flow pipe or tie a plastic bag from the survival kit over the pipe to catch the water. This obviously would work better with two people. Be very careful in climbing the tower. Some old wooden towers and ladders are rotten and waiting to crash to the ground with you. Some repair workers are lazy about putting braces back on steel towers, which creates further problems.

Windmill motors need periodic oiling, and through carelessness the ladder and platform may be coated with oil. Sometimes the platforms are rotten and have been shot up by vandals with guns, or attacked by woodpeckers. Test the platform carefully before committing your life to it. At the top of the tower it is best to take a length of strong rope to make a safety belt for yourself, like a electrical lineman. Loop it around the tower and tie it behind your back. Do not tie it to the tower! The brake must be off for the fan to engage, and should a wind come up you will need to be able to move freely out of the way. You may have to turn the fan a while to produce water, as the water column may rise less than one foot with each stroke. If water does come out, you may need to climb down and reposition your container to catch it, then climb back up to fill it. Remember, all this work is costing you water through perspiration and respiration. Because windmills are largely metal, very exposed, and well grounded, stay well away if an electrical storm threatens!

Sometimes you will find a mill turning in the wind, and nothing happening. This is usually a bad omen, but there are some things you can do that require little effort. Sometimes there is a pebble, dirt, or debris holding one of the check valves open at the bottom of the hole. Check valves look like cages with balls or thread spools in them that seal under pressure (see diagram). If the bottom check is stuck, the water will simply run back out the bottom of the pipe.

If the top check is stuck, it means the rods cannot lift the water to the surface. You can diagnose this by listening for the valves, which make a muffled buzz.

If you hold onto the rod where it comes out of the pipe, you should be able to hear a buzz on the upstroke and downstroke. If you only hear one stroke buzz, one of the checks may be stuck. There may be a hammer on site; if not, find a rock, pipe, or something else and rap sharply on the pipe—not the casing, which keeps the hole from collapsing. Do the same to the rod coming out of the pipe, but not too hard with wooden rods. This may dislodge the obstruction. Listen again for both check valves. If no buzz is heard at all, it probably means that a rod is broke down hole. If both checks are heard, but no water is being pumped, it most likely means there is a hole in the pipe or the leathers on the valves are not holding water. None of these can be readily fixed, but give the rods and pipe a few good whacks anyway, just for the satisfaction of it.

PUMPS AND PUMP JACKS

Sometimes you will encounter a pump and windmill combination—a hedge against windless days. If you see wires going down the hole, there is an electric submersible pump at the bottom. In this case there will usually be a power line to the well. Other setups have electric generators. Solar-powered submersibles are becoming very popular in remote parts of Mexico. You will need to locate the switch box on power lines, which is usually located on a power pole near the well. Turn the switch on. If nothing happens, you may need to reset the breakers or replace fuses, which are often found stored in the switch box. Be careful opening the box, as they are favored by venomous spiders and wasps.

The solar models will have photovoltaic panels wired to a battery bank. The switch will usually be located between the battery bank and the well. If the pump is connected to a generator, you will need to start the generator by a battery-powered starter, or manually, depending on the model. The switch may be directly on the generator, or between the power source and well. The generator may be run by gasoline, diesel, or LPG gas, and can require some tinkering to get running. Submersible pumps may also be found independent of windmills.

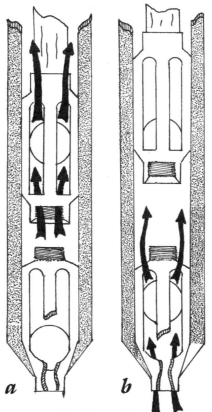

Check valves: *(a)* downstroke, *(b)* upstroke.

Pump jacks may be found alone on wells or in combination with a windmill. These also may be electrical, in which case it is a matter of finding a switch box or starting a generator. I have never seen a solar-powered pump jack. Other pump jacks will be powered by gas, diesel, or LPG. If they are found by themselves, there is usually nothing to do other than starting them, which may take some work with the internal combustion type. Pump jacks work down hole like a windmill, and the process for diagnosing and fixing stuck checks, broken rods, and holes in the pipe is the same as for a windmill.

If a pump jack is found in conjunction with a windmill, you may be in for some work. First, check to see if the jack or the mill is connected to the rods. If the pump jack is connected, then

Pump jack: *(a)* **walking beam,** *(b)* **horsehead,** *(c)* **bridle,** *(d)* **polish rod,** *(e)* **polish rod clamp,** *(f)* **engine or motor,** *(g)* **flywheel.**

proceed as above. If the windmill is connected, check the brake. If it is a windless day and the windmill is connected, you may want to try connecting the pump jack, which will require climbing up and down the tower at least twice if you are alone. Remember all safety measures when doing this.

First, give the pump jack a test run. There is no point in going through all this trouble to connect the pump jack only to find it won't start. If the pump is okay, turn it off and start your first climb with a stout piece of rope, chain, or wire. This stuff may be on site. Turn the fan until the rods reach full bottom stroke, and then turn it some more until the rods rise two inches. Tie the fan off securely to keep the rods in this position. This is necessary to keep the top check valve from hitting the bottom check and breaking the rods. Next, climb down the tower and manually turn the flywheel on the pump jack until the walking beam is on full bottom stroke. If it will not stay in this position, you will need to secure it with wire, rope, chains, etc.

For the next step you will most likely need tools such as crescent wrenches, which may be stashed somewhere on site. If the horse head is not on the walking beam, you will need to attach it. When the horse head is secure, attach the bridle to it and fit the polish rod clamp on the polish rod (the rod that comes out of the pipe or stuffing box). Take all the slack out of the bridle's cable, and tighten the clamp onto the polish rod. Above the polish rod will be the red rod, which is actually red sometimes. This will usually be a two-by-four board, or piece of pipe that is weaker than the rods. In case the rods jam, the red rod will break above ground and it will not be necessary to pull the rods and pipe. It is often painted red to be seen from a distance if it is broken.

Take your tools up the tower to where the polish and red rods meet and disconnect the red rod, tying it back out of the way to the tower. There will usually be a board laid across the tower braces to stand on while you do this. These are never wide enough and are usually rotten. Watch your step. Go to the top of the mill, untie the fan, then climb down and put the brake on. If you had to tie off the pump jack to keep it positioned, release it and start the pump jack. Pray, cross your fingers, and pull out any talismans you have. If water does not surface, listen to the checks and smack the pipe and rods with a rock. Good luck.

STORAGE TANKS, TROUGHS, AND PIPELINES

Chances are, if you find a serviceable mill or pump, there will already be water nearby in a storage tank or trough. Try to get your water directly from the flow pipe or storage tank. Even from the source, try to purify the water. Many livestock diseases are transmitted by saliva, and water troughs are a good place to contract them. If you come across a water trough on a pipeline that is dry, look to see if the float valve is tied up. If so, loosen it so that it drops and see if air or water comes out. Rushing air may mean water will shortly appear. Even if a trough looks clean, beware. Many troughs operate on the same pipeline, with water filling one and the overflow going down a pipe to fill the next.

In desert areas where freezing is not a problem, pipelines will be shallowly buried, or above ground. These can be followed to the source, storage tank, or trough. Sometimes along the way you may find a riser, which will be a small pipe connected to the line sticking up out of the ground. In high spots along the pipeline, risers are installed to release air. They often will have a plug in the end that will require a crescent wrench (which you most likely will *not* find stashed nearby), but sometimes will have a plain water faucet or pitcock like those found on gas lines. Opening a riser may create a bounty of water with little effort.

I am reluctant to talk about the next option. In places where
they use PVC (a hard plastic) pipe, it may be possible to break off a
riser or break the pipe itself with a large rock. This should be a last-
ditch measure only. You may solve your immediate water problem,
but you may not survive the wrath of the pipeline crew. Please don't
tell them I told you to do this. I could wind up being the Salman
Rushdie of the Chihuahuan Desert!

SPRING BOXES, DIRT TANKS, AND DAMS

Other artificial water sources include spring boxes, header dams,
guzzlers, and dirt tanks. A spring box is a natural spring with a box,
usually concrete or rock, built around it. These often have pipelines
running off them to troughs. The spring box will often be covered
to keep animals out, and this is where you should get your water
instead of the trough. Spring boxes may be filled with silt and
require cleaning to obtain water.

Header dams are large structures built across *arroyos* and creek
beds to catch rain runoff. Some have pipelines running from them
to troughs, while others allow direct access to animals. Guzzlers are
a smaller version of the header dam, sometimes only two or three
feet high, and are usually built to provide more wildlife habitat.
Animals have direct access to these.

Dirt tanks are usually big, built in drainages to collect rain
runoff, and are often shown on topographical maps. They are
scooped out by a bulldozer, and an earthen dam is built to hold the
water. These are nastier to drink out of than a lumberyard coffee

pot. Besides having mud bottoms, livestock wade out into them to drink, defecating and urinating in the process. If at all possible, filter and purify this sludge. I am really more afraid of human contamination than livestock, but dirt tanks can probably void your insurance.

CONDENSATION TECHNIQUES

What about the much heralded "survival tricks" for getting water through condensation? These usually include the solar still, reverse still, transpiration bags, and dew trap. First, let's talk realistically about the solar still. This is almost a cult item in survival lore. I have actually met people who have never made one heading out on long hikes with insufficient water expecting to use solar stills along the way. The way some survival books write them up, it is no wonder. Many books talk about solar stills in terms of maximum production under ideal conditions and do not discuss their failures.

You start a solar still by digging a hole approximately thirty-six inches in diameter and thirty-six inches deep in a location in full sunlight. It is best if damp dirt is found. You can put vegetation, urine, suspect water, etc. into the hole to evaporate moisture out of. A receptacle for water is placed in the center of the pit, with a six-by-six-foot piece of clear plastic sheeting spread over the top. The edges of the plastic are sealed airtight by piling dirt in a berm around the edges, and a smooth rock about the size of a golf ball is placed in the center above the receptacle, causing the plastic sheet to slant down toward the container.

The theory is, as the sun shines through the plastic, moisture from the ground, plants, and contaminated water evaporates in the greenhouse-type environment. As the vapor touches the plastic sheet, it is cooled and condenses on the inner surface, with the droplets running down the plastic to the low point where the rock is placed, dripping into the container. The result is purified water. Unfortunately, in practice the solar still usually falls far short of ideal conditions and maximum yields.

In every survival class I teach, we build a solar still. Even using shovels, we work up a sweat. Were you digging a hole a yard wide and a yard deep with a knife, digging stick, and your hands, the water loss would be considerable. We add chopped up prickly pear

Solar still.

cactus and dump about a pint of water in the hole to simulate urine before covering with plastic. The most we have ever salvaged was almost a quart in a day. The normal yield is about one cup. Some stills have provided absolutely no water at all.

Acknowledging that a person at rest is going to need about a gallon a day in arid lands, some authors have recommended building several stills. Consider this: For optimal performance you will need a sunny, hot day. The hole must be deep enough for the plastic to sag in at a steep angle or the droplets will fall off before reaching the point over the receptacle. You are going to dig several large holes with no guarantee of these providing more water than you sweat out, and not being at rest, your water needs will be higher.

Some defenders of solar stills say that failure is caused by the inability of the maker to properly construct one. Perhaps I fall into this category, but compared with my experimentation and earnest desire to make them work, can you imagine what happens when someone merely reads about stills and stakes their life on them? Before using them to carry less weight in water, find one of the books praising them and build one or two following their instructions exactly and see the results. If you decide I don't know what I'm talking about, please carry a larger sheet of plastic than the recommended six-by-six feet. That way, when we find you, we will have something to wrap you in so you won't smell so bad when we carry you out. There are times and conditions when I believe knowing how to make solar stills could be lifesaving, especially if the hard work was done at night or in cooler parts of the day. I do not recommend, however, that you depend on them instead of carrying sufficient water.

If you have plenty of water, but fear it is contaminated, a solar still can be an option. Containers of the suspect water can be placed in the pit (it still needs the same dimensions to work properly) with the receptacle in the center. The distilled water will not only be biologically safe, but free of most chemicals. Life rafts have special inflatable solar stills to desalinate water. You may want to experiment with one of these beforehand to see if they can be adapted to purifying chemically contaminated water. One thing I would not try to distill would be water from the radiator with coolants or antifreeze in it. These often have complex alcohols that are toxic. The alcohol can evaporate and condense with the water and still be harmful.

An easier way to distill suspect water is with the reverse still. This is done by pounding a stick into the ground, either in a puddle of suspect water or placing containers of bad water or chopped vegetation around the stake. The clear plastic is placed over the stick and allowed to hang like a tent. The edges of the plastic are rolled inward, being careful not to contact the impure water. The edges are sealed with dirt. The vapor also condenses on the inside of the plastic, but this time runs down to the edges and is caught in the rolls. By carefully lifting the edges, the water can be collected on one side and poured into a wide-mouthed container. I have had only limited success with the reverse still as well, but it requires much less exertion than digging a solar still.

Dew traps work in the opposite manner of stills. In this technique the plastic is spread in the bottom of a hole or depression, and smooth clean rocks are placed on top of it. At night the rocks cool, and moisture in the air condenses on them. Take the water out of the plastic by morning, or it will start to evaporate. Unless you need to dig a hole, this method requires minimal work. It can also be made in a cardboard box or similar containers. Water may also condense on your vehicle, and can be squeegeed off into a container with a credit card or like object.

Transpiration bags require the least work of the condensation techniques. This is where clear plastic bags, the bigger the better, are tied over vegetation. Plastic sheeting may be used if the edges are gathered up and tied like a bag. Plants also have respiration in which moisture is lost. The transpiration bag prevents this moisture from escaping and causes it to condense on the bag's inner surface. The

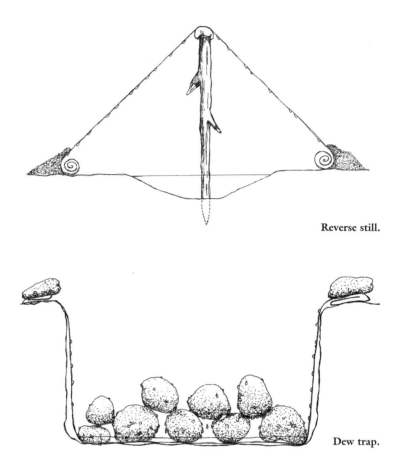

Reverse still.

Dew trap.

bag should be in full sunlight, and the branch should be tied down so the bag is drooping and not causing the droplets to run out the tied end. Mature trees with large root systems will give the best yields. Using paper, cloth, or plastic as a gasket in the mouth of the bag helps get an airtight seal. Water collects in the bottom corner of the bag. The upper corner may be punctured and then pulled down to drain the water. Tie off the corner when done and let the original corner droop. This will keep from disturbing the bag.

My best successes with transpiration bags have been up to two cups of water a day on cottonwoods and willows. It may take a lot of bags to get your gallon a day, but transpiration bags take much less sweat to place than digging solar stills. The water may not be biologically safe, as the bag is full of organic matter. And do not place the bag over poisonous plants, as the plant in the steamy environment may release toxins.

While I am skeptical of most condensation techniques, you should have plastic sheeting and bags in larger kits. In the event of rain, sheeting can be placed in a depression and weighted with rocks to catch water. It can also be used for shelter and waterproofing. Plastic bags are great emergency water containers, with several other applications. If you are alone and trying to turn a windmill by hand, tying one on the flow pipe will simplify how you catch the water. Another good trick is that if your vehicle is disabled, but the engine is still running, a plastic bag, clear or any other kind, can be tied onto the air conditioner's runoff tube or hose to collect the water that condenses and drips out.

NATURAL WATER SOURCES AND LOCATION TECHNIQUES

Desert water sources may consist of rivers, creeks, springs, catch basins, *playa* lakes, and *tinajas*. These may be as ephemeral as the rains; in many cases their presence is determined by local precipitation. It is always a good idea to check into water sources before preparing a backcountry trip. Most parks will have current information on water availability. Do not rely on maps, hearsay, or the

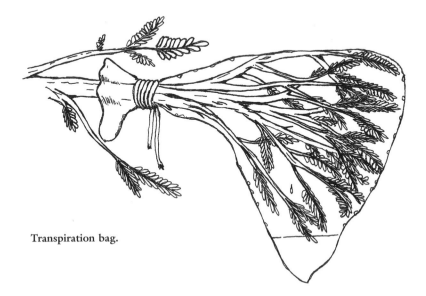

Transpiration bag.

information of someone who was there a few months ago. There can be situations where you are stranded in unfamiliar territory and will need to locate water on your own. Plants, animals, geology, and topography are means to locate water.

PLANTS AS INDICATORS AND SOURCES

An unusual green patch of vegetation is often an indicator that water is at or near the surface. Look for verdant plants in low areas, creek beds, or along mountainsides or cliffs showing different rock strata. Vegetation may also indicate some artificial water sources. Desert plants that make good indicators are cottonwoods, true willows, desert willows, seepwillows, ash, and introduced species such as retama (*Parkisonia aculeata*), tree tobacco (*Nicotiana glauca*), and salt cedar (*Tamarix spp.*). Large mesquites may indicate water, but due to their very deep root systems, it may not be near the surface.

Mature cottonwoods need upward of fifty gallons of water a day, and indicate water is close to the surface. Because of their water usage, cottonwoods also can affect the amount of water on the surface. The trees suck up water in the cool of the morning and release it midafternoon. Seep springs located at the base of cottonwoods may reflect this by not having surface water in the morning, and rising in the afternoon as the water is released. At any rate, water is usually close to the surface and can be reached with a little digging. Some other plants do the opposite, taking in water during the heat of the day and releasing it at night.

Much has been written about exploiting plants, especially barrel cacti, for water. The Hollywood scene goes like this: The dying cowboy crawls across the burning sands, delirious, with mirages ahead and impatient buzzards above. Making his way to a barrel cactus (usually in the genera *Ferocactus* or *Echinocactus*), he hacks off the top of the plant and mashes the inner pulp to free large quantities of water, disappointing his buzzard escort. One military manual I read went as far as to say that if the "cap" was replaced, the cactus would survive this treatment.

The main problem with this idea is that the water may contain chemicals that are extremely unpalatable or cause vomiting or diarrhea. As we shall see later in Chapter 9, some cacti flesh is toxic or causes hallucinations. While I have no personal experience, the liquid from the famous saguaro (*Carnegiea gigantea*) is reputedly toxic or at the very least extremely unpalatable. Barrel cacti may provide water, but I caution against using them except as a last resort. Some are over two hundred years old, and I question if putting the top back on them would result in their healing most of the time. Please do not cut them open just out of curiosity.

It Seemed Like a Good Idea at the Time . . .

A plant that has tragic consequences on desert springs is the salt cedar. These vegetational spring maggots were introduced by the U.S. government in the late 1800s and early 1900s to stop erosion, which they do quite well. Invading springs and creeks, they suck up huge amounts of water and dissipate it in the air, producing nothing more than a wood that, when burned, smells like someone urinated on the fire. The large output of water through the leaves does make it a good candidate for transpiration bags. While salt cedars may form a green stand in otherwise dry scenery, they may lower the water in a spring to such a point that it is unobtainable. Problem solved—no water, no erosion! Thanks guys.

ANIMALS AS INDICATORS

The movements of domestic and wild animals may be used to find water. Most larger animals will go to water morning and evening. Observing their direction of travel during these times can lead to water. Livestock, especially cattle, need large amounts of water daily. Cattle are not good at finding water themselves, and must be taken to it when they are put in unfamiliar pastures. If cattle are seen, water is near. It is merely a matter of following their tracks and manure to the source.

Wild and domestic animal trails often converge on routes heading to water. The trails combine at acute angles, just like freeway on-ramps. You don't need to be a tracker to follow such trails to water. Some animals not only can locate subsurface water, but they will actually dig it up for you. Javelinas (usually called collared peccaries by biologists) often will dig into dry creek beds, exposing subsurface water. Equines are very adept at smelling water, with burros (or "donkeys" for the Spanish impaired) seeming to be the best, over horses and mules. In some areas of the Southwest and much of Mexico, feral burros are responsible for digging water holes to the benefit of wildlife and the occasional human in trouble. When following equines, however, be aware that they often travel long distances to water. It is always a good idea to purify this water to diminish the chance of catching saliva-transmitted disease from these animals.

Birds are another way to get a general direction to water. Insect- and seed-eating birds may be seen flying to water in the early morning and late evening. Doves are especially useful in this category. Raptors and carrion eaters are not reliable indicators, as they do not water with the regularity of other birds, and often are solitary in nature. Remember that birds have the ability to go directly to water, whereas you may find yourself hindered by rough terrain or thorny vegetation while pursuing them.

RIVERS AND CREEKS

Desert people once respected rivers as the lifeblood of an arid ecosystem, and built whole cultures on their banks. Now many of them are used as waste dumps and sewers. Dams cross our desert rivers to divert the waters for important projects such as golf courses. Some desert rivers no longer reach the sea. Damn the dams. When found, the river will often create what is called "the green belt," with a diversity of plants not found on the arid terraces. Besides being a constant water supply (try to purify), desert rivers are often recreation areas for activities such as rafting. Your deliverance may be upstream and heading your way.

Creeks may or may not have surface water. Dry creek beds are often called *arroyos* in Spanish, and the Arabic term *wadi* is coming into popular usage after the Gulf War. What appears to be a dry creek bed, however, may harbor water. The sands and gravels found in most desert creek beds often allow water to pass through them, with the water table fluctuating with recent rain. In some places the creek will cross layers of water-impermeable rock or clay, forcing the water to the surface. Look for green vegetation in these areas and places where animals have dug. Rock outcroppings are another place to look. Generally speaking, the further downstream you go, the more likely you will find water.

It may be possible to dig to water. Look for a bend in the creek bed and dig on the outside, or concave curve. This is where the water current cuts deepest, and will be the last part to dry up. If there is a *cutbank* at this point, survey it well and dig carefully so it will not collapse on you. If you have not reached damp sand or gravel by two feet, especially if you are digging without a shovel, it is best to abandon the effort. Remember, ration sweat. If water is found, it may take a while for the hole to fill, and the water may be silty. If you do not have a way to extract the water from the hole, clarify, and then purify it, you can take a piece of cloth, like a shirt, and place it in the hole, which will force much of the silt to the bottom. Putting prickly pear pulp in the water is a Mexican trick for settling the silt. You are unlikely to drink the hole dry, as you are likely in a subsurface flow; but it may be necessary to wait for the hole to fill up.

Many survival books advise that following water courses will eventually lead to civilization. This may apply to most places, but in many deserts, water courses lead to huge barren basins, with dry, salt-encrusted lake beds.

Finding water in dry creek beds. Digging in gravel in the concave sides of binds, as indicated by arrows, may yield water.

SPRINGS

Springs occur when the ground surface intersects the water table. This may happen in creek beds, canyons, valleys, low depressions, or even on the sides of mountains and mesas. Springs rely on precipitation and often disappear in dry times. That a spring is named on a map is no guarantee it has water. Gullible hikers have died to prove this.

Springs often occur when a layer of water carrying rock or sediments, called a "permeable layer," is exposed to the surface. Examples of permeable layers are porous sandstones, fractured granite, limestone with joints, and loose gravels. Often a permeable layer overlies, or is sandwiched between, "impermeable layers" that do not allow water to pass through their structures. Examples of impermeable layers are shale and clay. While clay is porous, the water adheres to its tiny particles and free flow does not occur.

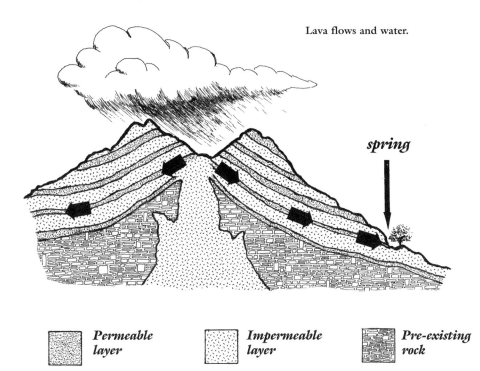

Lava flows and water.

spring

Permeable layer	Impermeable layer	Pre-existing rock

When permeable layers are sandwiched between impermeable layers, there is a lateral movement of water. In some parts of the Southwest, alternating layers of sandstone and shale are exposed on the sides of mesas, with water exiting via the sandstone layer. This is often indicated by green plants growing along the permeable strata. The water will sometimes pool at the base of the mesa.

Lavas can also create alternating permeable and impermeable layers. When lava flows, the outside cools faster than the interior of the flow, which forms a "skin" similar to molten wax cooling. This skin is often fractured, making a permeable layer. The interior of the flow cools much slower, making for a cohesive rock that excludes water. Subsequent eruptions and lava flows create alternating permeable and impermeable layers. As volcanic structures erode, the original vent may become a large basin and catch rainfall, channeling water into the permeable layers that are exposed elsewhere, forming springs.

Ways to find springs are to look for greenery in low-lying areas, along slopes or escarpments with stratified rock, along creek beds crossing bedrock, and at dikes and sills.

DIKES AND SILLS

Sometimes magma pushing its way to the surface will find or create a vertical fissure, intersecting previously existing layers of rock. When the magma cools in this fissure, it becomes an intrusive formation known as a "dike." Many times the dike is harder than the surrounding rock, and as time goes by, the softer rock erodes away, leaving a wall of rock, or dike, running across the desert. Some people find it humorous to have dikes in the desert, but sometimes they can be a vertical impermeable structure holding back water—in other words, a dike. Sometimes a creek has cut down through a dike, making a gap in the wall. Often digging on the upstream of the dike will expose water. However, as in the concave banks of creeks, do not dig far if promising damp sediments are not found. Sometimes dikes channel water *down* for hundreds of feet.

Sills occur when magma pushes its way between existing layers of rock. As the magma cools, it forms a horizontal intrusive formation that may be impermeable to water. Water may flow through permeable rock on top of the sill, and come to the surface where the sill is exposed, usually on a canyon or valley wall.

TOPOGRAPHY

It is often possible to locate natural water sources by surveying the terrain from a good vantage point or using a topographical map. Starting 24 million years ago, the American Southwest underwent a stretching of the earth's crust called the Basin and Range Extension. The result was massive earthquakes that dropped huge blocks of land and pushed up others, exposing the rock strata. This formed the Basin and Range Province, with its famous mesas and plateaus separated by broad low areas called basins.

As previously discussed, the sides of these mesas and plateaus may expose permeable layers to water. Water may also be found in the old fault lines at the base of these mesas, plateaus, and canyon walls. Close or convergent lines on a topographical map indicate a steep slope or vertical face, which not only may expose permeable layers, but also may indicate old fault lines. In some areas there were parallel fault lines where the land between them dropped, creating a "graben," which is German for grave. These areas, when located between mountain ranges, are called "bolsons," the Spanish term

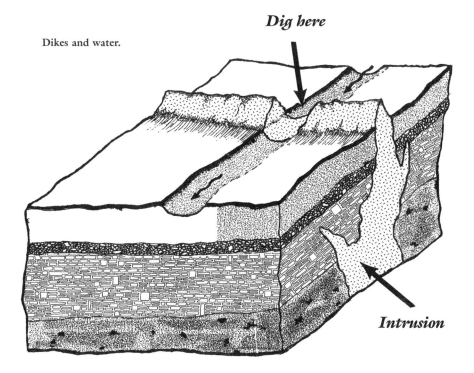

Dikes and water.

Dig here

Intrusion

for a large pocket. These areas may also collect water, but they may be miles across. Learning to read a topographical map will help you to identify possible catch basins or depressions holding water.

PLAYA LAKES

In some American deserts mountain ranges are separated by broad low basins called playas. These often collect water from intermittent creeks or rivers that flow into the basin with no outlet. This results in playa lakes, which can be very wide shallow bodies of water, or completely dry depending on the amount of recent rainfall. Because there is no outlet, the water from playa lakes may be extremely salty and undrinkable without distillation. The Spanish word *playa* (pronounced PLY-uh) means beach. Usually, playa lakes have a lot of beach and very little lake.

CATCH BASINS

This is a term used more by ranchers than geologists, but it indicates a natural depression that catches and holds rainwater. Some have drainages such as creeks feeding them (a smaller version of a playa lake), while others are broad depressions that collect rain at their lowest spot. Some examples, such as calderas, can be quite large. Calderas, Spanish for "cauldron," occur when there is a collapse. This often occurs after a volcano has spent its internal pressure, causing it to collapse in upon itself, making a depression. These may be completely ringed by mountains, making a large catch basin. These can also be identified with topographical maps.

TINAJAS

Tinaja (tee-NA-ha) is a widely used Spanish term for a waterhole or pocket. Tinajas are usually cut in solid rock by flash floods from heavy rains carrying sand and gravel as an abrasive, gouging pockets in the rock that may be less than a foot deep to very deep and wide pools. After the brief flood, the water left in these pockets are called tinajas, and are probably the most common water source in many deserts. Tinajas are often consistent enough to be named on maps, but they do have their shortcomings.

They may be dry, like any other desert water source. If found containing water, that water will be almost certainly stagnant, often with a good covering of algae. This can often be cleared away by tossing a shirt on it and slowly pulling to one side. Purification is highly recommended for water from a tinaja.

Getting water from a tinaja can be another problem. The same abrasive action that creates the tinaja can also polish the rock smooth as glass. Many tinajas are located below a lip in a creek bed, and at times of low water, the tinaja may be hard to reach. Tinajas readily trap animals that have gone down to get a drink, and they may drown or starve trying to get out. In these cases it may be prudent to lower an article of clothing down into the water on a rope or cord, and wring it out into a container.

Even if a tinaja is easy to enter, it may not be prudent to bathe in one. Although hygiene is important in survival situations, stagnant water can harbor harmful organisms. There is an increasing incidence of swimmers getting amoebic meningitis from still pools. Most people are also unaware that even desert water sources can have leeches.

There are some precautions as how to use water sources in the desert. The Apache never camped directly adjacent to a spring because they realized that animals also depended on it. Unless in critical circumstances, that is a good example to follow. Even if soap is labeled as biodegradable, do not use it directly in a water source. It is not intended to be left in a water source and can alter the delicate life in the water. Take the water away and dump it a good distance from the source. Never contaminate the water with human waste, food scraps, grease, and the like. Water is life. In the desert, water is your life.

5 Fire

Thank God I found a burning tree, and in the warmth of it
I passed the cold of that night. In the morning, loading myself with sticks,
and taking two brands with me, I returned to seek them [the Indians].
In this manner I wandered for five days, ever with my fire and load;
for if the wood had failed me where none could be found, as many parts
are without any, though I might have sought sticks elsewhere,
there would have been no fire to kindle them.

—Alvar Núñez Cabeza de Vaca, *The Narrative of Cabeza de Vaca,* 1542

While water is the first need in desert environments, fire-making is the skill that requires the greatest practice, especially when primitive techniques are used. A good fire will depend on proper selection of tinder and fuel, preparation, ignition, and building to economize fuel and labor. American Indians and Australian Aborigines were often critical of Europeans who built large fires to "roast on one side and freeze on the other." A look at primitive desert fire designs will help in survival situations. A fire is built with tinder, kindling, and fuel. An ignition source starts tinder burning, which lights small kindling, which in turn produces enough heat to ignite larger fuel to maintain a fire.

TINDER

Tinder is usually fine solid material that is loosely compacted, allowing for air space and causing easy combustion. For our purposes, flammable liquids and gases may also be considered tinder. Artificial tinder sources from survival kits include cotton balls, alcohol wipes, and candles. Natural sources of tinder in the desert include bird and mice nests, the stringy inner bark of cottonwood and juniper trees, and the old fibers from the leaves of the agaves and yuccas. Dried grasses also make good tinder. When starting a fire, especially with primitive means, make sure you have an ample and thoroughly dry tinder supply.

Quick fires can be started with gasoline and lantern fuels. Extreme care must be exercised when using flammable liquids. White gas, used to burn in many lanterns and camp stoves, is volatile at cool temperatures, and explosive in hot desert climates. Many moustaches and eyebrows have been instantly groomed by using white gas. Gasoline from the vehicle must also be used with extreme caution.

KINDLING

Kindling is smaller wood ranging from toothpick size up to an inch in diameter. Almost any dry wood can be used, but *quiotes* are often available and the right size. These can be shaved into a fuzz stick for easier ignition. Bark from the base of old ocotillos has a natural wax and will burn for quite a while. It is easily lit with a match. Kindling must be available and near the tinder and properly arranged to start burning as soon as the tinder is lit.

FUEL

Fuel is what maintains a long-term fire and is usually large wood. When signals are needed, motor oil, car seats, or spare tires might be used. In days gone by, dried buffalo dung was used in treeless areas. Cattle have replaced bison, and some ranches still use "meadow muffins" to fuel their branding fires, combining nostalgia with recycling.

Hardwoods burn longer and produce hotter coals, but give off less light than softwoods. Mesquite, acacias, oak, ash, and ironwood are excellent hardwoods available in many desert locales. Softwoods give better light for signaling at night and keeping animals away, but more fuel is needed, as they burn faster. Cottonwood and willows are good sources. As a rule, coals are best for baking and roasting, while flames are better for boiling.

You may want to collect both kinds of wood, keeping hardwood coals alive and ready to throw softwood on if needed. You may not have the advantage of an axe or saw and will need to collect downed wood or break off branches. Larger logs and branches need not be

Star fire.

cut and placed on the fire. Place one end into the fire and feed it into the fire as it burns. Remember to conserve energy by conserving your fuel. Keeping a good bed of coals will save relighting a fire.

IGNITION

Friction, concentrated heat, or chemical combustion are three methods available in survival situations to start a fire. Some igniters can be carried in the survival kit. Matches are an obvious source, but other means may be preferable, in order to save matches for when a quick fire is needed. The magnesium bar and flint is an excellent ignition tool. A knife is used to scrape magnesium shavings off the bar into a pile about the size of a dime. Holding the flint-striking insert over the pile, the edge of the knife is sharply scraped down, sending a shower of sparks onto the shavings, igniting them into a hot but brief flame. Tinder must be quickly added. It can be a problem on windy days to keep the shavings in one pile, but if you turn over rocks (being careful about uncovering scorpions, snakes, etc.), you may find insect or spider webs that you can scrape the bar over, which will hold the shavings together. The magnesium bar is very hard to use at night, but the striking insert may be used to signal with.

A magnifying glass can be used to start an ember with old charcoal, softwood, or, my favorite, rabbit droppings. The strip magnifier from the survival kit, or the lens from a binocular or a camera is used to focus the sun's rays into a fine dot to ignite the material. Some compass baseplates also have magnifying glasses. I have read about using a drop of water on a prescription eyeglass lens or a bottle with water in it to do this, but have never been successful with either method. The surface of the tinder needs to be fairly smooth to get a fine focus. This is why rabbit, goat, deer, or antelope droppings work so well. The "pellet" is placed in a nest of tinder, and the magnifying glass is focused until the dung starts to smoke. By slowly moving the dot into wider circles, a good ember will form that can be blown on to ignite the other tinder. Carnivore dung does not make a good ember and stinks to high heavens. Obviously, the magnifying glass is not good for overcast days or nighttime.

Potassium permanganate and sugar from the survival kit can be combined to start a fire. Mixing the two ingredients half and half into a pile about the size of a nickel on wood or a flat rock, a blunt stick can be ground into the mixture with a twisting motion at the edge of the pile. When a spark ignites, quickly scrape the rest of the pile to the burning part and add tinder. If the mixture is placed on a rock, a knife blade can be used to scrape the edge of the pile to start it. A magnifying glass will get it started quickly, as well as a drop of glycerine from advanced first-aid kits. Some antifreeze/coolants and brake fluids also have enough glycerine to get the mixture started. Dip a twig in the fluid and roll in the potassium permanganate. It will light like a match. Keep your face well back from the mixture, because as it ignites it can throw burning particles up about a foot high into your eyes.

In extreme cases, firearms ammunition can be used to start fires. Gunpowder from rifle and pistol ammunition can be extracted by inserting the bullet in the weapon's bore and wiggling the cartridge to loosen the bullet. Do not use pliers for this, especially with rimfire ammo. It could blow up in your face. By looking closely at plastic shotgun shells, you can usually see where the fiber wadding separates the shot from the gunpowder. By carefully cutting along the wadding, the powder can be exposed. The gunpowder is placed in a nest of tinder and carefully ignited using a magnifying glass or by spark or friction.

In extreme emergencies, flares can also be used to start fires. A hole is dug and filled with flammable energy-absorbing material such as dry grass and leaves. The flare is aimed at the hole with the firer turning their head, and the flare is shot into the hole. If the hole is not big enough and well padded, it is possible to bounce a burning block of magnesium back into your face. Flares should not be cut into for any reason. They are basically a magnesium block on top of a rocket and you could light yourself up. Using flares and ammunition for ignition sources should be a last resort only.

Another artificial ignition source is the cigarette lighter from the car. A loose ball of toilet paper or fine tinder can be dropped into the hot lighter and be blown into flames. Fine steel wool can be stretched across the positive and negative terminals of flashlight or nine-volt batteries to create glowing filaments to ignite tinder. I carry a small ball of steel wool wrapped in aluminum foil in the base of my flashlight. The lens and reflector can be removed and the steel wool put in as a loose ball across the electrical points. Turning the flashlight on, the steel wool will ignite. This can be enhanced by adding a potassium permanganate/sugar mixture or gunpowder, but don't expect to use the flashlight again! To save the flashlight, the steel wool can also be stretched thin and touched on each end of the battery to ignite, but this is more difficult.

Although too large for personal or expanded kits, Skyblazer makes an emergency firestarter called the Hot Shot that is self-igniting and burns at 1,200°F for two minutes. This is useful for quick fires, extremely cold weather, or with damp fuel. It could be included in larger kits.

PRIMITIVE FIRESTARTING TECHNIQUES

The primitive methods I will describe all rely on friction, and it is necessary to practice these diligently to gain the stamina, physical coordination, and skills in preparing the materials. It is hard to do this merely by reading. This is where you benefit from a class or

Blood, Sweat, and Tears

It is possible to start a fire with all natural materials, but it takes physical effort, sweat, and often in the learning stages —blood. In one of my classes I had both Air Force and U.S. Customs Service pilots in attendance. A spirited rivalry developed between the two groups, as the Customs group had several ex-Navy aviators. While learning to use a hand drill, an unofficial competition started to see which group would get their fire started first. One Air Force pilot was well ahead, his drill spinning rhythmically and smoke pouring out of the fireboard. Just when I was sure he had an ember, a blister earned from spinning the drill on the palm of his hand broke. Blood quickly ran down the fire drill, into the socket, and extinguished his lead.

having someone show you how to do it. If that is not possible, several videos show these techniques. A long time ago I saw a person demonstrate the hand-drill method. It took me much trial and error to get it right, but I did. And I now insist on doing the same with my students, so they know it can be done with enough practice. Some authors dismiss these methods as "impractical, unreliable, or not possible under extreme conditions." You can tell who practices and who doesn't.

All friction methods rely on proper material selection, preparation, and technique. The woods used must be fairly soft, with the *quiotes* of sotol, yucca, or lechuguilla being preferable for fireboards. The female sotol *quiote* is the best of the lot. While friction methods require some amount of speed to work, it is more essential to be rhythmic than fast. If a drill slips out of the hearth at the wrong moment, it may be necessary to start over.

THE BOW DRILL

This method uses a bow to rapidly turn a drill to create friction. Once it is set up, it can produce an ember rapidly, but it does take considerable time and a variety of material to assemble. It consists of a fireboard, drill, socket, and bow. The bow can be any nonflexible branch about two feet long with a bow shape. The string must be sturdy and able to take a lot of abuse. It is hard to find or create

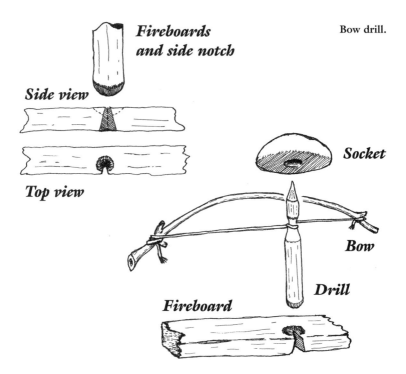

Fireboards and side notch

Side view

Top view

Bow drill.

Socket

Bow

Drill

Fireboard

natural strings that can withstand the rubbing without breaking. If you have some parachute cord or a tough bootlace, you may want to use it instead. Many natural fibers tend to break just as you start getting good smoke, wasting your energy and making you start over. The string must be perfectly adjusted. Too tight and it will bind the drill and be difficult to turn. Too loose and it will turn the drill in only one direction or not at all. It will take a while to get the feel. If too loose, you can grip the bow and string together, creating more tension.

The drill should be six to ten inches long and about three-quarters of an inch in diameter. It should be very pointed on top and blunt on the bottom. Some people like to thin the drill about two thirds of the way up, creating a "wasp waist" to hold the string in place and spin the drill faster. Other people cut flats down the drill, creating a hexagonal cross section, which helps the string grab the drill. The drill must be straight and of relatively soft wood. I prefer willow when available, but *quiotes*, cottonwood, and large seepwillows that are not too pithy can be used. Ash can work, but it is hard and not the best choice. The pointed end can be lubricated to help it spin in the socket. Ear wax can be used, or, if your hair is oily, run the drill through your ducktail. The glands along the side of the nose also give off a lot of oil and carefully rubbing the point there will add lubrication.

The socket is what holds the drill in place. It can be stone, hard wood, or an animal bone with a joint socket. The hole or socket should be deep and narrow enough to hold the drill in place, or in the middle of the process it will slip off and you will bore a hole into the palm of your hand. I prefer stone.

The fireboard is extremely important. Besides the materials listed above, cottonwood, willow, and juniper are good choices for the fireboard. The board should be split about one-half-inch thick for cottonwood and willow, and three-quarter inch for *quiotes* since they are softer and the drill bores through them more quickly. The board needs to be at least an inch wide. Make an indentation in the fireboard with a knife or rock to place the drill. Using the bow, drill in the indentation to see how the drill will set. This is the hearth. Its outside edge should be about one-quarter inch from the edge of the fireboard. Next, a side notch is cut as shown in the diagram. It should be cut in the shape of a V, with the point centered with the notch and extending well into it. In addition, the notch should undercut the hearth. This notch will collect fine dust created by the spinning drill and keep the dust in contact with the heat caused by the drill spinning in the hearth. Fireboards used in conjunction with hand drills from archaic archeological sites in the Texas deserts do not have side notches, the ember forming in the hearth and the fire-maker estimating when an ember was ready. Side notches speed up the process and cut out the guesswork.

Some people put the side notch over a flat object, like a wood chip, to catch the dust and eventual ember. I generally place the side notch over my tinder, first using my fingers to compact the part of the "nest" going under the fireboard. In this way, when I get an ember, I do not need to transfer it. With the side notch in position, wrap the bowstring once around the drill, and place the blunt end of the drill in the hearth and the socket on the pointed top end.

I find posture very important to the success of using a bow drill. Hold the bow in your dominant hand parallel to the ground. Place your weak foot on the fire board about six inches away from the hearth. Take your weak arm and brace your wrist at the front of your ankle, with the hand holding the socket and maintaining the drill perpendicular to the fireboard. It will be necessary to keep the fireboard very still so as not to disturb the pocket of wood dust forming in the side notch. With slight pressure on the socket, start sawing the bow back and forth. Try to keep a constant speed. If you try to go too fast, you will flip the drill out of the hearth and have to start over.

In a short while dust should start to creep out of the side notch. Smoke will start to appear around the drill. Keep a steady rhythm and watch the dust and side notch. When smoke starts coming out of the dust consistently (it will appear in puffs at first), stop spinning the drill and carefully pick up the fireboard. The dust should keep smoking and a red ember appear.

This is not the time to get excited and blow, this will only scatter the dust and decrease the quantity for the ember to grow. You

Proper bow drill posture: The wrist of the hand holding the capstone and drill is firmly braced against the ankle to minimize tilting the drill. Demonstrating is Jamie Clark, who summited Mount Everest in 1997 and trained with the author for a 700-mile camel trek in the Empty Quarter of Arabia, which he completed in March 1999.

can create a slight breeze by carefully waving your hand over it in slow motion. If you did not start your ember in a nest of tinder, carefully transfer it now. Wrapping the sides of the nest around the ember, start blowing with short, easy puffs. As the ember spreads to the tinder, increase the length and strength of the puffs. It is a good idea to hold the tinder nest up to the same height as your face, as leaning over the nest will cause you to inhale smoke (which by this time you should have a lot of) and cause you to cough, upsetting the process. Be ready for the tinder to burst into flames, and quickly put it into the tinder and kindling you have arranged nearby. Watch your fingers!

A variation on this method using two people is employed by the Inuit. Instead of a bow, the cord is wrapped around the drill once, with one person holding an end in each hand. The other person holds the socket and drill. The person with the cord saws it back and forth, spinning the drill.

THE HAND DRILL

The hand drill requires more skill and stamina, but it takes much less time to gather the materials and prepare. Because you will be spinning the drill with your hands, a fireboard of softer wood is desirable. Again, I prefer a female sotol *quiote*. The drill must be very straight, about two feet long, and three-eighths to one-half inch in diameter on the end to go into the hearth. Make a hearth and side notch the same way as described for the bow drill method.

Good woods for drills are seepwillow, willow shoots, the top ends of lechuguilla, yucca, or beargrass *quiotes,* and mullein stalks. I prefer seepwillow, as it is straight and the right diameter. The drill must be absolutely dry, but with no splits. For the sake of your hands, remove any small stubs or knobs as well as the bark, if present. Seepwillow bark is fibrous, and will come off the drill and scatter the wood dust. If the drill is tapered, put the small end at the top, as this will help you spin the drill faster and supply resistance to keep your hands from sliding down too fast. Again, form and technique are essential to your success.

Put a foot solidly on the fireboard and spit on your hands. No kidding, it really helps you get a grip. With your arms nearly extended, place the drill between your palms with the fingers completely extended. Hold the drill up straight. Unless you really enjoy large

Proper hand drill posture: demonstrated by Cathy Fulton, survival instructor and outdoor education specialist.

blood blisters, take off any rings before starting. Applying downward pressure, start spinning the drill using the entire length of your hands, fingers included. Move both hands; spinning the drill with one hand does not rotate it fast enough. As your hands get near the bottom of the drill the top end of the stick will whip around, which can cause you to lose control. Stop the drill, and, holding it between the thumb and palm of one hand, move the other hand to the top of the drill. When that hand has a good grip at the top, move the bottom hand up and start spinning again. It is very important to do this and keep the drill in the hearth, or you may have to start over.

Rhythm is all-important. It is more critical to have good rhythm and timing than speed. Smoke will appear around the drill, and then out the side notch in the wood dust. At this point, proceed the same as in using the bow drill.

There are two variations on this using two people. The first has the partners taking turns. As the first person's hands get near the bottom, the second person has their hands in position at the top to take over. When the first person says, "Go!" the second person starts spinning the drill. I like to take the brief time between my turns to spit on my hands again (which has been annoying to some of my partners sharing the same drill). It is important not to let go of the drill before the other person has it under control.

In the second method, the first person holds the drill in a socket with slight downward pressure, while the other person spins the drill between their hands. The advantage of this is that the spinner does not need to apply pressure, so the hands stay in one place on the drill, and there is no disruption. This can be done with one person, by holding a small socket in the mouth and spinning the drill between the hands. I do not do this, as I once saw a person using this technique lose control and let the drill slip out of the socket, nearly gouging his eye out.

THE FIRE PLOW

The last primitive method I will discuss is the fire plow, where a stick, the plow, is quickly rubbed up and down a groove in the fireboard to create dust ignited by friction. I find this the most difficult method, but I have seen documentaries showing Polynesians getting an ember glowing in under one minute using this technique. Using one of the same woods described earlier for a fireboard (again, a female sotol *quiote* is my preference), split a section two feet to two and a half feet in length.

The plow can be a stick about ten inches long and does not need to be perfectly straight. One of the plants described for making the hand drill will be a good choice. At one end on the split side of the fireboard, make a trench about one foot long and the same diameter as the plow. With softer woods, such as sotol, you can use the plow itself to rub a groove into the split side of the wood. Other woods may require you to use a knife. At the end of the trench, carve out a depression to catch the fine wood dust.

Kneeling, hold the fireboard between your legs, with the lower end against something immovable, like a rock. The fireboard must be at an angle to allow the wood dust to slide down the trench and into the collecting depression. Gripping the plow with both hands, thumbs up, rapidly rub the plow up and down the groove, pushing the dust into the depression, but not entering it with the plow,

Proper fire plow posture.

which would disturb the ember-forming pile. After a while, the groove will start to smoke, and hopefully, so will the dust pile. When it is smoking well on its own and an ember forms, carefully dump it into your tinder nest, and proceed as in the other methods.

Some hints about primitive firemaking techniques: Keep in practice. Not only do you need to hone your timing and coordination, but you need to keep up your stamina. You also need to keep your calluses tough for the hand drill. Be careful leaning over the fireboard when using any of these techniques. More than once I have had a drop of sweat roll off my nose and douse an infant ember. These methods are hard to learn, but if you can get a friction fire started, you can start one under almost any circumstances.

Why do I neglect flint and steel in discussing firestarting? When I was in Boy Scouts we started fires with flint and steel for our Pioneering merit badge, and had contests using flint and steel for our Camporees. My troop, Yucca Council 192, won the Camporee five years in a row and we were good at flint and steel. The problem is, it is very hard to ignite natural tinder sources with this method. The pioneers (both historical and merit-badge types) used charred cotton cloth to catch and hold the spark. Instead of putting flint, steel, and charred cotton cloth in your survival kit, I recommend a magnesium bar. I'll guarantee the pioneers would have used them!

BUILDING FIRES AND COOKING PITS

When building fires in survival situations, try to arrange the fire to best optimize your fuel. American Indians typically built small fires for personal use, sitting close and using small fuel. Some Australian Aborigines build two ground fires and sleep between them for warmth and to keep animals at bay. A look at Chihuahuan Desert archeological sites shows that the natives extensively used stone to conserve fuel. Stone structures can work as a heat bin, reflector, or windbreak. It is easy to tell recent fires from those of American Indians by the way they are constructed. Modern campers put rings of rock around fires built directly on the ground, which does little good other than containing the coals.

The Desert Archaic people, however, constructed hearths of rock the fire sat on top of. Using rock, a foundation was laid. Sometimes this was flat; or a shallow depression was lined with rocks to create a bowl-shaped hearth. The rock would absorb and retain the heat of the fire, and reflect it upward, taking less fuel for cooking. Imitating this type of structure will save the survivor time and energy in the search and collection of fuel. On windy days you may want to hybridize these structures by building a platform *and* placing a ring of rocks around it to help keep coals from blowing about.

When selecting rock for structures, you should exercise caution. Rocks from creek beds may contain moisture and explode when

Pit fire and reflector.

heated, sending hot razor-sharp shards in all directions. Some places have rocks that are hollow, such as geodes. Much sought after by collectors, geodes are hollow spheres that are often lined with crystals or banded agate. Cut in half, they are beautiful, but used in a hearth they become bombs. Limestone can also cause problems around a fire. The heat breaks down the rock, making lime, which can irritate the eyes, nose, and lungs, and cause caustic burns on the skin. In my area, many archeological sites indicate Big Bend natives showed preference for volcanic rock by carrying it hundreds of yards to make hearths near creek banks cutting through limestone.

An open fire radiates heat in all directions, but you can catch some of this by building a reflector, which is a short wall built on the opposite side of the fire from the person. In some places logs are stacked on the opposite side of a fire to do this, and some desert areas have large trees such as cottonwood that will serve as reflectors. In most desert environs, rock is usually easier to obtain. If you have a space blanket with you, this can be draped over a wall and be weighted down for an especially effective way to bounce heat back at you. You can make two reflectors, with you and the fire between them. If near a large rock, build the fire away from it and use it as one of the reflectors. Reflectors also have the advantage of sending smoke upwards and not into your face.

If you have found a *rock shelter* and have decided to stay in it, building a fire in the mouth of the shelter and a reflector behind it is the safest way to stay warm. Building a fire inside a rock shelter will heat the roof, often causing slabs to spall off, creating a hazard. Archeological evidence shows that most of the smoke blackening found in rock shelters was probably done by people of European

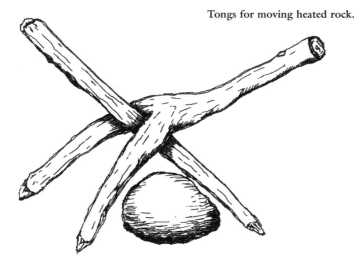

Tongs for moving heated rock.

descent. The Indians apparently knew better. Some people built low walls around the entrance to rock shelters to act both as a reflector and a windbreak.

Rock can also be used to supply indirect heat. Dense rock will retain heat and can be buried under areas where you sleep to keep the ground warm. If you are staying in a tent or have built a brush shelter, open flame may be dangerous inside. Rock can be heated in a fire outside and put inside the shelter to make it more comfortable. To move heated rock safely you will need tongs. These can be easily made by using a forked branch and a straight stick, as illustrated. Shed deer antlers can also be used as tongs or to scoop up hot rock.

Another way to heat a shelter with little fuel is a hobo stove. Take a large coffee can or small bucket and cut a door near the open end and punch holes around the closed end for ventilation. The can opener on combination tools is good for this. Fill the stove with sticks measuring three-quarters inch in diameter. Place a flat rock in the shelter and build a very small fire on it. When the fire is going well, set the can opening over the flames with the kindling inside. This will soon make a warm, but contained fire. You can even boil a cup of water on the top of the stove. Adding a few pieces of small kindling as the fire goes down will keep your shelter safely warm with little fuel.

Hobo stove made from large coffee can.

Cooking pits are another native method to utilize the heat-retaining ability of rock. Several of our desert plants are not edible unless cooked a long time to break down some of the chemicals in them. Agave pits are one of the ways that these plants can be kept hot enough to do the job. The Desert Archaic people up to the Apache cooked the hearts of plants from the family *Agavacae* in rock-lined pits. Some of these were huge and held hundreds of these hearts. In our survival classes we have scaled these pits down and have a good idea of how long different species need to cook.

If you find a depression in the ground to start with, you will save a lot of work. Otherwise you will need to dig a bowl-shaped hole. The hole should be four feet wide and three feet deep for one or two century plant or sotol hearts and three feet wide by two feet deep for a dozen lechuguilla hearts. Line the hole with rock. Flat rocks are best, about three inches thick, but they may not be available, so use what you have. They should be at least as big as softballs. Start a fire in the pit, using one of the hardwoods. Do not stand around and watch the pit, as it will get very hot, and the first time the rock is heated it will most likely send hot shrapnel audibly

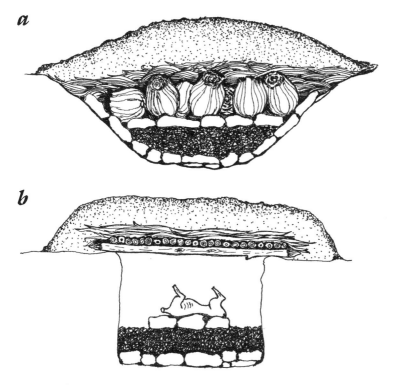

a

b

Cooking pits: *(a)* mescal/sotol/lechuguilla pit; *(b)* oven pit.

whizzing out of the pit. When a bed of coals forms, spread them up the sides of the pit and put some rock on top of them and let that heat up.

The hearts are laid on the top layer of rock, and the leaves that were cut off are laid around and over the hearts to add steam. Now bury the entire pit and tromp it down. Larger century plant and sotol hearts take forty-eight hours to cook by this method, and lechuguilla hearts, being smaller, need about twenty-four hours. If you have a good layer of dirt on top, a rainstorm will not bother the pit unless you built it in a drainage.

A pit oven is very effective for baking items like meat or young green quiotes that do not need such long cooking times. Dig a hole about two and a half feet square with straight sides, and line the bottom with rock. You will need to build a cover for the hole that will extend about a foot on each side. The cover can be made of *quiotes*, willow branches, etc. and thatched with brush to keep dirt out of the hole. A framework covered with a blanket or sheet can also be used. The plastic sheeting from the survival kit will *not* work, as it will melt.

Build a hardwood fire in the pit, and as it burns to coals, place some more rock on top. When this layer is thoroughly heated, place the cover over the hole and quickly bury it, starting at the sides and working your way toward the center. Make sure it is airtight. If you see smoke coming out anywhere, put more dirt on top and pat it down, as oxygen entering the pit can cause the cover to burn.

The shortcomings of pit cooking for the survivor are obvious. Digging pits, collecting rock, and making thatched covers are labor intensive, especially if you are using knives, digging sticks, or your hands. You should not even think about eating, let alone digging pits unless you have a large water source. They can, however, process large amounts of food that, as in the case of some species of the family Agavacae, have large amounts of sugars and carbohydrates.

Rock was also used by people to boil water. The Native Americans would do this in bison paunches, waterproof baskets, or even holes in the ground. The process is called stone boiling, and its application could be crucial for people in emergencies. Fist-sized stones are heated in a fire built near the water to be boiled. Using tongs, the stones are added to the water. As they cool they are removed, placed back on the fire, and replaced with hot stones. It takes quite a while, but with a lot of stones and patience it is possible to start and keep water boiling. This could be especially useful if you discovered a small tinaja holding five gallons or less of water. The water could be stone boiled directly in the pothole to make it biologically safe.

Smart survivors will guard and nurture their fire. They will keep a supply of tinder, kindling, and fuel on hand and keep it dry and ready. Fire requires thought of safety both for the environment and yourself. If you start a grass or brush fire accidentally, you could become its victim. Even small burns in stressful situations cause pain and nasty infections. Be careful in using fire for drying out your boots, socks, or clothes.

The Hot Rock Cafe

The type of rock selected for cooking pits is an important consideration, if there is a choice. I was once recording a hearth site with the Big Bend Archeological Society along a drainage called Comanche Creek, which is in a geological contact zone where both sedimentary rock (deposited by ancient seas) and igneous rock (formed from magma or lava) were both available. Although the creek cut through limestone, the hearth makers had hauled large cobbles of volcanic rock several hundred yards to make a fire near the water source. The work involved indicated a preference for igneous rock over limestone, which caused speculation among us. Perhaps igneous rock held heat better or did not crack from the fire as readily as the softer limestone?

Another explanation came from an article in a popular science magazine about the excavation of an 800,000-year-old *Homo erectus* site in Thailand. The inhabitants of a limestone rock shelter had hauled igneous basalt stones several hundred yards up a steep slope to build a hearth in their shelter. The archeologists in Thailand were as puzzled as we were in the Big Bend. The article went on to say that the archeologists had used limestone for the cooking fires in their field camp. After a few days the crew started experiencing a burning sensation in their sinuses and lungs. Fearing they had contracted a tropical fungus infection, they were preparing to leave for medical attention when the Thai camp workers pointed out that when you burn limestone, it breaks down into lime. In the normal cooking chores, water and coffee were being spilled on the hot limestone, creating caustic clouds of lime dust in steam to be breathed in, causing the irritation. The archeologists soon followed the 800,000-year-old example and started cooking on basalt. Following examples as practiced by indigenous cultures or from archeological sites can save us from having to "reinvent the wheel."

6 Shelter

Enkidu prepared a sleeping place for him for the night;
a violent wind passed through so he attached a covering.

—The Epic of Gilgamesh, *Tablet IV, 2000 b.c.*

Because deserts can exhibit climate extremes and sudden weather changes, shelter is an important consideration, whether in an emergency situation or not. Shelter is as basic as what we wear. People enjoying the desert as outdoor recreation should prepare by wearing proper clothing, eye protection, and sunscreen. Most typically we are concerned with shelter from the sun, but wind, rain, hail, snow, and cold can also be considerations.

CLOTHES

Clothing is our first line of defense. Take the example of the Bedouin Arab, whose billowing clothes allow air circulation but protect the body from head to toe from constant exposure to the sun. Military BDU (battle dress uniform) is loose fitting, durable, has a lot of pockets, and is well adapted to hot desert wear. The trouble is that it is also usually of a khaki color, or camouflaged to blend in with the environment, making it hard for rescuers to see you. I can also tell you from firsthand experience, from when I worked as a dispatcher for the National Park Service, that if you show up in full camouflage wear in a park, an enforcement ranger is going to call in a license plate check on your vehicle. I like BDUs and wear them on searches, but I wish manufacturers made them in blaze orange for visibility.

A hat is a necessity. Protect your brain first. Hats with wide brims or something along the style of the French Foreign Legion protect the scalp, cheeks, back of the neck, and shade the face. I see people who show up in all kinds of headwear they think will be cooler but are neither sensible nor stylish. Plastic visors that clamp to the forehead and hats without crowns come to mind. Another head cooker is the popular baseball cap with the front made of foam rubber lining and the back of plastic mesh. These usually come with some smart aleck slogan that is not especially funny when the wearer is being put into a body bag.

Choice of hats will depend on the season, but most of the time straw or breathable cloth is preferable. In hotter times, one that can be soaked in water will keep the head cool. If you choose the straw cowboy style, get one with a good fit or you will be chasing it with every gust of wind. Caps can be modified by taking a bandana or other large cloth, tying two corners together, putting the tied end over the head and securing it with the cap to make a Legionnaire-style of headwear. You can also purchase Legionnaire-style desert

Good choices of hats for desert use: Demonstrating left to right are Big Bend Ranch State Park survival course alumni Tim Jurek, Dana Jepson, Rick Edgington, and Curtis Smith.

caps. People have improvised desert hats by draping a bandanna over their head Arab style and making a brim out of cardboard by cutting a hole in it to fit over the crown of their head. Some of the "baskets" found in our archeological sites may actually be conical hats woven from yucca leaves.

Another addition is a cotton neck scarf, which can be used in conjunction with a hat for sun protection, or wrapped around the face in dust storms, or to keep the ears warm in chilly weather. A scarf can also be dipped in water for cooling or can be used to mop perspiration out of the eyes. In some areas with light sand or dirt that reflects light upward, you can find the bottom of your chin and nose sunburned. The neck scarf can be used as a face veil to prevent this.

Sunglasses are another aid, especially for people with light-colored eyes. It is possible to become "snow blind" in the desert where there is reflective soil, sand, or rock. New research is also indicating that not using eye protection may later lead to cataracts. When selecting sunglasses, get some that block UV (ultraviolet) light. Ordinary sunglasses will cause your pupils to dilate, opening them to even more of the damaging UV rays. The glasses should be durable. I like lenses that are gray tinted because they do not distort colors as much. I identify many plants from a distance by the color hues of their foliage or blossoms. Sun goggles can be improvised by putting tape on regular glasses or sunglasses without UV protection, leaving a slit to see out of but limiting the amount of light reaching the eyes. The Inuit made snow goggles that I have imitated by carving some out of sotol *quiote* and making tie strings from lechuguilla fiber.

Goggles: Although these were made by the Inuit people to prevent snow blindness, they also work well in desert conditions. This pair is made from a sotol *quiote*.

I am a fair-skinned person, and I like to wear a long-sleeved shirt and long pants in the desert. Sunblock is good, but it can run out or be lost. There is no better sunblock than clothing. Dark-skinned desert people live their entire lives in full desert sun wearing practically nothing, but light-skinned people should think about sunburn in the present and skin cancer in the future. In most desert situations, cotton is the coolest fabric available. In cold situations, the saying goes, "cotton kills" and wool is preferable. Synthetics and blends are very dangerous in hot climates —they seem to absorb solar radiation and turn your clothes into an oven bag. The only BDUs I ever found in blaze orange for SAR work were 100% polyester, so I am still wearing khaki and desert camouflage. Take heed you folks out there in outdoor clothing manufacturing: there is a need for durable cotton military-cut clothes in bright colors.

Many people are amazed at me wearing long pants on days at 115°F. I am amazed someone would wear shorts out in the direct sun, surrounded by thorny vegetation. Pant legs bloused into the top of high-topped boots will help keep insects such as ants off of your legs. While long pants will not stop a snake's fang from penetrating, there have been many cases where a snake struck a loose pant leg and missed the leg itself. I am a big believer in long, loose-fitting pants. I think blood on top of a sunburn is so déclassé.

Let's talk candidly about underwear. To wear, or not to wear, that is the question. T-shirts can be beneficial in that they catch and retain perspiration, allowing it to evaporate slowly and cool more effectively. At times when the humidity level is low and the temperature is high, perspiration may vaporize the moment it comes out of your pores, negating the advantage of a T-shirt. In this case, a T-shirt only makes you hotter. T-shirts can make a cool evening more comfortable, so I recommend wearing one and taking it off if you think you will be cooler without it.

I can speak about underpants with authority only from a male perspective. In desert situations, men are often better off without any at all, especially where briefs are concerned. While T-shirts may absorb moisture, briefs tend to concentrate it in the crevices and folds of the groin. If you are subject to fungal infections, this can lead to raging cases of jock itch that can become virtually incapacitating. Cotton briefs are the worst. While cotton may be preferable for hot weather outerwear, it will chafe when tight fitting and damp. If for some reason you need the support of briefs, those of silk or silklike synthetics do not chafe as bad. While I do not recommend synthetics for outerwear, under the garments synthetics are shielded from direct sunlight and do not heat up so much. If underwear is desired, boxer shorts allow for much more air circulation.

As for women, my advice would be entirely theoretical, so I consulted Cathy Fulton, who teaches wilderness survival classes. According to Cathy, panties, bikini briefs, and panty hose also increase the risk of rashes and fungal infections. Because a women needs no support in this area of anatomy, not wearing panties may be best for desert excursions. An exception to this rule is when a woman must use expedient menstrual pads in emergencies, as discussed in Chapter 9. Brassieres, however, may be of benefit. With buxom women, perspiration can be trapped between the underside of the breasts and the rib cage, encouraging fungal infections, rashes, or prickly heat. A bra will lift the breasts and not allow perspiration to accumulate. Many outdoor clothing manufacturers make bras especially for outdoor active women, designed not to chafe.

Socks are important to keep feet cool, dry, and to cushion the foot. When hiking long distances in rough terrain, the sock must be thick enough to keep blisters from forming, not be of a material that makes the foot hot, and wick perspiration away from the foot. There are many socks on the market for rough terrain and hot climates, made from special blends of synthetic and natural fibers. Socks must be kept clean to protect the feet. An extra pair in a larger kit will help. One pair can be rinsed out and drying while the other is in use.

I used this method in Australia, rinsing out the socks I was wearing when we reached water, while changing into a dry pair. The wet socks were secured to my belt with a diaper pin and dried as I walked. My feet stayed in good shape this way. If you take care of your feet and keep the brain hydrated and in the shade, it's a pretty good bet that everything in between will follow along.

Footwear is very important, and the market is so wide that your choices are limited only by your budget. The following are some of the things I look for in desert hiking boots. High lace-up tops give optimal ankle support. These also can give some protection against snakes (although most are able to strike well above the ankle). The sole should give a good grip on rock surfaces but also be of a durable material so the rock does not quickly wear them down. The entire boot, and the sole especially, should be able to keep thorns out. The sole should also not be extremely flexible, so it can span the spaces between rock. Otherwise the toes can be bent backward and the foot injured. Light colors will be more comfortable, while black boots will cook your feet. I made the mistake once of going cheap and buying Army surplus Vietnam jungle boots for the desert, which are black and have vent holes to let water out. The boots become almost too hot to keep on, and the vent holes, which I thought would allow air circulation, let fine sand in instead. The Army issue Desert Storm boots are built on the same pattern but are light colored and without the vent holes. When buying your boots, make sure the store has a ramp to stand on so you can feel where your toes will be going downhill.

You may find a jacket necessary in winter and almost any night. March and April are busy months where I work, and the weather can range from near freezing to the mid-90s. I try to explain this to persons calling me on the phone, some wanting to know what the weather will be like on *specific* spring dates two months in advance! After living here all my life, the best advice I can give is to bring both parkas and bikinis. Remember, even if the temperature is cool, clear days in the desert will still grill you with UV rays. Hats, sunglasses, and sunblock are needed as much for the winter as the summer.

SHELTER

While dressing properly will enhance your survival strategy, it will often not be enough. It may be necessary to construct a makeshift shelter for protection from the elements. Shelter construction has several requirements. The shelter must be located in a safe place, out of drainages and washes, away from terrain prone to rockslides, and not on a high, windy point. Conversely, it needs to be visible. While a shelter in a grove of trees will be shaded, it will be hidden from searchers. In locating a shelter, you must balance protection against visibility. A shelter near water is desirable. The shelter must also be sturdy. If you build something that blows down around your ears in the night, you have wasted your time, energy, and have compromised your safety.

ARTIFICIAL SHELTER

There are many shelters that can be built from items carried in the car or airplane. One of the best options, of course, is a tent. The problem with tents in desert days is that they prohibit air circulation and become portable hothouses. In some circumstances the car can be used if the windshields can be covered, the windows are rolled down, and if a cross breeze is coming through. A car without a breeze on a hot day, especially with the windows up, can be a death trap. Many pets and, most unfortunately, a few children have died of hyperthermia when left in cars. In this case, a tarp strung up as a shade may be your best bet, as it will catch a breeze coming from any direction. It is important that you not sit on the hot ground, as ground temperatures will be much hotter than the ambient air temperature. I have had Mexicans tell me that sitting on hot rocks causes hemorrhoids! Shade shelters will allow the ground to cool and allow air circulation.

Tarps, space blankets, wool blankets, unzipped sleeping bags, etc. can be suspended from brush to provide shade. Plastic tube tents are included in many survival kits, and will provide some protection, but because the ends are open, they must be positioned properly to keep out wind and rain. On many desert nights, the only shelter you need will be a blanket to keep off the chill. I often sleep without a tent to enjoy the night sky that is increasingly disappearing to city lights. Blankets can be folded as illustrated into makeshift sleeping bags that insulate over and under you.

Emergency sleeping bags are now being made out of space blanket material designed to reflect your body heat back. The advantages of using space blankets is that they are highly visible. Even the plastic bags or sheeting from your kit can be used as a wrap for instant protection from freak storms.

These same blankets, bags, and tarps can also be rigged into lean-to shelters. Any of these items can have one end slammed in a car trunk and the other end anchored with rocks to make a low shade quickly. Many books advise to dig down into cooler soil, place sticks over the trench, and lay a blanket with the edges weighted down by rocks, for a cool subterranean refuge. This is similar to what many desert animals do, but take caution that the excavation does not cause dehydration or undue fatigue. I would not recommend using a natural depression for this unless located on high ground, because of flood problems in case of rain. It may be much simpler to build a U-shaped rock wall about three feet high to cover instead of digging down.

People have shown great architectural resourcefulness by using things like airplane wings as a basis for shelter. The parachute is a great standby in military survival training for creating teepee-like

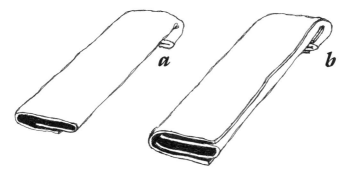

Blankets as sleeping bags: *(a)* one blanket; *(b)* two blankets.

shelters. Most of us will not be carrying parachutes, and if you are, chances are you have had quite a bit of training on how to make shelter from them.

NATURAL SHELTER

You may be blessed to find natural shelter, which will save you a lot of work. Sometimes this can be as simple as finding natural shade. For instance, you have found a creek bed with a cut bank about ten feet high that looks stable. Going to the shady side of the creek, you scoop away a shallow depression and find some cool, damp sand a foot below. Remembering that if you can keep your skin temperature below 92°F you will minimize your body's water loss, you sit in the damp sand with your back to the bank and relax. You have shelter. Sleeping there is a hazard, however, because you are in a drainage; so you leave the spot at night.

> ### Good Sense Overcomes Poor Preparation
>
> One woman lost in the Big Bend for two cold November nights found a small pocket in a steep rock face near a pool of water. Having found water, she wisely chose to stay at that spot and wait for help. With only a light jacket and an orange poncho, no matches, and no knowledge of how to start a fire from natural materials, she stuffed the hole full of dead grass and burrowed in at night. She was spotted on the third day, waving the brightly colored poncho to attract a helicopter. While her preparation was lacking, her instincts were good.

Rock shelters are exactly what their name says, a shallow rock cave that is a ready-made shelter. Many of these are prime archeological sites and I do not advocate campers using them except in life-threatening emergencies. Many rock shelters require no modification, but they can be made more comfortable by building a windbreak and fire reflector in front of them. Long poles such as *quiotes* can be leaned against the opening with their butts anchored by rocks, and be used as a frame for a brush windbreak and shade. In selecting a rock shelter, make sure that you are not putting yourself in a Goldilocks situation. Javelinas love them and you will see their scat. Look for signs of occupation such as large cat tracks or gnawed bones. Also look closely for things such as wasp nests, snakes, and rodents that may carry parasites. Be aware that some diseases such as Hantavirus are transmitted through contact with feces of mice, squirrels, rabbits, etc. Rock shelters may house these animals and diseases. Check the overhanging rock for stability. Once while surveying a rock art site with the Big Bend Archeological Society, I was using a stadia rod while measuring the height of the ceiling and accidentally dislodged a rock, which came down on my head and gave me a full-thickness scalp laceration. An hour and a half later when I was being sewn up by our local paramedic, he asked how far the rock fell. "Three point five meters from height of instrument," replied the archeologist who was working the transit at the time. In the previous chapter I warned how such rock falls can also be caused by building a fire in a shelter. Rock shelters also have the distinct disadvantage of being hard to see from the air and not especially significant to ground searchers from a distance. In this case you will want to make your location distinct and visible.

Brush shelters are traditional to deserts in North America, southern Africa, and Australia. These can be simple lean-tos built up beside a boulder, structures with ridge poles, or conical shaped. The conical-shaped shelter, often called a wickiup, is ideal but time consuming. I prefer the Apache term *kowa* for these shelters, and while they take some effort, they are ideal for making a brush shelter. The conical shape has several advantages. An open-faced lean-to can be destroyed should the wind shift and hit it from the front. *Kowas* can be made on open ground for visibility, but offer wind resistance no matter the direction. In addition, if you cover the *kowa* with something reflective like space blankets, the conical shape will reflect

Emergency shelter: This type of brush hut is modeled after the Apache *kowa*.

from virtually any angle during most of the day, while a lean-to reflects from only one side. The Apache built *kowas* in two ways. One was to bury the butts of flexible willow poles and bend them into arches to make a frame. The other way was to take nonflexible poles and lash them together like teepee poles. The latter is easiest and best suited for our purposes.

The *kowa* pictured was made of sotol *quiotes* and seepwillow branches and tied together with strips of heated yucca leaf called pita (see Chapter 9). It is extremely sturdy and has weathered winds of fifty-plus miles per hour and stayed relatively dry inside during cloud bursts. Three poles are tied together with pita to form a

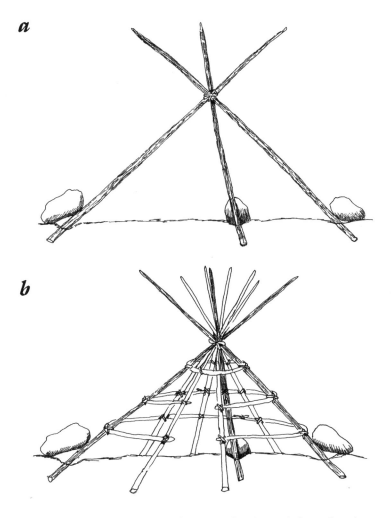

a

b

tripod. The poles should be about ten feet long. A forty-five-degree angle is optimal for stability, floor space, and water-shedding ability. These poles are placed to form an equilateral triangle for further stability. The butts are placed in shallow holes, covered, and a good-sized rock placed on the hole. More poles are added and tied in at the top with pita. These need not be buried.

Next, take long flexible branches, such as willow or seepwillow, and tie them in three hoops around the poles. Cut a good supply of branches from leafy plants such as willow and seepwillow. The Apache used bundles of beargrass when available, but watch for the sawtooth edges, which can cut you. The more foliage on the branches, the more waterproof your shelter will be. Take the longer

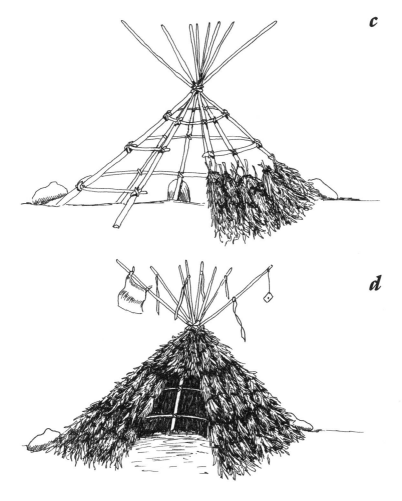

Constructing a *kowa:* *(a)* Tripod poles set; *(b)* extra poles and hoops placed; *(c)* thatching tied on in layers starting at bottom; *(d)* complete *kowa* with streamers, flag, and signal mirror tied to poles for visibility.

branches and start tying bundles of them to the hoops and poles at the bottom of the frame, leaving a space for the door. You will want to position the door away from prevailing night winds or toward the east where the hot afternoon sun will not be shining in. When that is completed, start a new row above and overlapping the previous layer. Do the same until the top is reached. After these rows are tied in, you can go back and fill in thin spots with more foliage merely by jamming the branches upward into the tied foliage. You can make a door that can also double as a covering for the cooking pit shown in Chapter 6.

The *kowa*, being built of natural materials, is also hard to see. You can enhance this by hanging unused clothing, a signal mirror, strips of aluminum foil, etc. from the poles. Covering the *kowa* with a blanket, especially an aluminized rescue blanket, will make a very noticeable air signal as well as waterproof the structure. *Kowas* produce good shade, allow air circulation, and, while they will leak some, are much better than standing out in the rain.

In Mexico I have seen *jacales* (huts) covered with leaves cut from century plants that have used the natural curve of the leaf to lay like Spanish tile. When the leaves dry, they are very hard, and if you allow for shrinkage, make a waterproof shelter. I never cease to be amazed at the ingenuity of my Mexican neighbors, and have learned that knowledge is not always found with a diploma.

There are some additional things to consider when seeking shelter: On hot days it is best to sit in the shade with air circulating all about you. If you can sit on something that keeps you off the ground, so much the better. You can add comfort to your shelter with a bedding of plants such as grass or broomweed. Be sure to take it apart and inspect it for critters before retiring for the night. Also take care not to set your bedding on fire. Shelter is not something you want to try to build when freak weather hits. By then it is too late. It is like the cowboy that didn't fix his roof because he couldn't when it was raining and he didn't need to when it wasn't. It takes less energy for two or more people to build a group shelter than individual ones. You can also economize firewood this way and share body heat on cold nights. Make the shelter your temporary residence. Remember, in emergencies, "Home is where the heart is still beating."

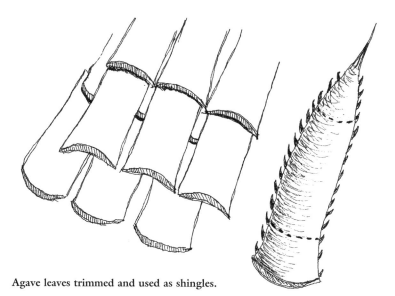

Agave leaves trimmed and used as shingles.

7 Aiding Rescuers

The sentinels were provided with bits of mirrors to flash warnings. When General Miles wrote of his campaign against the Apaches he assumed we knew nothing of the heliograph. He was mistaken.

—Eve Ball, as related by James Kaywaykla,
Warm Springs Apache, *In the Days of Victorio*

Once you have your physical necessities taken care of, you will need to devise ways to make yourself known to searchers. While I do not like to see people in trouble, search and rescue (SAR) operations are some of my most rewarding duties. I get to use my knowledge of the terrain, pursue clues to unravel mysteries, and actively help someone who truly needs it. SAR personnel are normally highly trained people, often volunteers, who follow strict procedure. Gone are the days where mobs of local citizens took to the field walking abreast, often destroying valuable evidence. SAR is now a science, and knowing how searchers work will help your rescue.

First, you must make preparations before you go into the desert. Appoint someone as your contact person and give them a detailed itinerary of your trip, including times and routes, and stick to it. If you are out alone, give someone a time you *will* be back, and leave instructions to call for help immediately if you do not return before then. Too many times I have been called out as it was getting too dark to start a search. If you are hiking in a national or state park, get the required permits and fill out a solo hiker form if you are going alone. Leave an example of your footprint with the rangers or your contact person. A footprint of record can be made by dusting the sole of your boot with baby powder and then standing on a piece of carbon paper. You can also lay a square of aluminum foil on a carpet or rug and step on it. These can be photocopied so every searcher will have an example of your footprint. Photocopying is more effective with the carbon paper print.

In the event you are lost, make sure your family or friends will cooperate fully with SAR personnel. There will be a person assigned as an investigator who will have some questions that sound outlandish but have their purpose. These questions are for helping to find the lost person, not for legal ends. Examples: "Does he/she have any fictional or real heroes?" If they say, "Cabeza de Vaca," I may believe that they are using de Vaca's ordeals for inspiration to persevere. If they say, "Rambo," I get worried. Your family will be asked about any alcohol, drug, and tobacco consumption. Your experience in the terrain you are in will be noted. Personnel will also want to talk to your friends, in case you have started a "Bastard Search."

Train and prepare your children before you venture out. One of the problems facing SAR people these days is that children are being taught not to talk to strangers. This is certainly good advice, but it has led to instances where children hid from searchers. For this reason, most SAR teams try to have uniforms that will make them

The Bastard Search

Despite its name, a Bastard Search is a legitimate SAR term. It comes about when SAR volunteers are out braving terrible weather when the subject's friend admits to the investigator that the so-called victim is actually in a nearby town at the No Tell Motel with another person not recognized as a family member. That is when the investigator gets a passkey, opens the door, and says, "You bastard!" Sometimes a real search becomes a Bastard Search when the lost person makes it out on their own, and forgets to notify someone. Some needless searches have been fraudulently started for amusement. In these instances the person has hid, usually on a high spot, where they can watch the action. Extreme forms of Bastard Searches have involved people faking their own death, insurance fraud, and covering criminal activity. I know *you* wouldn't do any of these things, but it happens often enough.

recognizable to children as authority figures, but this is not true everywhere. Teach your children that if they are lost, and especially if someone is calling their name, that it is okay to go to that person.

Your family and friends may also need to deal with psychics offering advice. You should make a decision beforehand whether to accept their help or not. If your family agrees to a psychic's help, at least one person will be sent to look at any area the psychic identifies. This can divert valuable personnel away from the search area. Some people do seem to have an amazing ability to direct searchers to lost people through precognition. Others are simply charlatans who are looking for publicity or seeking payment.

When a search is initiated, special teams will be sent out rapidly to patrol where you said you were going to be. If you have stayed on your route, you should be found quickly. Next, they will send perimeter searchers out to "contain the area" where there is the greatest probability you are. At night the SAR people may start a "passive search" using lights and sounds. In the event you are moving, these signals will lead you in the right direction. It may be best to only note where the lights or sounds are coming from instead of going toward them at night, because of the dangers of terrain, vegetation, or snakes. If you see or hear what you think is a passive search, try to signal back. You will need to make a decision whether to stay or leave. For the reasons previously mentioned, the best advice is usually to stay in place. If you must leave your vehicle, aircraft, or place where you realized you were lost, leave many notes and signs such as rock cairns. Make it easy on the SAR team.

Signals are generally visible, audible, and to a lesser extent olfactory. The key to signaling is to call attention to searchers' senses stimuli that are distinguishable from natural surroundings. Distress signals, whether visual or audible, are generally sent in groups of three. This can be three flashes from a signal mirror, three blasts from a whistle, or three fires in a triangle. Groups of three should be done in a steady, rhythmic pattern, and then repeated after a pause. Nature is chaotic and random; signals should not be.

VISUAL SIGNALS

Avoiding camouflaged clothing and gear is a start. Visual signals should stand out in color from their general surroundings, which is why I recommend blaze orange for everything from ponchos to smoke bombs. The best piece of gear for visual signals is the mirror. The majority of successful air searches are brought to an end by sighting a reflection. Many signal mirrors are visible for over twenty miles on a clear day, and have some limited use on overcast days. My father-in-law is a U.S. Border Patrol pilot, and as an experiment had ground agents signal to him with mirrors from different locations. He spotted one over fifty miles away in desert terrain from the air.

Signal mirrors are made of glass, metal, or plastics. The new acrylic ones are unbreakable and also reflect much more light than does metal. Some have sighting holes with various techniques on how to direct the reflection where you want it. Follow the directions and practice until you have it down pat. Some of the new ones are made with a silver and a red side. The red side is for using at night for reflecting artificial light sources, such as car headlights, skyward. I have no personal experience as yet with sighting a red mirror beacon, but the manufacturer claims that red is more visible at night than white light. Red does evoke a sense of emergency.

Signal mirrors are so effective that you should get yours out at the first sign of problems. If the one in your kit has a lanyard hole, hang it around your neck and inside your shirt so it will be handy while going to water, collecting firewood, or building a shelter. If you do not have one, you must improvise. Most vehicles will have at least two mirrors on them, and the rearview mirrors attached to the windshield are so easy to pull off that a three-year-old can do it. (I know this because when my son was three he did exactly that to my Ford Explorer.) Cathy Fulton is another fair-skinned Celt who takes special care of her skin conducting desert safety workshops. She carries a makeup compact that has a normal mirror and a magnifying mirror that would certainly get an aircraft pilot's attention. As a matter of fact, the beam would probably melt birds in the way! Any bright, reflective object flat enough to direct a reflection can be used.

If you are using a mirror or expedient that does not have a sighting hole, it is still easy to direct the reflection, with a little practice. Hold one of your hands outstretched with the index and middle finger extended. With the other hand, hold the mirror toward the sun and angle it until you illuminate the outstretched hand. Now, keeping the outstretched hand illuminated, move it and the mirror in conjunction until the aircraft or rescue vehicle is seen between

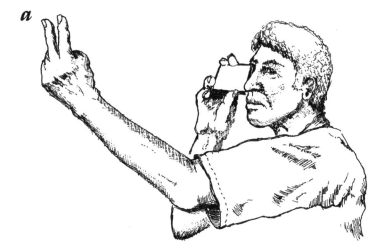

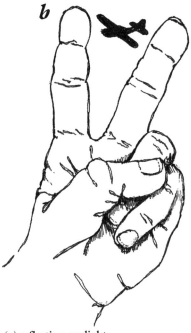

Using signal mirror: (*a*) reflecting sunlight on hand; (*b*) placing target between fingers.

the fingers. By wagging the mirror up and down, you can make flashes to attract attention. If you are signaling an airplane that is not searching for you, and do not flash, but keep a steady beacon on it, it may mistake you for a water reflection or a parked car, and not investigate.

If you see a dust cloud on the horizon, flash at it. It could be a vehicle on a dirt road. It is not a bad idea to periodically scan the horizon with your mirror. This may well attract searchers you do not know about or hikers in the area unaware of your predicament. If you have built a shelter such as a *kowa*, you can hang a mirror by its lanyard off one of the frame poles. It will twist and turn in gentle breezes, making a constant daytime beacon for a shelter that may be hard to see. Do not tie it in such a way that you are not able to remove it quickly to direct a reflection.

Other visible signals for aircraft are ground markers. These can be made of aluminum foil from a car kit, rescue blankets, or even pages of newspaper spread out and weighted down with rocks. You can align rocks, brush, or tramp a signal in sand. A giant X, about forty feet by forty feet, is a good air signal. There are at least eighteen military emergency symbols for aircraft, but many civilian pilots will not recognize them. An X, which means "unable to proceed," is usually all you need. However, for circumstance calling for relaying special information, official ground-to-air signals are illustrated here. These should be at least twenty-five feet long. Aircraft receiving ground-to-air messages will wag their wings.

Rescue blankets are great because the silver side designed to reflect body heat also reflects sunlight for a signal. They also come with a red or orange side, which is more visible than the silver side on overcast days. These make very visible shelters. Some makers of these blankets claim they are radar reflective, but so is everything else on land. For air-to-ground radar to pick up an object, it must be moving. Waving the blanket, or using it like a flag, especially if it can be mounted high away from ground clutter, will increase the chance of detection. Unfortunately, air-to-ground radar is not really designed for search and rescue.

After you have been spotted by aircraft, it is possible to relay certain messages by body signals, such as a need for pickup or medical attention. It is important not to make gratuitous arm waves or gestures at aircraft, as you may send the wrong signal. Not all pilots will

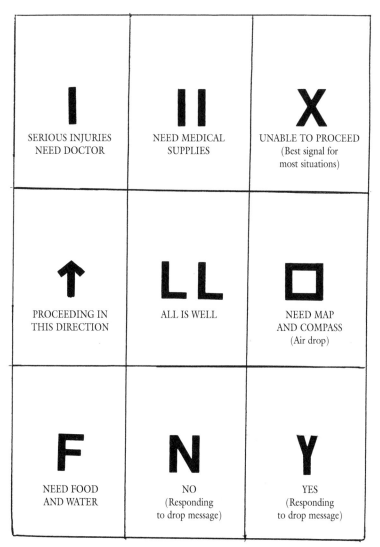

I	**II**	**X**
SERIOUS INJURIES NEED DOCTOR	NEED MEDICAL SUPPLIES	UNABLE TO PROCEED (Best signal for most situations)
↑	**LL**	**□**
PROCEEDING IN THIS DIRECTION	ALL IS WELL	NEED MAP AND COMPASS (Air drop)
F	**N**	**Y**
NEED FOOD AND WATER	NO (Responding to drop message)	YES (Responding to drop message)

Ground-to-air signals.

recognize body signals, but most rescue, law enforcement, and military pilots will get the message. The "yes" and "no" signals illustrated are responses to written messages dropped from an aircraft unable to land. Drop messages will generally have a streamer attached so the person on the ground can see their descent and locate them.

Smoke is a daytime way to attract both air and ground rescuers. It has the additional advantage of having a distinctive odor, which

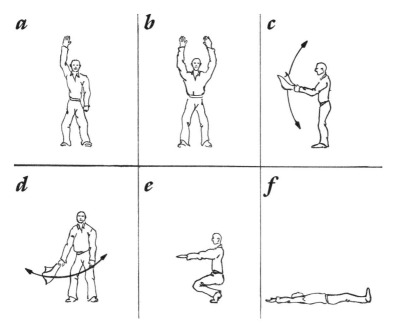

Body signals for aircraft: *(a)* all is well; *(b)* need help—pick me up; *(c)* yes—affirmative; *(d)* no—negative; *(e)* land here; *(f)* urgent medical assistance needed.

is useful at night. Smoke can be generated through artificial fuels, many from automobiles, which will be discussed in the next chapter. Smoke bombs, especially those in orange or red, are very effective if you know rescuers or aircraft are near. Their main problem is that the kit-sized ones have a rapid burn time, usually under one minute. Other smoke fuels, such as auto tires, send up huge smoke columns for several minutes.

Natural fuels do not send up as much smoke as artificial sources, but they may be all that is at hand. A smoky fire can be generated by adding green vegetation to a fire or bed of coals. Freshly cut creosote bush will generate copious white smoke if laid on hot coals. It also has the advantage of producing a curious odor that will not be mistaken for a natural state of affairs. When putting natural smoke fuels on hot coals, it is important not to let them burst into flames. This accelerates combustion and the fire will not give off as much smoke as a "smudge" fire. This can be accomplished by adding the fuel and smashing it down with a long stick to close air gaps in the fuel and decrease its oxygen. Laying a wet blanket over the fire for a few seconds at a time will also inhibit oxygen and make smoke.

Crossed Signals

Confusion between those stranded on the ground and pilots has caused more than one tragedy in survival situations. One such story concerns a man that had planned on staying several months in the Alaskan wilderness, living off the land. He was dropped into a very remote area by an amphibious airplane at the edge of a lake in March of 1981. As his departure time in August passed, he concluded he had forgotten an important point in his adventure—to contract the bush pilot to return and pick him up! One day in September as his rations, ammo, and meat were dwindling and cold weather was approaching, he heard a plane and managed to attract its attention by waving an orange sleeping bag cover. The plane acknowledged by circling, but could not land, as it was equipped with wheels and not pontoons. The fellow was certain that his location was established, however, and raised a fist in the air as a victory salute to his rescuer.

A few days later, when no help arrived, the man looked on the back of his hunting license, which showed air-to-ground body signals. It was only then he realized that one raised hand means "all is well." The account was found in his journal at his camp in February of 1982, along with his body. Near frozen and starving in late November, his last entry in the journal was a plea to God to look after his family. He then used one of his rifles to take his own life. The omission of arranging a flight out is a monumental example of poor planning, but even more disturbing is the sheer irony of an upraised fist in triumph sending rescue away.

Another problem that can cause confusion is that in water rescues, a raised hand is a signal for help, while two uplifted arms are the "all's well" signal. The reason is that persons on watercraft such as rafts may, in an emergency, be able to raise only one hand, using the other to stabilize oars or to hang on. If the pilot does not know the difference, it could cause a helicopter to leave when needed, or to come in closer when it is not desired.

Smoke will rise and be most visible on calm, warm days when the air is heated and rising. This should produce a tall column visible to both air and ground searchers. On cool days, especially mornings, the smoke may not rise, but spread out in a blanket hovering above the ground. This makes it hard to see for ground searchers, but the smell is still valuable. A blanket of smoke along the ground can be seen from the air, and will help.

Fires are also used to attract attention by light, especially at night. You should build three signal fires, ideally in a triangle one hundred feet on each side and ready to light at a moment's notice. These should be constructed and kept sheltered from the elements if possible. Make the fires carefully, with an additional supply of fuel. Stack green fuel or keep artificial smoke fuels near each one for optimum daytime signaling. If you have small containers, you may want to fill them with gasoline from your vehicle or plane and put one by each fire set so it can be ignited quickly. You should always have at least one fire going at all times to add smoke fuels or to take brands to light other signal fires. Try to use soft woods on signal fires at night to produce more light.

The sotol is an extremely useful plant for both emergency signaling and warmth. The base of the plant is surrounded with dead leaves that can be easily ignited with a match. Sotol burns for several minutes, and the green leaves smoke and make an unusual odor. This is an old Mexican and cowboy trick I have used in freak storms to warm up. A dead sotol will burn longer than a living one, but not smoke as much. This technique will also burn off many of the sawtooth leaves and make it easier to harvest for food. Be careful that you do not start a wildfire. Sotol often grows in grassy areas on hillsides, and once on fire is hard to put out. The fire can spread easily. Sotol are also notorious for spreading wildfire by burning off at the base, allowing the flaming heart to roll downhill in a ball of fire.

Another reason to maintain fires is a search system known as FLIR (Forward Looking Infra-Red). This system creates a visual image from the differences in heat between objects and their background. On a hot desert day, 100°F and up, a human will appear as a cooler object against the ground. On cooler days and nights, people will be seen as objects hotter than the background. The forms can be easily identified as human. A fire, or several fires, will be very noticeable to FLIR systems, whether used by air or ground searchers.

Flares are another way to attract attention. Aerial flares are most effective at night, when their movement and brilliance are best seen. They are less noticeable in daylight, but often leave a smoke trail that can call attention to the sender. Kit-sized flares burn for six to eight seconds and go about 500 feet in the air; so timing in their use is critical. Parachute flares dangle under a parachute, and stay aloft longer at higher altitudes, but their size limits them to large kits. You will also need to use caution, especially on land, to use the right flares. Flares made for land use burn out before they hit the ground, while marine flares are designed to burn throughout their trajectory. They are not a hazard on large bodies of water, but if used on land the burning magnesium could fall to the ground and start a wildfire.

When using aerial flares, or any other signal for aircraft, remember that pilots cannot see directly below them unless they have an observation bubble. Neither can they see behind. Flares must be launched far in front of the aircraft. Never fire a flare directly at an aircraft! You could hit the aircraft and damage it or harm its occupants. If you should find yourself in a combat zone or area of political unrest, be advised that aerial flares have been mistaken for anti-aircraft fire. The plane could return not to rescue you—but to retaliate! Road flares are also good for signaling an aircraft that is headed your way, especially at night. Aerial and road flares come in different colors. I recommend red as a color that is unusual in most desert surroundings and indicates an emergency. An exception to this would be much of the Australian outback, which is very red. After walking for several days in the Pilbara, even my teeth were red.

A strobe is very handy for signaling at night, and newer ones are being made in small packages. These produce regularly timed flashes of bright light and are a standard distress signal. These will flash all night on a single battery set, and if placed on high ground can be seen up to twenty miles away.

Other visible signals can be improvised by flashing a car's headlights, a flashlight, using a signal mirror in front of a camp lantern, or striking the flint on a magnesium bar or similar firestarter. You can alert others that your vehicle is incapacitated by raising the hood and tying a rag to the aerial, if the car has one.

AUDIBLE SIGNALS

Audible signals do not have the range that visual signals have, but they are important nonetheless. Audible signals should be sent in rhythmic groups of three in order to be identified as distress signals. The Morse Code distress call, SOS, is not an acronym for anything, but takes advantage of the use of groups of three. It consists of three short bursts (S), three long (O), and three short (S again). This can easily be done with car horns or whistles. SOS can also be relayed with certain visual signals, such as flashlights.

Whistles are a highly recommended item for any kit. They can be used if a person is incapacitated and unable to make a fire or signal with a mirror. If you can breathe, you can usually blow a whistle. It is not necessary to blow SOS on a whistle. Three sharp, timed blasts with pauses between will be recognized as a distress signal. Do not blow long, single blasts. These are easily mistaken for hawk screeches at a distance. Many times SAR personnel will be trying to signal you with whistles. Searchers usually blow their whistles in sets of two to attract your attention and to keep track of each other. You should respond by blowing a set of three.

Firearms can be used for signaling by firing regular shots in groups of three. Stop and listen between sets for a response. Always practice caution and safety.

Car horns can be used to signal, but it may be better to repeat SOS, as many urban people are so used to hearing them that they may ignore a simple group of three. This even occurs out in the sticks where I live, where people are constantly using their horns to move livestock off the road. Raising your hood will allow your horn to be louder, and is a distress signal in itself. Shouting is not the best option, because it takes energy and does not carry far. At small distances the human voice becomes distorted, and cries for help may be interpreted simply as someone calling someone else.

All audible signals can be distorted by echos, air density, wind, and background noise. They are next to useless to attract aircraft. Sound can be a great ally, however. It often is better received at night and is used in passive searches. Such a message could reassure you that help is on the way. You will often hear aircraft before you see them, and the advanced warning can give you time to get your mirror in place or a fire lit.

There are a few miscellaneous ways to help searchers find you. Aircraft not involved in a search will be flying in a straight line and you will need to act quickly to attract their attention. Search aircraft will often fly a baseline search, which means they will fly back and forth over the search area in an overlapping pattern to cover the zone thoroughly. Often these will be airplanes because they have a longer range than helicopters and can stay up for more time. While they may not be able to land and help you, they can relay your position to a helicopter or ground personnel. If a plane passes you by, do not drop your guard in disappointment. If they are flying a baseline, they will be back around; so be ready with everything you have. Some planes, such as wildlife researchers using radio tracking devices, will fly over several times, even if they are not looking for you. Try to get their attention with visual signals. If an airplane spots you, it will usually circle a few times, or fly by and wag its wings before leaving the area. Many times the plane will return and keep circling. If this happens, stay put. The pilot is most likely using the wing to point your position to ground searchers. If you believe you have been spotted, do not let your guard down. In some cases, stranded persons have thought that passing aircraft had spotted them, and abandoned their survival plan, expecting a rescue in the near future that did not materialize.

Stick to your survival plan. Keep your fire going and fuel piled. Every time you see an airplane or dust cloud, signal to it. Keep alert for noises searchers are making, and be prepared to answer back. Never assume you are rescued until the SAR people are shaking your hand.

Never Assume Anything

An air-to-ground misreading of signals occurred in the famous events of a South American airliner crashing in the Andes with a rugby team, inspiring the book and movie *Alive*. Shortly after the crash a small plane flew near the survivors, who frantically signaled by waving their arms. The plane seemed to wag its wings as it passed, encouraging the stranded people that help would arrive soon. That night, sure of their salvation, some of the survivors ate all of the groups' meager rations of candy bars. Help did not return, and the group's subsequent resorting to cannibalism of the dead passengers and the walk to rescue is now legendary. The moral is to never let your guard down until SAR personnel are shaking your hand.

8 Expedient Vehicle Repairs and Uses

"So we were driving by the clinic and saw smoke pouring out from under the hood. I ran into your wife's office, grabbed the fire extinguisher and yelled to her, 'Your Jeep's on fire!' Bob and I tried to pop the hood, but you had one of those locks on it, so we tried to shoot the extinguisher up under the grill. Apparently it was an electrical fire, because the starter engaged—it was in gear—and the thing started chasing me and Bob! It was kinda like a Stephen King movie."

—David Claypool recounting the demise of my Jeep CJ-7, *1994*

Remember back in Chapter 3 when I talked about how tools have a psychological allure to them? Let's take that thought a step higher. A hypothetical person has a new four-wheel drive that is loaded. It has an extra gas tank, heavy-duty winch, oversized ten-ply tires with tread deep enough to make a science fair mouse maze, and extras like a great air conditioner and a stereo with 200-decibel speakers. It also has a postfactory gun rack and CB radio. Now let's make the driver young with a self-image driven by testosterone. Let's say that the payments and insurance eats up a good portion of his income. He loves this truck. We have just constructed the opening to a myriad of survival scenarios.

If tools seem to project power, then it is easy to see what a big four-wheeler can do. There is an adage that four-wheel drive trucks and extra gas tanks can take you in twice as far, get you in twice as much trouble, and make you walk twice as far out. Preparation and caution are not extras available at your dealer. These types of vehicles, however, when used properly are one of the best ways to get around the backcountry.

DRIVING SENSE

Do Not Go Off-Road: Deserts are very fragile and any damage done is a long time healing. You could also damage your vehicle. Respect private property and leave gates as you find them.

Be Prepared: Carry extra spares, parts, water, etc. Make sure your car is in good condition and the tires can handle rough use. Carry extra gasoline in a rack outside the vehicle.

Scout Ahead: If in doubt about the way ahead, get out and look. This includes creek crossings, washes, sandy areas, ruts that can cause high centering, and treacherous slopes. Look for wide places to turn around. Leave the engine running to help prevent over-heating while looking around. If the vehicle will be idling for over a few minutes, open the hood.

Use Your Equipment: Some people like to let the road get pretty bad before they shift into four-wheel, to show off their driving "skills." This puts a lot of strain on your vehicle. By using four-wheel drive you can ease through spots and make an easier ride on the truck, you, and your passengers.

Don't Use Your Equipment: Some items, like air conditioners, can cause overheating if used while the vehicle is in lower gears. That loud stereo can mask noises that could warn you of trouble. It also destroys the serenity of the desert.

Use Your Head: Always keep alert and think about your driving. While a big four-wheel rig may give you a feeling of power, your ego will be pretty deflated when you knock a fist-sized hole in your oil pan. Just because you are driving on a backroad is no reason to forego sobriety. There may not be any police around, but you are still responsible for yourself and your passengers. As a medic I have had to respond to several single-vehicle accidents on remote roads resulting from intoxication.

EMERGENCY REPAIRS AND PROCEDURES

Despite all of your caution, vehicles are mechanical things and can break. They seem to have a complete understanding of Murphy's Law and fail at the most inconvenient times. Many people are stranded because they do not know some simple tricks to get their cars running again or unstuck. Know how to use the jacks and other equipment supplied with the vehicle. Better yet, throw the factory-supplied junk away and get heavy-duty jacks, tire tools, etc. Become familiar with your vehicle and know where everything is and how it works. This is really important with the newer models that are electronic. I was once very embarrassed when I offered a jump from a new department vehicle I was driving and could not find the battery! One of my friends from Mexico drove up in a vintage Bronco and said, "If you want to move your computer, I'll give this guy a jump."

Overheating is one of the biggest problems in hot climates. It can be caused by not having sufficient coolant in the radiator, poor circulation, a blocked radiator (e.g., the spaces full of bugs or a spare tire mounted on the grill), the radiator needs flushing, leaks, driving with the air conditioner on, a stuck thermostat, or a broken fan belt. Obviously most of these can be avoided by prevention. If your car overheats, stop the vehicle but leave it running. Turn off the air conditioner if it is on. To help bleed some of the heat off the engine, turn on the heater with the fan on high. You will probably want to be outside the car after this move. If possible, point the car into the wind and open the hood. Let the car idle and watch for the temperature gauge to drop. If this does not happen, it may be necessary to turn the car off and wait for it to cool. Try to be patient and do not attempt to open the radiator while the engine is hot. You could severely scald yourself and others.

After the engine cools, you may take off the cap and try to add more water or coolant. If you have an overflow container (and you should, both for ecological and water conservation reasons) take the liquids out of there. This is a good time to put in unnecessary items such as beer from the ice chest. Do not commit your entire water supply to the radiator, as it may not work. Small leaks can be pinched off with pliers, and ones that cannot be seen or repaired can often be temporarily stopped by using commercial additives found at auto parts stores. While it takes a long time, you can drive the car until it heats up again, shut it down, wait for it to cool, and repeat the process. You may be risking damage to the engine, but we are talking about a situation where your life is more important.

Leaky hoses causing overheating can sometimes be fixed with special tape available at auto parts stores. Sometimes a liberal wrapping of duct tape will work, but it is temporary at best. Weak hoses can also explode and scald you, so take care.

Vapor lock occurs on hot days when the gasoline in the fuel line, usually between the fuel pump and carburetor, turns to vapor and creates a blockage. The car acts like it is running out of gas, and will not restart. This is often a problem when the weather starts to warm up because many oil companies think the entire country lives in one climate zone and distribute gasoline during the winter and early spring that has a lower flashpoint for easier starting in cold weather. Generally you must stop the car and let it cool for half an hour or more. You can sometimes help the process along by wrapping a damp cloth around the fuel line between the fuel pump and carburetor.

Your air conditioner can be a liability while driving but it could be useful later. If for some reason the vehicle cannot move, but the engine will run, the air conditioner can be used to cool. This can be very important to the elderly or small children. Make sure they are in the shaded side of the car. Run the engine and air conditioner off and on as needed. Don't forget that the air conditioner has an outlet pipe near the grill to release water it condenses from the air. Place a container under this or tie a plastic bag to it to collect this water.

Flats are a constant problem because of thorny vegetation and sharp rocks. Many desert travelers like to carry two spares. A quick remedy is to use the canned tire sealers and inflators on the market today as a temporary, but quick fix. It is also a good idea to know how to fix flats and carry the tools to do so. The new plug type repair kits work well for tubeless tires. Some people carry tubes, so that if they get a flat on a tubeless tire, they can break it down, pull out the offending object, and put a tube in. I know of people in Mexico who have had flats and broken the tire down and crammed it full of leafy creosote branches to keep the rim off the ground. How they kept the tire on the rim without inflating it to set the bead is still a mystery to me.

Getting stuck is one of the most common problems in the desert, especially with inexperienced people. My theory is that if you are moving an inch in any direction except down, you are not stuck. You may need to dig the car out, jack it up and put rocks or brush under it, or place under the rear tires the carpet strips I recommend carrying. It helps to deflate the tires and drive out. Obviously you need an air pump to reinflate the tires after you do this and also after you fix a flat. Carrying a Come-Along can winch you out, as well as an electric or power take-off winch. A trick for sandy ground that will not hold a stake to anchor to is to pull the winch cable far ahead, hook it to the rim of your spare tire, and bury the tire. It is a lot less work to scout ahead and not get stuck. As you gain experience, you get tired of getting stuck and stop doing it.

A highlift jack is standard off-highway equipment for changing flats in rough terrain or getting unstuck. It is critical that you use these with extreme care, as they can become unbalanced if the car is lifted too high and cause it to fall. Stand aside while lowering the car because the handle can slip out of your hands and fly up, hitting you under the jaw and causing serious injury.

Holes in the gas tank or oil pan are common on rocky roads. The epoxy putty in the vehicle kit can repair some of these, but other holes may be too large and require fashioning a plug from a stick or like material. I once saw a gas tank hole plugged with a potato, but there wasn't enough gas left to do much good. If you see a rock you have doubts about clearing, throw it out of the road. Kids are real handy for this and I like traveling with them for that and their ability to open gates.

Hot weather is especially hard on car batteries, and you need to check the water in them frequently. Remember that items like CB radios may not turn off when the engine is shut off but ignition left on. Leaving the headlights on or the radio or tape deck playing on ACC also will run down the battery. Make sure the battery is solidly mounted or it may bounce off, break, or short out. You can remount a battery temporarily using things like pieces of inner tube or rope. Wire is a last resort because if it is not placed carefully it can short across the battery posts. Follow the rules strictly in the owner's manual if you are using jumper cables. Hot weather can cause an increase in hydrogen gas from a battery, which could explode from stray sparks.

Spare gas is a good precaution, but carrying it inside the vehicle can be very dangerous. Hot climates increase gasoline vapors, which are not only explosive but can make you very intoxicated or ill. In this case an extra gas tank or an outside carrier is a good idea.

Water crossings can cause problems, especially with newer electronic ignition systems. I had a four-wheel drive that would not start after I washed it because water would run down the fire wall into a bad seal on a control box and prevent it from starting until it dried. Spraying WD-40 on wet electrical connections often displaces water and gets things going again. An old trick of desert travelers to keep distributor caps dry was to remove the fan belt before crossing water, and put it back on after the ford was completed. This kept the fan from throwing water up onto the engine. Another good reason to remove the fan belt is that if the water is deep enough to get into the fan, the fan acts like a propeller and pulls water into the radiator, damaging both fan and radiator.

Speaking of belts, always check them for wear before a back-country trip, and carry spares. There are some on the market that can be fitted with a sliding clamp. This keeps you from needing several different-sized belts and also lets you put it on without loosening things like the alternator. A true expedient I have used is to twist a pair of panty hose and tie it on like a belt. These don't last very long, but it might hold just long enough to get you back to the pavement. Too bad I recommended in Chapter 6 that they not be worn.

Beware of driving through or parking in tall grass or brush, especially if you have a catalytic converter. These become very hot and can ignite dry vegetation, burning your car up. People have hit large tumbleweeds blowing across the road and had their catalytic converter start the weed, and then the car, on fire. Should your vehicle catch fire, exit immediately, taking your kit and water if possible. Do not worry about things like stereos or other junk. While the CB radio may be of great help in normal situations, it will be no good without a power source. If you have a fire extinguisher, take it out. Do not do like my well-meaning friends trying to save my Jeep and get near the vehicle to shoot the extinguisher under it. The recommended procedure is to pull the pin on the extinguisher, push down the handle, and quickly reinsert the pin to keep it discharging. Throw the entire extinguisher under the car like a bomb and get far away. Burning automobiles can blow up and easily kill you.

EXPEDIENT USES OF A VEHICLE

The more complicated and computerized that vehicles become, the harder they are to fix in the field. In cases where the car has become hopelessly disabled, it may be necessary to use it for other purposes. Because vehicles take such a large part of most peoples' incomes, many are reluctant to cannibalize them in emergencies. It seems that some people would rather die than do some of the things I am about to discuss. Let's look at it from another angle. If you are in a fix because your vehicle is incapacitated, you owe it no loyalty. It has betrayed you. Take it apart and use what you need from it to be rescued. Find a reason to live. Decide to make it out alive so you can sue the manufacturer!

Various parts and fluids from your vehicle can be used for firestarting, signaling, even furniture. Gasoline or diesel from the vehicle has already been discussed as a firestarter to be used with caution. While it may not be feasible to use your vehicle as a shelter on a hot day, unless you have a good cross breeze or are using the air conditioner, it can be used as such in cooler weather, rain, or dust storms. Cars have very little insulation and will become extremely hot or cold in severe weather. You can run the air conditioner or heater, but you must have a good muffler system and not fall asleep while doing so, to prevent carbon monoxide poisoning from the exhaust.

On hot days you can take the seats out and into shade to allow air circulation underneath you. The seats can also be burned as a distress signal should you see aircraft or vehicles in the distance.

This should be a last resort and be done with caution. The modern foam padding used in car seats can produce cyanide gases when burned; so make sure you are well upwind after you put such items on the fire. They will make a lot of smoke.

The spare tire will make a monstrous black smoke column unless the day is especially windy. To burn the tire you must first slash the sidewall, cut the valve stem, or remove the valve core. Setting an inflated tire on fire will cause it to swell and explode, possibly injuring bystanders. It will do no good to merely let the air out and leave the valve core in. The heat will cause the air left in the tire to expand and eventually rupture it. Once the tire has been made safe, lay it on a fire and it will soon produce smoke, even after it bursts into flames.

Motor oil is another smoke producer. It can be drained from the oil pan, and poured onto fuel ready to ignite for a signal. It can be distributed onto your three signal fires to put up smoke. Another trick is to drain the oil into a hubcap and set it on hot coals to make thick smoke. The hoses, fan belts, or any other rubber parts can be added to fires to produce smoke, but they will not yield as much as seats, tires, or oil. When burning any artificial product for smoke, stand well upwind.

Headlights can be used at night as a signal, but they point in a horizontal direction. You can take off the side or rearview mirrors and use them to reflect the beam upward if an aircraft is heard. Alternatively, with a few simple tools you can remove the headlights from the car, wiring still attached, and rest them on the hood pointing towards the sky. Don't forget the horn as a signal.

In most of these applications you are not damaging your vehicle beyond repair, but you will probably have some problems and expense getting it out to be fixed. That should not concern you at this time. You should be developing a plan and taking care of your physical needs. The vehicle is only an object that is presently not of use to you except for its parts and fluids.

⑨ Chihuahuan Desert Plant Resources

Urshanabi, this is a plant against decay
By which a man can attain his survival.
—*The Epic of Gilgamesh*, Tablet XI, 2000 B.C.

WARNING!

Tere are inherent dangers in using plants for food, beverages, or medicine. Plants are described in this chapter to give you a basic understanding of those that can be used in emergency situations. Common sense is necessary when utilizing these plants. Many plants are edible only by careful preparation. Some plants can be found both in books on poisonous and medicinal plants. Like any medicine, plants must be used in proper dosage and should not be indiscriminately mixed with other plants or drugs. Do not be fooled by the current attitude that "natural" is without its hazards. Remember, death is how nature recycles.

Many survival books delete plant uses because most survival scenarios are for a period of a few days or less, and the risk of using plants for food or medicine is not worth it. I include plants for emergency uses for several reasons. I believe in being prepared for the worst situations. I have made a study of plant uses for over two decades, and many of my students attend my classes for that very reason. The U.S. Air Force is interested in long-term survival strategies and started sending me their pilots as a result of a class I did on *ethnobotany* attended by one of their instructors. However, *this chapter is not intended to be a bible for plant uses or identification*. It is merely a springboard to give those persons interested in more advanced desert survival techniques a start and an understanding of some basic emergency uses of plants.

A survival situation is not the proper time to start learning how to identify these plants. One survival book currently on the market is advertised as user friendly because it omits Latin names because "that is the last thing you want to read when you are hungry." I haven't read the text yet, but it sounds like a recipe book for poisoning. If you do not have the time or patience to deal with scientific classification and proper plant identification, please skip this chapter.

If you have an interest in using plants, please start ahead of time by taking courses, questioning knowledgeable people, reading authoritative books, and visiting botanical gardens. Try plants before a crisis to test for allergic reactions. Persons using any wild plants must take the following precautions:

Be certain of a plant's identification and its application. Do not guess at a plant's identity or associate it with another because it looks similar. Do not rely on techniques such as the "doctrine of signatures," which uses quasi-voodoo associations such as "plants with heart-shaped leaves are good for the heart." Be aware that common names vary from place to place. This is especially true in Mexico. There are also notable inconsistencies in scientific classifications in some species. *If you are not completely sure about a plant's identity or application, do not use it!*

Know how to prepare any plants to be used. Just because a plant is listed as edible does not mean it can be readily consumed. Some must be cooked for long periods of time to break down harmful chemicals. Others must be thoroughly ground before they are digestible. Even if a plant is edible, it may not be right for you. It is possible that you have allergies you don't know about. Also, the body may react to strange plants by vomiting or diarrhea to quickly remove a potential hazard. This can cause dehydration, nutrition loss, and death. Some medicinal plants are for external use only, some must be dried, while others must be used fresh.

Be careful in harvesting. Many desert plants have thorns or spines, and in survival situations any infected wound is potentially dangerous. Whenever possible, especially in experimentation, harvest plants with concern for the ecosystem. Do not cut all the leaves from a yucca or destroy an entire colony of plants for their roots.

Some plant roots are exposed in cut banks and can be harvested without digging up the plant. This economizes your energy and spares the plant's life. Do not harvest more plants than needed.

Below is a listing of plants found in the Chihuahuan Desert and their uses. Many will be found in other North American deserts and have the same uses. Some of these are introduced species, but are prevalent and useful nonetheless. I have not included plants other than what I have firsthand knowledge of, which excludes most plants particular to other deserts. The plants are listed below in alphabetical order in capitals by the most common English name in the Chihuahuan Desert, followed by other names, often in Spanish. Scientific names are italicized. The plants are described in groups according to general use.

ACACIAS: catclaw, gatun, *Acacia gregii;* whitethorn, largoncillo, *A. constricta*
ALGERITA: agarita, agrito, palo amarillo, *Berberis trifoliata, B. haematocarpa*
AMARANTH: pigweed, *Amaranthus spp.*
APACHE PLUME: *Fallugia paradoxa*
ASH: fresno, *Fraxinus spp.*
BARREL CACTUS: *Ferocactus spp., Echinocactus spp.*
BEARGRASS: basketgrass, sacahuiste, *Nolina spp.*
BICOLOR MUSTARD: *Nerysyrenia camporum*
CANES: giant cane, *Arundo donax;* river cane, carrizo, *Phragmites australis*
CATTAILS: *Typhus spp.*
CENIZO: (say-NEE-so) *Leucophylum frutescens; L. minus*
CENTURY PLANT: mescal, maguey, *Agave spp.*
CHOLLA: (CHOY-ya) cardenche, cane cactus, *Opuntia imbricata*
COTTONWOOD: alamo, *Populus spp.*
CREOSOTE BUSH: greasewood, guame, hediondilla, *Larrea tridentata*
CROTON: *Croton spp.*
DESERT WILLOW: mimbre, *Chilopsis linaeris*
FALSE AGAVE: guapilla, aguapia, *Hechtia scariosa*
FOURWING SALTBUSH: chamiso, *Atriplex canescens*
GUAYACAN: (gwy-a-KHAN) *Guaiacum angustifolium*

Beargrass, *Nolina erumpens*

Apache plume, *Fallugia paradoxa*

Cholla with fruit, *Opuntia inbricata*

Creosote bush, *Larrea tridentata*

Century plant, *Agave havardiana*

HACKBERRY: spiny hackberry, *Celtis pallida;* netleaf hackberry, *C. reticulata*
HOREHOUND: marrubio, *Marrubium vulgare*
JUNIPER: cedar, tascote, *Juniperus spp.*
LEATHERSTEM: sangre de drago, sangrada, *Jatropha doica*
LECHUGUILLA: (leh-chu-GHEE-ya) *Agave lechuguilla*

False agave, *Hechtia scariosa*   Guayacan, *Guaiacum angustifolium*

LOTEBUSH: tecomblate, condalia, *Ziziphus obtusifolia*; javelina bush, *Condalia ericoides*; Warnock condalia, *C. warnockii*

MAIDENHAIR FERN: culantrillo, *Adiantum veneris*

MESQUITE: *Prosopis spp.*

MEXICAN BUCKEYE: monilla, *Ungnadia speciosa*

MEXICAN WALNUT: nogal, *Juglans microcarpa*

MORMON TEA: popotillo, canutillo, *Ephedra app.*

MULLEIN: gordolobo, *Verbascum thapsus*

OAK: encino, *Quercus spp.*

OCOTILLO: (oh-co-TEE-yo) *Fouquieria splendens*

PITAHAYA: (pee-TIE-ya) purple pitahaya, *Echinocereus dubius*; strawberry pitahaya, *E. stramineus*

PRICKLY PEAR: nopal, *Opuntia spp.*

PRICKLY POPPY: cardo santo, *Argemone spp.*

SAGE: *Salvia spp.*

SEEPWILLOW: jara, *Bacharis spp.*

SOTOL: *Dasylirion spp.*

TASAJILLO: (tahs-ah-HEE-yo), Christmas cholla, *Opuntia leptocaulus*; candle cholla, *O. kleiniae*

TEXAS PERSIMMON: chapote, *Diospyros texana*

THELESPERMA: cota, greenthread, *Thelesperma spp.*

TOBACCOS: tree tobacco, *Nicotiana glauca*; desert tobacco, *N. trigonophylla*

WILLOW: sauz, *Salix spp.*

YUCCA: spanish dagger, palma, palmilla, *Yucca spp.*

Leatherstem, *Jatropha doica*

Lechuguilla, *Agave lechuguilla*

Mesquite with chirrupes,
Prosopis glandulosa

Mexican buckeye, *Ungnadia speciosa*

Mormon tea, *Ephedra spp.*

Oak, *Quercus spp.*

Pitahaya, *Echinocereus stramineus*

Ocotillo, *Fouquieria splendens*

Prickly poppy, *Argemone spp.*

Prickly pear, *Opuntia engelmannii*

Sotol, *Dasylirion leiophyllum*

Tasajillo, *Opuntia leptocaulis*

Yucca, *Yucca faxoniana*

Above left: **Yucca sandals.** *Above right:* **Fiber and cordage.** *Left to right:* Yucca pita strips, two-ply yucca rope, two-ply lechuguilla twine with lechuguilla ixtle fiber.

EDIBLE AND BEVERAGE PLANTS

There are at least two hundred species of edible plants in the Chihuahuan Desert. Some of these are seasonal producers, such as fruit or seeds, and will not be available at all times. Harvest times fluctuate because the plants are opportunistic and bloom when rains come and it is warm enough. Yuccas may produce a profusion of edible flowers in January. This is called the "fifth season" and cannot be predicted. While the land may appear barren, desert harvests are often more productive than forests or woodlands. Desert plants often produce huge quantities of flowers, and conversely fruit and seeds, to ensure that a few find the right circumstances to germinate. Many desert plants rely on the fruit and seeds being consumed to help in germination.

While strict identification is advised, not all people have the time to become thoroughly familiar with all the edible plants. There is a method that is time consuming but will help identify plants without toxicity. Some edible plants will be discarded using this method, but it is better to err on the side of caution. Discard any plants that have the following:

1. Red seeds and those from prickly or hairy pods.
2. Leaves shaped like an open hand.
3. Milky sap (can be very caustic in some plants).
4. Trumpet or pea type flower shapes.
5. Odors that are pungent or similar to peach or almond.
6. Leaves that grow opposite to each other on a stem.
7. *Avoid all fungi.*

Harvesting pitahaya fruit: Ruben Hernandez finds a snack.

If the plant passes this inspection, take a small piece and rub it on the inside of the wrist and wait fifteen minutes for any reaction. If there is none, rub a small piece in one corner of the mouth. Discard if there is any burning, tingling, or dryness. If there is none, take a dime-sized piece and put it in the mouth, and swirl it around and over and under the tongue, checking for the same sensations. If it passes these tests, swallow a dime-sized piece and wait four hours, not eating anything else, and check for stomach cramps, stomachache, nausea, diarrhea, sweating, etc. If the plant passes this test, it should be safe.

Do not use this test on mushrooms, toadstools, or any other fungi. These plants often taste fine and have agreeable odors, but have toxins that take effect much longer than four hours later. One general survival video claims they are a step above other plants in nutrition. This is not true. They have no calories, take calories to digest, and other than B complex vitamins, have no nutritional value at all. It takes considerable skill to identify the edible varieties and knowledge of when to harvest and proper preparation. Because so many are toxic and/or hallucinogenic, the risk of poisoning is great. *Fungi have no place in your survival strategy.*

The following plants are found in many desert regions and are frequently available as a food or beverage source.

ACORNS: The acorns of some OAKS are highly edible as they become mature and are called *bellotas* in Spanish. Others have high amounts of tannins and must be leeched by placing in running water or boiling and pouring off the water several times (retain this water for medicinal uses described later). White oaks tend to produce acorns that are mild, while some black oaks have acorns that are so bitter that several changes of water will not make them palatable.

ALGERITA: The small fruits of this plant are quite tasty, but the spiny-tipped leaves make them hard to get. Placing a blanket under the bush and beating the bush with a stick is the quickest method.

AMARANTH: The seeds and leaves are high in protein, lysine, and calcium. The seeds may be popped like corn, boiled into a mush, or can be sprouted. The seeds are rubbed between the hands over a receptacle to remove the chaff. The young leaves make a good pot herb boiled and are called *quélites* in Spanish.

BICOLOR MUSTARD: Leaves are edible and spicy tasting like mustard greens. Eat raw or as pot herb.

CACTUS FRUIT: Some books say that all cactus fruit are edible, but use caution. Some species, such as TASAJILLO, have fruit that are hallucinogenic in large amounts. While they may be not be toxic, do you really need to have an

Elvis sighting in a survival context? Others in quantity can cause diarrhea at first. Most cacti fruit are eaten fresh or dried. PRICKLY PEARS should be scorched over flames to rid them of the small but vicious thorns called *glochids*. All larger fruit should be peeled. Species with small seeds, such as PITAHAYAS, can be eaten whole, while ones with large seeds, such as PRICKLY PEAR and large BARREL CACTI should have the seeds removed. The seeds can be ground into flour or saved to bait bird traps. The fruit of some BARREL CACTI are waxy but edible, and can be stewed and the seeds ground into meal.

CACTUS PULP: Contrary to some sources, all cactus flesh is not edible. Some cause severe vomiting, while others, such as peyote (*Lophophora williamsii*) and long mamma (*Mammilaria macromeris*), are hallucinogenic. PITAHAYA flesh causes severe gastric reactions in some people, and none in others. Most *young* prickly pear leaves are edible. They are best scorched to remove the thorns and glochids. They should be peeled and cooked on coals. They can also be fried or boiled. Leaving them out in the sun for a few hours will help get rid of their slimy texture.

CANES: The seeds are parched and ground into flour. The young shoots are boiled.

CATTAILS: These can be found around consistent water sources. The spring roots are boiled or eaten raw (the water they grow in, however, may be contaminated, so cooking is preferable). The core of young stalks can be eaten raw, but because they usually grow in stagnated water it is safer to cook them. This is done by placing the butts in coals for three to four minutes, then peeling the leaves back to reveal the white inner core, which is eaten. It tastes much like asparagus. While the green bloom spikes are still in their paperlike sheaths, pick and remove the sheaths, and boil.

CENIZO: Leaves and flowers steeped in hot water for palatable tea.

CENTURY PLANT: Both century plant and SOTOL are difficult to harvest. Taking a hardwood stick with a fire-hardened point on one end, jam in the sharp end of the stick at the base of the plant just above the dead leaves

Cattail shoots cooking in coals.

and hammer with a rock on the blunt end. Prying up will cause the "heart" to dislodge. Leaves are cut off and the plant is cooked in a rock-lined baking pit as described in Chapter 5 for up to forty-eight hours. The leaf butts are pulled off the heart and eaten like artichoke. The center pulp is also eaten. Leaf bases can be scraped and the pulp dried and ground into a meal for later use. The heart contains much sugar and the food yield from mature plants is high. The budding *quiote* can be roasted and the seeds can be sprouted and eaten raw. The juice of some species can cause dermatitis. Handle with care. If the plant is very bitter, it has not been cooked long enough to break down the harsh chemicals in it. Do not eat if bitter.

CHOLLA: Fruits are edible fresh, dried, boiled, or fried. Burn off the glochids and remove seeds. Peeling the fruit is almost impossible. The fruit is high in calcium and tart when fresh. Dried, it tastes similar to artichokes.

FOURWING SALTBUSH: The seeds are ground and used as baking powder.

HACKBERRY: Spiny hackberry has juicy fruits that taste like cantaloupe. Because of the spines, the berries are best harvested by placing a blanket under the bush and beating it with a stick. Netleaf hackberries have no spines, but the fruit are drier than spiny hackberries and have a large, hard

Left: **Sotol heart (left) and century plant heart ready to bake;** *right:* **baked and split sotol heart.**

seed. The berries can be boiled and the juice drank, or the berries with seeds can be dried, ground and mixed with water, and baked on hot stones like crackers.

LECHUGUILLA: Some authors claim that LECHUGUILLA is inedible, but the archeological record shows differently. Archeologist Jeffrey Huebner, who has done extensive isotope analysis of American Indian skeletons, has found that LECHUGUILLA and PRICKLY PEAR were the two main plants consumed by southwest Texas natives. LECHUGUILLA does require cooking in a hot baking pit for about twenty-four hours, as described in Chapter 5. It is always served on my courses, but is not usually the favorite wild plant food. SOTOL and CENTURY PLANT are much more palatable. The juice of the plant can cause dermatitis in some people. Handle with care.

LOTEBUSH: Fruits of the genera *Condalia* and *Ziziphus* listed here are edible but hard to collect among the thorns. The seeds can be squeezed out of the fruit and the remaining pulp mashed together and dried on a flat surface to make fruit leather.

MESQUITE: The ripe pods (called *chirrupes*) can be dried or roasted and ground into flour, sifting out the hard seeds and fiber. The *chirrupes* can also be boiled and mashed to make a nourishing broth. The pods are high in both sugar and protein.

Sotol in cooking pit.

MEXICAN WALNUT: The nuts of this tree are small and hard to crack. The entire nut can be crushed between two stones and dumped into water. The hulls sink, while most of the nutmeats float and can be skimmed off.

MORMON TEA: The green or dried firlike needles can be steeped in hot water to make a good-tasting tea that is also a stimulant.

OCOTILLO: The flowers can be steeped in cool water overnight to make a tangy beverage. The seeds can be ground into a meal, but have an alumlike taste and were used by American Indians only in starvation times.

PITAHAYAS: See CACTUS FRUITS and CACTUS PULP. These are some of the most delicious and easy to prepare of all cacti fruit, but are not as common as PRICKLY PEAR fruit.

PRICKLY PEAR: There are numerous species, the fruit of all of which is edible. See CACTUS FRUITS and CACTUS PULP. It is best to use young pads called *nopalitos* in Spanish. Larger pads can have the spines scorched off and be stuffed with meat and placed on the coals to steam. The flowers are also edible as they are.

SOTOL: Harvested, cooked, and eaten like CENTURY PLANT. Sotol is high in sugars, and each plant produces a large quantity of food. The young *quiotes* can be baked and eaten. It is imperative not to confuse SOTOL with BEARGRASS, of the same family, which is toxic.

TASAJILLO: Not recommended for consumption. See CACTUS FRUITS.

TEXAS PERSIMMON: Fruits are edible and tasty, but will turn the tongue and gums a weird green color. Great for Halloween!

YUCCA: The flowers and baked young *quiotes* are edible. The flowers may be eaten fresh or dried. In some species the fresh flowers can cause an itching sensation in the throat. The dried flowers can be reconstituted with water or ground into flower flour. Only the petals should be eaten, as the centers are bitter. The fruit of some species are edible, while some are too "woody." Take ripe fruit that are somewhat soft and boil for one-half hour, then peel and remove seeds. The cooked fruit pulp can be eaten or mashed into a layer and dried for future consumption. Banana yucca (*Yucca baccata*) fruit is especially palatable.

MEDICINAL AND FIRST-AID PLANTS

A great number of desert plants are used in pharmaceuticals and folk medicine. The examples listed below are those with emergency applications or first-aid uses. Like any medicine or treatment, they are to be used sensibly. Where teas are referred to, the indicated part and quantity of the plant is steeped in water that has been brought to a boil, but the plant is not boiled unless directed.

ACACIAS: The powdered dried leaves and seed pods are used to treat chafed skin, rashes, and abrasions. Also has the same uses as MESQUITE.

AMARANTH: A tablespoon of the dried chopped leaves steeped in a cup of hot water and drank every three or four hours will help with stomachaches and mild diarrhea.

CENIZO: A tea made from the leaves and flowers helps relieve cold and flu symptoms. *It will cause sweating.* The tea has a slight sedative effect and will aid in sleep.

CHARCOAL: The charcoal (not ash) from a campfire is powdered, mixed with water, and drank to control diarrhea. It can also be used this way if you suspect you have ingested a toxin, to bind to it and help it pass on through.

COTTONWOOD: Cottonwoods, willows, aspens, and poplars are all closely related and have the same medicinal values. All contain salicin, a precursor of aspirin. A tea made of the bark (dried is best) will help reduce pain, fever, and inflammation. A hot poultice of the leaves can be used for swelling.

CREOSOTE BUSH: A tea of the leaves applied externally is antiseptic and antifungal. Fresh leaflets can be put into boots to prevent athlete's foot. The tea can be used to treat fungal infections such as athlete's foot, jock itch, and ringworm.

DESERT WILLOW: This is not a true willow and cannot be interchanged with willows for medicinal purposes. The tree is actually a catalpa. The flowers are steeped as a tea for coughs, and a hot poultice of the flowers is applied to the chest for congestion. The dried and powdered bark and leaves make a good first-aid dressing for wounds.

FALSE AGAVE: In Mexico the mashed pulp of this plant is sloshed in water and the water drank as a preventative against kidney stones, which are common in hot arid lands.

FOURWING SALTBUSH: The leaves of the plant are chewed with a little salt and swallowed with water for stomachache.

HOREHOUND: Introduced from Europe, the plant is now widespread, especially in disturbed ground. A tea of the plant is good for lung congestion. The hot tea will cause sweating, while the cold tea promotes stomach secretions.

LEATHERSTEM: The sap is highly astringent and will stop minor bleeding when applied to a wound. It may also be applied to hemorrhoids for relief. The sap will contract gums and tighten loose teeth. The sap is also analgesic and will help stop the pain of toothache and mouth sores on contact. The stems can be chewed for a sore throat. A tea of the whole plant taken in small frequent doses helps control diarrhea.

LOTEBUSH: The fresh roots of *Ziziphus obtusifolia* (called *Condalia lycioides* in some references) are pounded into a pulp (not an easy task) and are added to hot water and briskly stirred to wash wounds, blisters, and ulcerations. It is also used against ringworm and as a shampoo for seborrhea. It will make a good medicinal sudsing shampoo with the addition of YUCCA root.

MAIDENHAIR FERN: Drinking a tea of the leaves soothes sore throats, laryngitis, and bronchial infections.

MESQUITE: Internal use of the tea made from twigs, bark, seed pods, and/or leaves helps control diarrhea and gastrointestinal inflammation. A handful of the green leaves boiled in a pint of water with one-half teaspoon salt added is an excellent skin disinfectant. A good eyewash can be made by boiling six crushed green seed pods in a pint of water and adding one-quarter teaspoon of salt. Let cool to body temperature before use. This is good for wind-burned and sand-irritated eyes, conjunctivitis, and pink eye. The sap can be diluted and put on exposed skin, turning it a dark brown for a sunblock. Be aware, however, that you are going to stay that color for a long time.

MULLEIN: Flowers when available, or leaves for a second choice, are steeped and the tea drank for lung congestion. The dried leaves may be smoked (a few puffs only, not held in the lungs for long) for coughing or asthma.

MORMON TEA: A strong tea of the needles is a stimulant and also helps bronchial dilation for easier breathing. It is especially good for allergies.

OCOTILLO: A tea of the fresh bark taken internally is useful against pelvic congestion of the lymph system and prostate inflammation. The Apache powdered the dried root as a wound dressing and made a tea of the fresh root to drink and bathe in to counteract fatigue and sore muscles. The tips of the branches can be roasted over coals and the juice expressed onto a cloth for a wrap around swellings and sore joints.

PRICKLY PEAR: The peeled, heated pads make a good poultice for drawing abscesses. The gel from the pads acts similarly to aloe vera juice for minor burns, sunburn, and skin irritations. The gel can also be mixed with powdered charcoal from the campfire and applied to the skin as a sun block. A peeled piece of the pad placed between the cheek and gums will ease the pain of mouth sores or infected gums. A teaspoon of the fresh juice taken every two hours will ease the pain of (but not cure) urinary tract infections and ease stomach cramps. A tea of the dried flowers will help strengthen capillaries.

PRICKLY POPPY: The sap can be diluted and used directly on sunburns for pain relief and to aid healing. The seeds can be smoked with regular tobacco as a sedative and to aid in sleep. The leaves may be steeped as a tea and taken to relieve menstrual cramps and helps calm PMS symptoms.

SENNA: Two leaflets steeped in hot water make a strong laxative—something usually not needed in survival settings. They can cause cramping and should be used with an anti-spasmodic such as a teaspoon of PRICKLY PEAR juice.

THELESPERMA: A tea of the entire aboveground plant is antiseptic to the urinary tract. It is also quite good merely as a beverage.

TOBACCO: *The wild tobaccos are for external use only!* The fresh leaves can be bruised and wrapped in a hot moist cloth to make an analgesic poultice. The same treatment can be applied to ease hemorrhoidal pain.

YUCCA: The *thoroughly* dried root can be powdered and added to hot water at the rate of one-quarter teaspoon per cup and drank for arthritis. This should be done no more than once a week or it could block the absorption of B vitamins.

PLANTS FOR CONSTRUCTION

ASH is a good hard wood, well suited for tool and weapons construction, and is a good choice for bows, rabbit sticks, atlatls, digging sticks, and the pointed tools used to harvest CENTURY PLANTS and SOTOL.

Quiotes are useful when long straight pieces are needed. Those of LECHUGUILLA are good for atlatl darts. SOTOL *quiotes* are long, straight, and suitable for shelters. The female SOTOL produces the stronger *quiote*, and can be identified by its larger size and greater number of flowers than the male. CENTURY PLANT *quiotes* can be quite long and are useful for shelter construction. The leaves of the plant can also be used as natural shingles.

CANES, depending on size, are useful for arrows, atlatl darts, and fishing poles. They can also be used to thatch shelters and, if tied in bundles, as support poles.

Tarahumara woman in the Sierra Madres of Mexico
weaving a basket from split sotol leaves.

WILLOW can also be found in long, straight pieces, and is flexible when green, making it useful for support arches in shelters. WILLOW also makes an acceptable bow. WILLOW shoots are good for arrows and darts. SEEPWILLOW is good for arrow shafts, and makes a good thatching for a *kowa*. Almost any dense brush can be used in the same manner.

FIBER PLANTS

All of the YUCCAS, SOTOL, and CENTURY PLANTS have useful fibers called *ixtle* in Spanish, which make strong cordage. These are best extracted by heating the leaves over coals, lightly pounding the leaf with a round stone, and scraping the pulp from the fiber with a dull edge of a stone or knife. LECHUGUILLA produces a very strong fiber that is readily extracted by the same method. Two to six fibers with the needle left intact can be twisted together for sewing. Some YUCCA leaves must be boiled in water with hardwood ashes to extract the fibers.

The leaves from the above-mentioned plants, as well as BEAR-GRASS, can be split and used for weaving.

SOTOL and BEARGRASS have sawtooth edges, so be careful when harvesting. The leaves of the broad-leaved YUCCAS are heated over coals until the skin blisters, and split into lengths for tying. These are called pita, and shrink tight as they cool and dry, making a firm lashing that is useful in shelter projects.

The inner bark of COTTONWOOD and JUNIPER can be used for cordage, although it is inferior to the above species and should be used for light tying jobs only.

PLANTS FOR HYGIENE

Hygiene and sanitation are extremely important to people under stressful conditions. While overall bathing is not necessary, being clean will help morale. The roots of YUCCA, LECHUGUILLA, and CENTURY PLANTS contain soapy substances called saponins. The fresh root, with the bark in place, is pounded and mixed with hot water and whipped into a lather for an excellent shampoo. The pulp from the leaves of LECHUGUILLA, which is a by-product of fiber extraction, is called *xite* in Mexico and is used to wash laundry. Add the pulp to hot water. It can also be used to wash cookware. In both applications, rinse thoroughly.

Fresh GUAYACAN root, called *amole* in Mexican markets, is sold to wash woolens. Prepare the same as YUCCA root shampoo. This is a good plant to wash socks with to keep them clean and so keep the feet in good shape.

LEATHERSTEM has hygienic as well as medicinal uses. It is common in backcountry Mexico for people to chew on the end of a cut stem to make a brush to clean their teeth. At first the taste is bitter, but the sap's numbing properties take care of that. LEATHERSTEM whitens teeth and constricts the gums. Nine out of ten Chihuahuan Desert dentists recommend LEATHERSTEM for their patients who chew desert plants.

Besides CREOSOTE's antibacterial and antifungal uses, it makes a good deodorant. A tea of the leaves removes body odor and can keep it away for up to a week. It is locally well known to remove foot odor. It can be used as a body wash to mask human smell while hunting, and traps and snares can also be washed with it to remove human scent. Be advised, that CREOSOTE stains the skin yellow and, like MESQUITE gum, is very persistent.

Women may have special problems, especially if they are separated from birth-control pills. Depending on the time of the woman's cycle, stress, environmental heat, and other factors, a woman may start menstruating three to seven days after the last dosage. Women without tampons or sanitary napkins may need to make menstrual pads from plant sources. The shredded inner bark of COTTONWOOD and JUNIPERS was used by American Indian women. JUNIPER bark prepared the same way was also used to diaper babies. The shredded leaves of MULLEIN can also be used for menstrual pads. The whole velvety basal leaves of MULLEIN make an acceptable toilet paper substitute.

Women may also have problems with vaginal irritation or yeast infections. A tea of dried AMARANTH leaves applied as a douche or by soaking and inserting a tampon soaked in the tea will help itching and irritation. *Candida* yeast infections may be helped in the same manner with DESERT WILLOW bark tea.

In Mexico, CROTON is placed under mattresses to repel bed bugs. It may be used similarly against some insects in the wilds, but take care not to have it directly against you, as some species with glandulous hairs cause skin and eye irritation on contact.

FISH POISONS

Plant-based fish poisons work by blocking the ability of the fish's gills to assimilate oxygen. The plant materials are mashed or pounded, mixed in a container of warm water, and then are slowly stirred into still pools where fish rest. MEXICAN BUCKEYE seeds are ground and added to water. These contain cyanide compounds that inhibit oxygen absorption. The pulp from LECHUGUILLA leaves and many other AGAVE species contain saponins that give it its soapy quality, which also coats the gills and blocks oxygen intake. Because these plants inhibit oxygen transfer, they do not get into the bloodstream of the fish and leave them safe to eat. Both of these plants are currently used as fish poisons by Mexican Indians. *Keep in mind that this is very illegal and should be used as a last resort.*

Chihuahuan Desert Animal Resources

The school he learned in was a hard one. The plants and animals he lived with were armed with thorns, fangs and claws. Everything lived on something else, and every existence had to be bought with another. Kindness and pity were luxuries the desert could not afford.

—C.L. Sonnichsen, *The Mescalero Apache*, 1958

Hunting is a major part of the survival fantasy game. People dreaming of living off the land usually picture themselves as big-game hunters. Such is not usually the lot of desert people. The Desert Archaic people of the Chihuahuan Desert seemed to rely heavily on small game, especially rodents, for most of their protein. They weren't very picky, either. Archeologist Jeffrey Huebner relates the find of a human *coprolite* (a dehydrated and preserved fecal specimen) that contained an entire vole—hair, bones, and all! It was simply chewed and swallowed. Not exactly in line with the romantic notion of the great hunter.

Animals can supply the survivor with food, hides, tools, bindings, and glue. Animals are almost indispensable for long-term survival. In most situations, however, they are not needed. As stated before, food is not a high priority in most scenarios these days. Still, there are relatively simple ways to acquire game with little effort, and it should not be neglected if the opportunity arises. There are exceptions. Some people do not eat meat for religious or ethical reasons, and the psychological discomfort caused by eating meat may be of greater harm than the lost nutrition from not eating it.

Also, people who have been vegetarians for a long time may also experience extreme gastric discomfort or diarrhea if they attempt to eat meat.

Also be aware that taking game has its share of risks. I am not referring so much to animals returning your attack as to the transmission of disease. Animals can directly transmit diseases such as rabies, leptospirosis, histoplasmosis, and tularemia. They also can harbor parasites that carry diseases such as Rocky Mountain spotted fever, Lyme disease, and tick-borne relapsing fever. I went to college with a fellow who died from bubonic plague after running a trapline over Christmas break.

If you decide you need to use animals in your survival strategy, obligate yourself to some ethics. Dispatch the animals as quickly as possible by the most humane means. Check any traps regularly and do not leave an area (even if rescued) without collecting traps and hooks. I hunt and have no qualms about people taking their rightful place as predators. I do not, however, condone torture and waste.

Hunting and stalking require a lot of energy and may take you away from your camp and lessen your chances of being found, but there are some techniques to gather in game that require little skill or energy.

The fishhooks from the survival kit can bring in fish, birds, and on occasion, small mammals. The hooks can be baited with small scraps of foil for birds and fish. In Australia we saved the foil from the bouillon cubes as lures. Bait found along the bank such as worms, grubs, maggots, insects, and even bits of plants can be used for fishing. Certain seeds such as from cactus, leatherstem, and croton can be used to catch tastier birds such as dove and quail. Old meat or offal from other animals can catch fish, birds, and mammals. If fishhooks are unavailable, certain barrel cacti have thorns that are well suited for the purpose. For catching birds, select species with smaller thorns.

FISHING

While fishing in the desert may sound ludicrous, many rivers, creeks, pools, and even larger tinajas contain fish. While a pole can be cut from cane or a *quiote*, a more effective method is with trotlines and nightlines. These are stout lines, such as parachute cords, with hooks dangling from smaller strings tied at spaced intervals.

The ends are secured on both banks, or one end is secured on the bank and the other is weighted with a heavy object like a rock. Floats are not used. These lines catch fish while you go about other tasks.

If hooks or cacti thorns are unavailable, you can still fish with gorges. These are slivers of bone or wood about three-quarters of an inch long that are sharpened on both ends. A small groove is cut around the middle to hold the line. The gorge is placed parallel to the line and the bait impaled upon it. When the fish swallows it, the gorge sets crosswise in its gullet.

Some fish can be attracted at night by lights. A flashlight beam, lantern, Cayalume stick, or nearby campfire can bring them close to shore. You can also attract fish by using the discarded innards of other fish or animals. These can be chopped and put into still water near the bank, while the same material is used as hook or gorge bait. Offal can also be tied in a bundle and suspended over the water for a couple of days to become flyblown. As the maggots develop, they fall in the water, attracting fish. Ant and termite nests can be broken up and tossed on the water. During the nesting season a good place to fish is under cliff swallow nests. These birds build mud nests on rock faces over water, and unfortunate young periodically fall out, becoming a meal for catfish.

Larger fish can be snagged or speared, although many desert water sources are not clear enough to see very deep. In dry times the fish congregate in sluggish pools and can be seen at the top, especially large carp. Big fish hooks can be lashed to a pole as a gaff to snag fish. Spears can also be used, but be advised once again to carve a spear point and not to lash your knife to the pole. It is much too valuable to damage or lose.

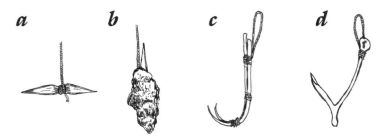

Expedient fishhooks: *(a)* **Bone or wood gorge;** *(b)* **bait placed on gorge;** *(c)* **cactus thorn hook (two thorns tied together);** *(d)* **bird wishbone hook**

Bottle trap for small fish.

Small fish can be caught for bait or food if a large plastic bottle is handy. Cut the top off the bottle at the shoulder. Place bait in the bottle and invert the neck, securing it by cutting holes at intervals and lacing the two together. Tie a string to it and submerge the trap. Fish swim into the funnel to the bait, but most cannot find their way out.

Poisoning fish is a last resort, but in some cases, the only viable one. Many desert ecosystems have more varieties of fish than forests, but they are often small minnowlike creatures that do not take hooks or are too small for most nets. In this case they can be poisoned using the plants and methods covered in the previous chapter. When they float to the surface, they are skimmed off. Before you do this, consider several things. You are going to kill all the fish, large and small in the pool. Many of the smaller desert fish species have a very limited range and are considered threatened or endangered species either on state or federal lists. The potential for damage is great and the legal consequences could be severe. *Make sure there are no other options before you poison fish.*

HUNTING

Animals can also be harvested as the opportunity arises. While gathering firewood, attending to the latrine, or moving from place

Throwing sticks: Expedient throwing sticks for small game, and large jaw bone thrown as a nonreturning boomerang.

to place, always arm yourself. If you get a glimpse of a cottontail running from you, it will be too late to locate a rock to throw. Better yet, carry a stick, which twirls end over end and covers more area. It should be thrown overhand and vertical at ground animals. If it falls short, it will tumble and still may hit the target. A sidearm throw is best for rising birds such as coveys of quail that often explode in front of the desert hiker. Rabbit stick and boomerang designs enhance the effectiveness of a throwing stick.

In areas where there are mounds of sandy soil held together by brush on top, you may find a network of rabbit tunnels. Often you can see a cottontail flee into one of these openings. Cut a bundle of switches and drive them down through each entrance to the warren like jail bars. If you know which tunnel the rabbit entered, start collapsing that entrance with a stick and follow the tunnel. Be ready to club the animal quickly when you encounter it. Cottontails often seek refuge in other animal burrows. So do rattlesnakes. Be careful in unearthing the quarry lest you dig up an angry badger or a nest of vipers!

Another way to extract mammals from burrows is with a skewer. In many places a supple pole, such as willow shoot with a small fork on the end, was inserted into burrows until an animal was encountered. The pole was forced into the animal's skin and twisted, wrapping the hair into the fork. With the torque held, the animal was

pulled out of the hole. The Chihuahuan Desert can provide an even better skewer. If willow is not available, exposed green mesquite roots that are long and flexible may be used. *Quiotes* are long enough, but not flexible to follow curves in a burrow. Taking small branches from thorny vegetation, especially catclaw acacia, tie several in hoops at the end of the skewer. These will readily grab an animal's fur and hold it better than a mere fork. As in digging out animals, be careful that what you pull out of the hole won't be more than you can handle!

Hunting and stalking consume much time and energy, but circumstances may require them. In areas where water is not abundant, game can often be taken at a watering spot. Hunters should conceal themselves downwind from the water early morning and late evening. If using an atlatl, bow, or small-caliber firearm, it will be necessary to be close for a clean shot. Blinds are often built near waterholes to conceal hunters. Keep in mind, however, that this works only a few times. After a few ambushes the animals will seek water elsewhere.

If you are traveling and hunting, keep wind direction and air current in mind. In the cool of the morning, air generally flows down mountain slopes. As it heats later in the day, it rises. It is best to hunt uphill in the morning and downhill later in the day to keep downwind of prey.

A final caution about animals. Most animals will fight viciously if cornered. Javelinas, however, do more than that. These intelligent animals are well known for setting ambushes. Many domestic dogs have been maimed when they chased a javelina running as a decoy by others concealed and waiting to attack. They will also hide near a wounded or trapped member of their group and attack en masse. They generally will flee if you give them lots of room, but if you decide to hunt them, you'd better be good at it.

TRAPPING

Traps and snares are much more energy efficient than hunting. They work all the time while you are at other tasks. A comprehensive discussion of the styles of traps and snares is beyond the scope

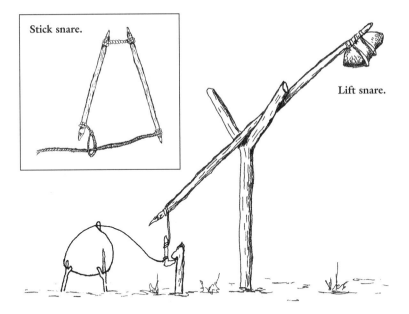

Stick snare.

Lift snare.

of this book, especially since we are not considering food a high priority. For those interested in advanced techniques, I suggest publications listed in the Selected References at the end of the book. Baiting hooks is the simplest and most energy-efficient method for catching smaller animals. There are four traps that I find work well in my area. They are the leghold snare, lift snare, Ojibwa bird snare, and ocotillo quail trap.

Leghold snares are nooses set in game trails, often for larger game. A hole is dug and covered, with the noose concealed on top. Most large-game snares are not anchored, but attached to a heavy drag or long pole to tire the animal. Most people are thinking of deer when they set these, but mountain lions and bobcats are often caught by this method. Big animals are hard to dispatch without projectile weapons when caught in snares. After roping a javelina from horseback in my younger (and not-so-wise) years, I would hate to encounter one in a leghold snare. Some animals will chew their leg off when caught in such devices.

Lift snares are designed to catch smaller animals around the middle or neck when they try to pass through the noose. The noose is set vertically on the trail and closed shut by a bent sapling or counterweight when the trigger is released. Wire works well because many rodents can chew through cordage. If wire is unavailable, a stick snare, as employed by desert American Indians, can be used.

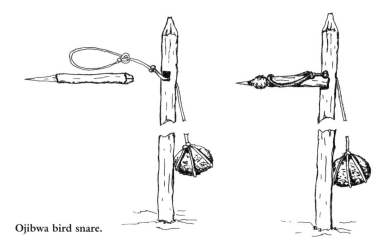

Ojibwa bird snare.

These are built out of two sticks as shown in the diagram and placed like snares. They are especially good when placed over the exits to burrows that show signs of occupation.

An animal that is rather easy to snare with wire or stick snares is the pocket gopher. These dig a maze of tunnels from one plant to another, eating roots. The tunnel systems can be identified by the mounds of dirt they use to cover the tunnel openings. By digging between two mounds you can often break into their tunnel less than a foot down. The gophers don't like this and will come to fix it. Placing the snare in the break will often catch them. The counterweight may not pull them out of the hole, so you may need to do that yourself.

The Ojibwa bird trap is from the woodlands, but it works well in the desert. You will need a stake about four feet long that you can sharpen on one end and bore a hole in the other. Once again, *quiotes* are perfect for the job. Bore a hole about ten inches down from the top and square it on one side. Make a trigger from a stick about six inches long and sharpen one end and whittle the other end square to loosely fit in the hole on the stake. Take a string about three feet long and make a noose in one end long enough to cover the trigger and tie a knot behind it. Tie the other end to a rock as a counterweight. Bait the trigger on the sharp end with something shiny, some offal, cactus fruit, or whatever the birds are eating in your area. Drive the stake into the ground and assemble the trap as shown in the diagram. The bird cannot reach the bait from the top of the stake, and jumps on the trigger, letting the knot

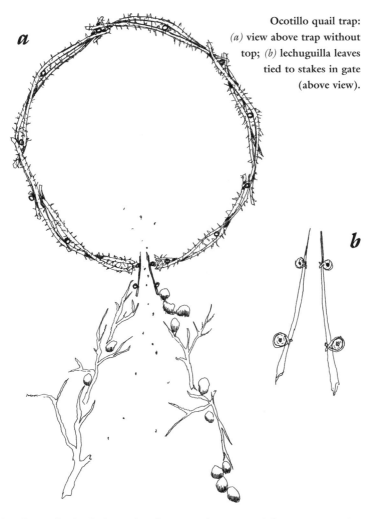

Ocotillo quail trap:
(*a*) view above trap without
top; (*b*) lechuguilla leaves
tied to stakes in gate
(above view).

a

b

slip through the hole and tightening the noose. This snare can be built and set in about twenty minutes.

A more complicated trap is the ocotillo quail trap, but it can catch large amounts of quail and some small mammals. Take a number of one and a half foot stakes and drive them into the ground in a circle about four feet in diameter. Weave ocotillo branches or other thorny brush around the stakes, leaving about a ten-inch gap for the entrance. The idea is to have the weave tight enough that the birds cannot escape, but loose enough so that they can see out and not be afraid to enter. The gate is built by driving a pair of stakes in the entrance gap about four inches apart. Several inches back, drive another pair of stakes about six inches apart from each other. As shown in the diagram, take six to eight lechuguilla or stiff yucca leaves with the end points intact, and tie them to the stakes so that there is about a two-inch gap between the points. If lechuguilla is used, trim the spines off the margins that would snag the birds passing through. Fill in around the gate with thorny sticks.

An ocotillo or thorny brush top is built that can be lifted to extract the birds. Using loose branches, rocks, etc., build a large V-shaped alley to funnel the birds toward the gate. The alley, gate, and inside of the trap can be baited with seeds previously described. The birds pass through the gate, but the angle of the points do not allow them to get back out. The captured birds can be frightened toward the back of the trap, and long sticks (such as seepwillow) can be run through the sides of the trap to make it smaller. Carefully lifting the top, the quail can be grabbed out as needed. The beauty of this trap is that quail can be kept alive in it for several days and removed as needed. Another benefit is the fact that quail cannot seem to tell the difference between one having a good time or being trapped. After one is caught, the rest will follow thinking the leader is getting all the good food. *The downside is that trapping birds, especially quail, is illegal almost everywhere.* This trap will occasionally catch small mammals, but they can usually dig out if not removed soon.

REPTILES AND AMPHIBIANS

Eating rattlesnake figures very prominently in desert survival lore, and I have served it in some of my classes. The amount of meat you get from a rattler, however, does not balance out the risk of envenomation. Many species of nonvenomous snakes can also inflict vicious bites with high risk of infection. There are few lizards large enough in the Chihuahuan Desert to pay much consideration to, but their bones are found in archaic human coprolites, which indicates they were eaten whole. There are no venomous lizards in the Chihuahuan Desert, but the Gila monster of the Sonoran and Mojave Deserts and the beaded lizard of Mexico should be avoided. Turtles, which are easy to catch on land and will take hooked bait in water, can be eaten. Frogs can be found in some waterholes, and the legs are tasty. Some frogs and toads have toxic skin secretions, so handle carefully and skin them without contaminating the meat. Tadpoles were often on the Apache menu.

CRAWLING CREATURES

Insects, worms, grubs, larvae, and such other fare are not looked upon with favor by industrialized people, but they are a valuable protein source to some cultures. Texts often describe the larvae and pupae of insects such as bees and wasps as edible, but obtaining them would be very risky. Many grubs and worms can be cooked on a hot stone until crispy and powdered to add to soups. Avoid furry caterpillars, bright-colored species, bad smelling ones, or those found on the underside of leaves. Grasshoppers and locusts with the wings and legs removed are also roasted. Ants and termites can be boiled to break down any formic acid they may use for defense. Avoid insects, grubs, etc. that are feeding on carrion, refuse, or dung. If you can't get over the cultural barrier of going that far down the food chain, use them for bait.

COOKING

All game should be cooked to avoid diseases. Skin and clean the animals well away from camp to keep flies down. Kill only healthy animals and cover any open sores or wounds while handling. Boiling is the safest method of cooking to kill any parasites or germs. This is especially true with carrion-eating birds. After boiling meat, it is important to drink the broth so that nutrients are not lost. If it is not possible to boil water, there are other cooking methods.

Cooking whole fish on coals: Southern Cross survivor Terry Gadean prepares a meal in the Pilbara of Western Australia.

Roasting meat on a spit is wasteful of nutrients, because the juices drip off into the fire. The baking pit described in Chapter 5 is excellent for cooking meat. A chicken-sized animal takes about an hour and a half. Cottontails take an hour. Some animals can be buried directly in the coals. Fish less than a foot long are put in the coals whole. The heat gels the guts, which can be removed before eating without a loss of moisture.

Before placing the fish on the coals, put a finger in one gill and your thumb in the other and reach up high toward the fish's spinal column, pinching it and bending it upward. This breaks the fish's neck and, besides being humane, keeps the fish from flipping hot coals into your eyes.

Fingerling-sized fish can be cooked on a hot rock until crisp and then eaten whole. If clay is available, larger fish and birds may be cooked in it. Gut the animals, but leave the scales, feathers, or skin on. The animal is wrapped in wet clay and placed on the fire. When the clay shell is dry and hard, it is broken off. If the animal is done, the scales or feathers come off with the clay casing.

Small pieces of meat or quartered rodents can be stuffed into large prickly pear pads that have had their spines singed off for handling. The pads are buried in coals, protecting the meat from burning. Turtle and tortoise meat is excellent when boiled, but the animal (killed by cutting off the head) can be placed whole on the fire on its back. When the shell splits, the animal is ready. Carefully remove the bottom shell, then the innards. Burned turtle plastrons are often found in archeological sites.

OTHER USES FOR ANIMALS

The by-products of hunting should not be neglected. Larger animals will have leg tendons and a broad strip of tough membrane running down the backstrap, both containing sinew. Sinew makes some excellent bindings, and is preferred for bowstrings. Leg tendon is lightly beaten with a smooth stone to break it down into the individual fibers. The back sinew is scraped clean and pulled apart as needed. Moistened sinew has its own glue, and will stick to itself when wrapped, such as binding a point to an arrow shaft. Sinew also makes excellent sewing thread, especially for leathers.

Animal hooves can be boiled for long periods of time until the water thickens into a glue. The glue is twirled on the ends of sticks and allowed to harden. When the glue is needed, it is moistened and rubbed on the object needing adhesives.

Animal skins can be prepared through lengthy processes. Rawhide, however, is easy to prepare and makes good bindings. A skin can be scraped clean on the flesh side and soaked in water with hardwood ashes until the hair begins to "slip." The hair is scraped off and the hide stretched to dry. Re-wetting the hide, strings can be cut off that will shrink tight and be very strong after they have been tied and dried. Rawhide holds its shape when dried. Wet rawhide can be sewn into containers, filled with sand, and will keep the shape when dry. In emergency situations it is not necessary to dehair the hide. Cut the green hide into strips and use it like that.

Bones have uses for everything from clubs to sewing needles. The lower leg bones of larger animals are extremely strong, but can be shattered with large rocks. They break into long sharp pieces that can be used for projectile or spear points, awls, and needles. Antlers shed by deer can often be found. They can be used for fire tongs, handles, and knapping stone tools.

Fats from animals can be used to help preserve wood and keep it from breaking. It is very desirable to rub onto primitive bows in dry climates. Almost every animal has some fat on it that can be scraped off the hides. Fat can also be rendered down into oils for cooking and for making salves with medicinal plants.

I am aware of two medicinal properties of animals. A Mexican cure for boils I once saw involved plucking and cleaning a roadrunner, and boiling the bird. The flesh was then eaten and the broth drank, and within two or three days the patient (who with so many boils had looked like Job from the Bible) was showing rapid progress. Local Mexicans call the comical bird *paisano* (fellow countryman), and many believe it to be very bad luck to kill one except for medicinal purposes. How does it work? I don't know. I can tell you a lot about the chemistry of medicinal plants, but I have never seen a list of chemical properties of roadrunners!

Another palliative with good repute is snake oil. I once had the privilege of showing baseball great Nolan Ryan (a Texas Parks & Wildlife commissioner) around my park. In talking about folk cures, Commissioner Ryan told me that when tendonitis was giving his pitching arm problems, he would rub it down well with snake oil for relief.

Expedient Tools and Weapons

With two stones, you can make one into a tool with sharp edges that can be used to work other materials like wood.

—John C. Whittaker, *Flintknapping*

A steel knife is one of the most desirable tools to have in a survival situation, yet the human species spent most of its past living in the wilderness without it. What our ancestors did have, however, was considerable skill in tool manufacture. When historical contact was made with people who made stone tools (e.g., American Indians, Australian Aborigines), little attention was given to the methods used in their production. Twentieth-century archeologists had to relearn how to make stone tools through trial and error. This brought about the specialized field of experimental archeology. Primitive toolmaking is not of major importance in most survival strategies, but it certainly does not hurt to know some techniques. My greatest reward in indulging in experimental archeology is to gain an insight into the lifestyles of the people who have lived before me.

KNAPPED STONE TOOLS

Knapping is the process of making stone tools by driving off flakes to form a cutting edge, as opposed to grinding. Making fine stone tools is a complicated process, requiring a variety of tools and a lot of knowledge and practice. Whole books and videos (which

I refer you to later) have been produced on the subject. With a little practice, however, you can make crude but functional tools and projectile points. First, you must encounter the proper stone. Minerals based on silicon dioxide, in the quartz family, are by far the best. These break with a *conchoidal fracture*, in which the fracture surfaces are curved like a clam shell. The common analogy is a BB hitting a window. With practice, these fracture lines make it possible to predict a break in the stone. The best materials are

Losing the Edge

How could any modern outdoors people be separated from their knife? It could have happened to me once in a remote spot in Mexico when I came across two men trying to remove some porcupine quills from a dog's muzzle. My only knife was a Leatherman combination tool with pliers, which I loaned them, hastening the job considerably. Having never seen a tool like that, they pooled their money to buy it from me, but came up very short. I refused the offer and one became angry, trying to convince the other that with two to one they could just take it from me. This behavior was very uncharacteristic of most of my experiences in Mexico. The other man disagreed and prevailed, but had he not, I could have been stranded, with injuries perhaps, in the desert without a knife.

Knapping tools. *Left to right:* Leather palm protector, hammerstone, wooden billet, deer antler billet, deer antler tines for pressure flaking.

quartz based and include flint, chert, obsidian, agate, silicified wood, chalcedony, jasper, onyx, quartzite, and even glass. The material to be knapped is called the *core*. For knapping tools you will need a hammerstone, billets, and if pressure flaking is to be done, a flaker.

Safety is very important. You will be hitting rocks and creating what amounts to glass shards flying off. Many times these small bits of shrapnel make a "zinging" sound in flight. Protect your eyes with glasses, goggles, etc. If gloves are available, use them first for the hands, and when pressure flaking, as pads for palms or thighs. Without protection, your hands will receive cuts ranging from small nicks to some pretty good bleeders. All have the potential for getting infected. You can also mash fingertips, or bruise your legs in the process. Long-term injuries include tendonitis from the strain put on muscles and joints in pressure flaking. Silicosis is another long-term problem, where the fine dust created from the fracturing rock gets in the lungs. Clean up afterward and be careful where you walk. You should not walk around a knapping site barefoot unless you want to collect the small flakes in the soles of your feet.

Knapped stone tools are generally classified as unifaces and bifaces. In unifaces, the flakes are knapped off from one side of the tool's edge, making a chisel-like cutting surface. This is used for tools that will take a lot of punishment, such as scrapers in which the edge cuts broadside instead of in line. In bifaces, flakes are removed from both sides of the edge, giving a symmetrical cutting line along the tool's median plane. These are used for tools cutting in line with the edge, such as knives or projectile points.

The most basic step in knapping is percussion flaking. This is usually done starting with a hammerstone. It should be fairly round, fit comfortably in the hand, and be durable but lighter than the core. A flat section is needed on the core, which is called the *platform*. If the core is a cobble, this can be achieved by striking the core sharply with the hammerstone and breaking it in half, or knocking off one end. While seated, the core is held in the non-dominant hand, platform up, and braced against the inside of the thigh. To remove usable flakes, the core is struck sharply with the hammerstone near the edge. To get large flakes, it is necessary to strike the platform obliquely, usually by holding the core at an

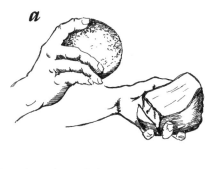
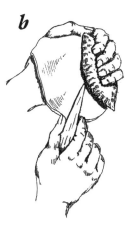

Stone knapping techniques:
(a) percussion flaking; (b) pressure flaking.

angle. It often helps to take the hammerstone and abrade the area to be struck first for good contact. With practice, sharp flakes are readily made like this.

Thin flakes are very sharp and usable for cutting just as they come off the core. Larger projects, such as choppers, scrapers, and axes may need smaller flakes removed in order to thin and refine the edge. Although smaller hammerstones of soft rock such as limestone are sometimes used for this, it is generally done with a billet. Billets can be made of bone, fire-hardened wood, or the base of a deer antler, which is the best material available in most North American deserts. The large flake is held like the core, but padding is best used in the palm holding the flake to prevent it from being driven into the hand and cutting it. The edge is usually abraded with another stone and struck with the billet, again at an oblique angle, to remove a series of flakes along the edge. This method works well for turning the bottoms of glass bottles into sharp knives or scrapers.

Pressure flaking involves taking a pointed tool and pushing at the project's edge to remove smaller flakes. Pressure flaking is done when more control or finer work is needed, such as shaping an arrowhead or dart point, making a serrated edge, or resharpening a dulled flake tool. This is most often done with a tine from a deer antler, but bone and fire-hardened wood flakers have also been used. Pressure flaking in Australia, which lacks native animals with antlers, was often done using a split kangaroo leg bone as the flaker. Start by abrading the edge of the tool being manufactured. This creates a small platform and prevents the edge from being crushed under the initial pressure. Pad the flake to protect the hand and brace it against the leg. The flaker is pressed against the edge with increasing force and then simultaneously pushed slightly downward. Done properly, this will dislodge a long, thin flake. The process is repeated around the flake until it takes the desired shape.

FIRE-HARDENED WOOD

Some woods can be bent, shaped, or hardened by heat. This process is especially useful for spear and projectile points made of wood, and for digging and sotol harvesting sticks. Hardwoods are the most receptive to fire-hardening. The wood is not actually burned in the fire, but heated over coals or on a hot stone until it starts to darken. Hardwood arrow and dart foreshafts can be sharpened and treated this way to be used in lieu of stone points for small game. Some woods, such as willow, can be heated, bent and held in position until cool, and retain that shape. Spiny hackberry has a local reputation for this quality. Arrow and dart shafts are straightened by heating and bending out the crooks with a shaft wrench (a stick with a hole through it) or by using the teeth for a vise.

A digging stick has a pointed end and a chisel-shaped end for digging holes, gathering roots, and other chores. The ends are fire hardened. The sotol harvesting stick has a pointed end and a flat end, with both ends hardened. The point is driven into the plant at its base by pounding the flat end with a rock, and pried up to remove the sotol (or century plant) from its root. Both of these are three to four feet long and are best made of a strong branch such as ash, mesquite, or acacia.

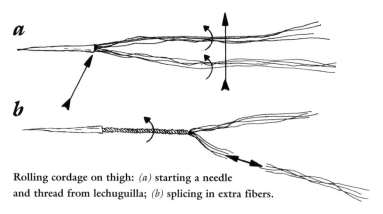

Rolling cordage on thigh: (a) starting a needle and thread from lechuguilla; (b) splicing in extra fibers.

CORDAGE

The Chihuahuan Desert supplies the materials for some of the strongest natural cordage anywhere. Fiber is extracted from plants as described in Chapter 9. It may be used fresh or dried. The easiest for expedient use is two-ply cordage, which means it is twisted from two groups of fiber. An easy example is a lechuguilla needle and thread. The end of the leaf is cut about two-thirds of the way through just below the thorn. The thorn is then pulled backward down the leaf, ripping out the longest fibers and pulp. Two, four, or six fibers are freed from the pulp with a knife point or fingernail and left attached to the needle. The rest are cut off. The fibers are cleaned by scraping with a thumbnail and divided into two sets, with an equal number on each side. If you intend to make a long thread by splicing more in, trim one group of fibers an inch shorter than the others, so the splices will not be in the same place and weaken the cordage.

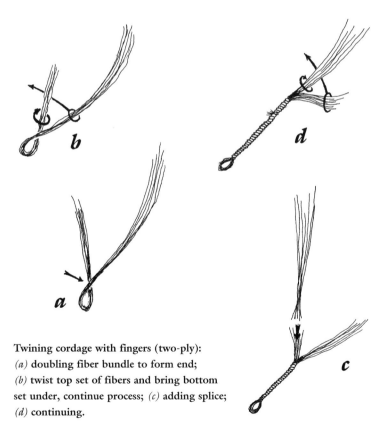

Twining cordage with fingers (two-ply):
(*a*) doubling fiber bundle to form end;
(*b*) twist top set of fibers and bring bottom
set under, continue process; (*c*) adding splice;
(*d*) continuing.

Holding the needle firmly between the thumb and index finger, lay the divided fibers on the leg. Moving down about three inches, lay the palm of the other hand flat on the two sets of fibers, and roll both forward at the same time. (This often works better on a bare leg than pants, but it also rolls your hair up and pulls it out!) When the fibers are well twisted (but still in separate pairs), roll the needle forward between the thumb and index finger, allowing the two groups of fibers to twist around each other, making a two-ply cord. With the thumb and index finger, grab the spot where the fiber pairs separate again, and repeat the process. When you get to the end of the shorter strand, lay in the same number of fibers with about an inch overlap, and keep rolling. It will splice itself together as it rolls. When you reach the desired length, tie the plies together.

For really strong string, such as a bowstring, a slower method is preferable. Take a bundle of fibers, about half the number of what you want the string to be, say about fifteen. Two-thirds of the way down, give the bundle a twist and make a small loop, with the ends out in a sideways V. You now have two groups of fifteen, which will be twisted to make a two-ply cord of thirty fibers. One set is shorter than the others, again for splicing. Holding the loop tightly, take one set and twist it forward, and then lay it over the other set in the opposite direction. Do the same with the other strand, alternating as you go (see diagram).

When you get to the end of the shorter strand, take a new bundle of fiber, and push the end into the working end about an inch, and keep twisting, splicing it in. When done, you may have some short fibers sticking out at the splices that can stick in you. By passing the string quickly through a flame, these can be burned off.

Simple ties can be made by using pita. The broad-leaved yuccas, century plants, lechuguilla, and sotol can be split for tying by heating the green leaves until the skin blisters, and then cutting them into long strips. The strips are used for lashings before they dry. As they dry, the strips shrink and become very strong. They must be cut off to remove. This method is by far the easiest and least time consuming of cordage methods, but I offer a word of caution. While heating the leaves, steam and hot juices can come out the cut end and scald you. Some yuccas, such as the giant dagger, have much moisture in the leaves and will pop, spraying you with hot juices.

The Desert Archaic people made sandals from a variety of fibrous, tough-leaved plants. There may be circumstances where

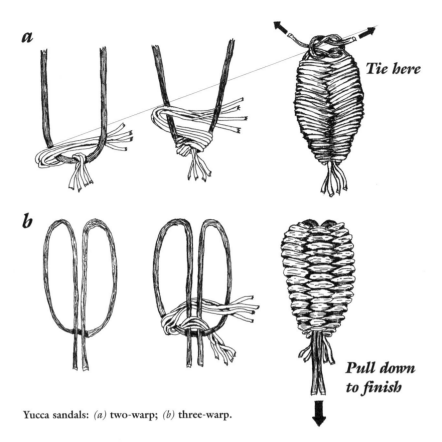

a

Tie here

b

Pull down to finish

Yucca sandals: *(a)* two-warp; *(b)* three-warp.

the stranded person "dressed to arrive" and has unsuitable footwear. An example would be a person wearing heels in an airplane that went down. Using the illustrations as a guide, two types of sandals can be made from century plant, lechuguilla, or especially the longer-leaved yuccas.

Cut a long strip from a leaf to be used as a framework (called the *warp*). Next, pound leaves with a smooth rock to break them down so they can be torn into strips for weaving. These are called the *weft*. It helps to heat the leaf and make pita for a good strong sandal. Using several strips together, weave the weft about the warp, using your foot for a pattern, and tie off as shown. Allow for some shrinkage.

While I was making some sandals, one of my customers told of being in the Peace Corps in India, and having trouble climbing a muddy slope in his slick-soled boots. His Indian friends wove similar sandals from grass to go over his boots and give him a grip. It takes me about an hour and a half to weave a pair of three warp sandals, and they last about two weeks.

RABBIT STICKS AND BOOMERANGS

These weapons are a step above the hand-thrown stick in that they are thinned down for better distance and truer flight. The most common types have a curve like a shallow V or U, but some Southwest examples were S-shaped. The branches of the curves are not necessarily symmetrical. The best kind are flat on one side and convex on the other, to create an airfoil like an airplane wing. This gives a sidearm throw more lift and makes for longer flight. Many boomerangs are nonreturning, and these are the easiest type to make. The boomerang with an airfoil will actually fly further thrown into the wind because of the added lift. American Indians used a nonreturning boomerang called a "rabbit stick" to hunt small game. Other cultures, however, have attacked larger animals with these weapons.

Large boomerangs, such as the Western Australian type pictured, were thrown sidearm at larger animals to break their legs. A large boomerang (approximately two and a half feet long) with a slight curve was found in an Ice Age archeological site in eastern Europe. It was made from mammoth ivory and had sharp tips. It is believed it was used to hunt reindeer, with the twirling weapon good for stunning the animals, breaking legs, or impaling the prey with the

Boomerangs. *Top*: Western Australian nonreturning boomerang for kangaroos and emus; *middle and bottom*: Southwest Native American-style rabbit sticks.

Sling.

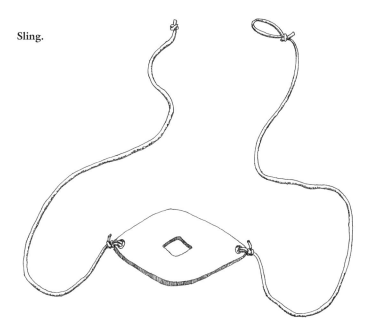

sharp points. I have modified the style out of ash, and fire hardened the sharp tips for a style that could be used on birds, smaller game, or larger animals if the opportunity presented itself.

Like a stick, the rabbit stick should be launched vertically at small game to tumble into it should the throw fall short, and horizontally into flocks of birds. A horizontal throw may also be used against the legs of larger animals. If sharp tips are to be used, however, an overhand throw would set the weapon in a vertical flight and make deep penetration between the ribs more likely.

SLINGS

Slings are easy to make and not hard to learn how to use. They can be made from natural cordage, a boot tongue, shoelaces, even strips of cloth. The sling greatly increases the velocity and distance over a hand-thrown projectile, and can be used on various-sized game. The length of the cords and size of the pocket depend on the length of the thrower's arm and projectile size, but I like one with eighteen-inch cords and a seven-by-five-inch pocket. You will need to experiment. I highly recommend reading Cliff Savage's *The Sling for Sport and Survival,* listed in the Selected References.

One cord (the retention cord) is tied into a loop that goes over the middle or ring finger, while the other (the release cord) has a

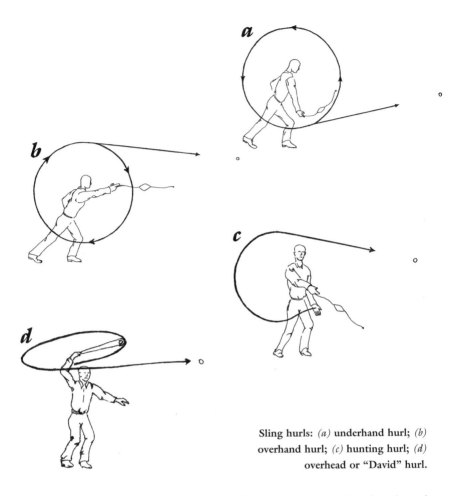

Sling hurls: *(a)* **underhand hurl;** *(b)*
overhand hurl; *(c)* **hunting hurl;** *(d)*
overhead or "David" hurl.

knot tied in the end that is held tightly between the thumb and
index finger until the projectile is released. The pocket is usually
diamond shaped, and if it has a diamond-shaped hole cut in the center, it will hold the projectile more securely. A smooth rounded
stone the size of a goose egg makes a good projectile. Look for
them in creek beds and save the ones you like.

There are several ways to hurl the projectile, and all should be
practiced far away from people, pets, buildings, and automobiles.
You must understand that in any throw, when the knotted cord is
released, the stone will fly immediately in a straight line at that
moment. In other words, if you are twirling the sling over your head
clockwise (looking up) and release it when the stone is directly to
your right, it will fly straight forward. A release to your left will fly
straight back—the stone flies tangential to the direction of sling's

arc. Until you figure this out, you must never use a sling around others. I still demonstrate only overhand and underhand throws, with everyone seated to my left, lest I accidentally release a deadly projectile head high in the wrong direction. Please be careful. No matter the style, most hurls are performed by making one or two windup spins, followed by one quickly accelerated, and then the release.

The easiest hurl to learn and the one with the longest distance is the underhand throw. The sling is twirled clockwise (if right-handed) to the side like a softball throw and released just a little past the bottom of the circle, letting the stone go forward and slightly upward for range. Be careful not to release too late, which will send the stone straight up and leave you apprehensive for a few seconds about where it will land!

The overhand throw is also done at the side, but with the rotation reversed and the stone released at the top of the circle. This is more accurate for shorter distances. An excellent variation for hunting starts by holding the pocket with the nondominant hand, letting the stone and pocket drop, and with a forceful snap, making only a partial circle, releasing the stone as soon as it comes to the top. This is an accurate throw and does not frighten prey quite as much as a couple of windup twirls.

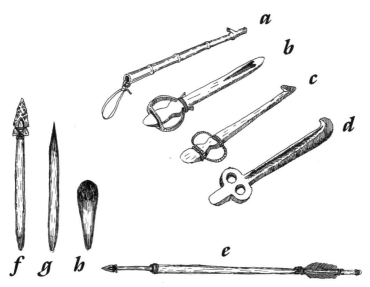

Atlatls and darts: (a) expedient cane atlatl; (b) female type (Anasazi);
(c) male type (Lower Pecos River); (d) mixed female and male (Aztec);
(e) dart; (f) foreshaft with stone point; (g) fire-hardened wood foreshaft;
(h) bunt foreshaft for stunning small animals.

In the overhead hurl (picture David facing Goliath), the stone is twirled like a lariat and released, combining power and accuracy. It is also the most dangerous basic hurl, especially for bystanders.

Variations on the sling include a stone tied to a cord, which is thrown cord and all when released. Bolas tether two or more stones together to hit or wrap up an animal. Slings mounted on staffs were once used to hurl larger stones over castle walls at attackers below, but have little application for the wilderness.

THE SPEARTHROWER, OR ATLATL

A relatively easy weapon to make, but harder to master is known as the spearthrower, or by its Aztec name, *atlatl* (at-LAT-ul). This is a compound weapon that can propel a slender spear (hereafter more correctly called a dart) six times farther than a hand-thrown spear and with 150 times the foot-pound energy. It is so effective that many archeologists believe its use is responsible for the extinction of elephantlike mammals in the Western Hemisphere! It predates archery by perhaps 10,000 years in the Americas.

The atlatl is a stick up to thirty inches long with a hook (called a male type), or an inletted area (female style), to engage the butt of the dart. The atlatl is held at the opposite end and used to propel the dart, artificially lengthening the thrower's arm. The atlatl can be carved from a tree limb with a small nub of a branch left intact for the hook, or a piece of wood that has been inletted to accept the dart. Ash makes a strong atlatl, but other woods are also useful. One of the easiest ways to make an atlatl is to cut a stout piece of cane to length, leaving a leaf node in place as the hook. Finger loops are desirable to keep from throwing the atlatl with the dart.

The dart is five to six feet long, and may have a foreshaft or have the projectile point lashed directly to the mainshaft. *Quiotes*, cane, and willow shoots are all good for the mainshaft. When tapered shafts are used, the large end should go forward. For greatest accuracy the mainshaft should have fletching toward the butt end. Split feathers are best, but even things like credit cards can be used by inletting the shaft or splitting it and tying it back together. A depression is made in the butt to engage the atlatl's hook. The mainshaft should be stoutly wrapped with cordage at each end to discourage splitting.

a

b

Atlatl throw: *(a)* proper stance; *(b)* holding atlatl and dart together.

A foreshaft is a hardwood piece, about three-quarters of an inch in diameter and about ten inches long. It may be notched for a stone or bone projectile point, be simply sharpened to a point itself, or be a "bunt." The foreshaft is slightly tapered on one end, which is inserted into a receiving socket at the forward end of the main-shaft. Foreshafts are for two purposes. They allow you to exchange projectile points to match the prey. If you are throwing at a rabbit, there is no reason to risk a fragile stone point when a fire-hardened foreshaft sharpened to a point will work. Other foreshafts are merely wooden balls with a stem, called "bunts," that fit in the mainshaft socket and are used to stun small animals. Another advantage is that when a projectile point or sharpened foreshaft hits a large animal, the mainshaft usually detaches and falls away. The quick hunter can pick up the mainshaft, reinsert a foreshaft, and make another throw. Some people, such as Aborigines, attached their points directly to the main shaft instead of using foreshafts.

Using the atlatl takes no small amount of practice. Unless you have used them before, I recommend you forego them in survival situations until you have all of your other priorities taken care of and are just killing time. The easiest way to use the atlatl is to hold it

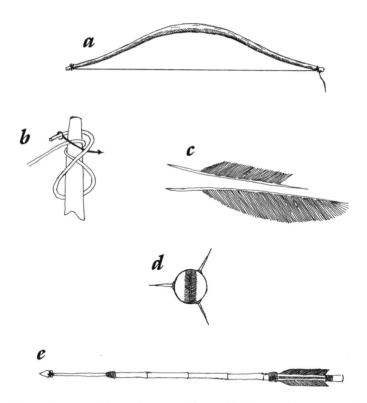

Bow and arrows: (*a*) expedient round bow; (*b*) tying on a bowstring without an end loop; (*c*) splitting and trimming a feather for fletching; (*d*) placing the nock in relation to fletching; (*e*) composite cane arrow with hardwood foreshaft and stone point.

with the little, ring, and middle finger around the handle end. If you have finger loops on it, put the thumb and index finger through them. Place the butt of the dart in the hook or inletted area, and lay the dart across the fingers holding the spearthrower. Grasp the dart between the index finger and thumb, using slight backward pressure to keep the butt engaged with the atlatl.

The atlatl and dart are held with the arm back and slightly flexed. The nondominant arm is held forward, pointing at the target, with the weight on the dominant foot. The throwing arm is brought forward with a snap, much like casting a fishing line with rod and reel, while the body's weight is transferred to the other foot. Releasing the dart is all important: too soon and it falls aside harmless; release it too late and you can drive it into your foot. As the atlatl reaches the two o'clock position, the dart is released and the wrist given a flick with complete follow-through. Do not try to power it at first. A graceful flick will send it farther and straighter than trying to power throw it like a football. As a matter of fact, I find that women often catch on faster than men, having graceful moves and no macho drive to set a new distance record. Spear throwing is a fun sport with several competitions. I recommend you give it a try—before you get into trouble!

ARCHERY

Making a bow and arrows requires a lot of time and skill. I made my first primitive bow using the instructions in *Outdoor Survival Skills* by Larry Dean Olsen, and I still recommend that book for a thorough review in bowmaking. I like to use true willow or ash for my desert bows. I find willow somewhat easier to work and to have a little more snap than ash. Most of the time you will find it necessary to start with a green piece of wood. Find a shoot or limb about one inch in diameter, straight as possible, with as few twigs growing on it as can be found. Holding it up to your right shoulder, measure a length to the tips of the fingers of your outstretched left arm. Always chop, saw, or cut the bow stave. Trying to break it off will crack the wood. Peel the bark off and let it dry for twenty-four hours out of direct sunlight. The curve of the bow is determined by putting the larger end on the ground, a hand on top of the smaller end, and pushing in the middle. This will show you how the bow will be held when done.

After the minimum drying time has passed, the bow can be shaped by scraping only. Trying to whittle out the bow with a knife will not give a consistency in diameter. Scraping can be done with a knife, but broken glass or stone flakes are better. Starting at one end, start scraping away wood, working up toward the center of the bow to make an easy taper. Follow the natural cross section of the wood and make a round bow. Do not try to make a flat one. Twice I ignored Olsen's advice and made flat bows—both broke as I was trying to string them. The handgrip should be about an inch in diameter, tapering down to a tip about five-eighths of an inch. Make the other limb of the bow the same way. Nocks can be cut in at the ends to hold the string. After the bow has been completed, it should be rubbed down vigorously with animal fat, preferably hot. Snake oil works well. Oils boiled from wild nuts and gourd seeds also can be used.

Arrows can be made from several different plants found in desert environments, including small cane, cattails, seepwillow, and willow shoots. If using cane, make the small diameter end the one that engages the string and smooth down the segment joints on the shaft, or they will be sliding the wrong way across your hand and take a chunk out of you. Cane and cattail are brittle and require a foreshaft made of hardwood like an atlatl dart. The difference is that the foreshaft on an arrow is glued and/or tied in so it will not separate from the mainshaft. The foreshaft may be notched to receive a point, or be merely fire hardened and sharpened. The foreshafts are about three-eighths of an inch in diameter and six inches long. The arrow should be about thirty-two inches overall. Cut a nock in the base to accept the string. The fletching should be made of small split bird feathers, tail feathers working best. These can be tied and glued on. I use fine lechuguilla twine and mesquite gum for this and for attaching the foreshafts.

Position the first split feather so that it is at a ninety-degree angle to the nock. Place the other two at thirds around the shaft. When the arrow is nocked on the string, the fletching at ninety degrees is placed to the outside of the bow. In this way it will not hit the bow going by and will be truer in flight. When attaching the fletching, make sure the forward tips of the quills are well covered with cordage, or they may skewer your bow hand as they fly by. Some American Indians placed the arrowhead in line with the string nock while hunting animals and perpendicular to the nock for war. This was supposedly to keep the point in line with the animal's or person's ribs, to make it easier for the arrow to pass between them. My arrows are fletched pretty crudely, and have some spin in flight anyway. Arrows with stone points do seem to fly straighter and hit harder than ones with sharpened foreshafts.

The easiest obtainable string material in the Chihuahuan Desert is lechuguilla fiber. By following the above directions in the section on "Cordage," you can have a string in about two hours. When you finish the string, make another one! They tend to break at bad times, so always have one in reserve. The string can be tied in a noose to go on one limb of the bow. Place the end with the string already tied on the outside of the right foot, and put the left leg over the middle of the bow. With the left hand, bend the bow and tie the string onto the free end using two or more half hitches. Reverse the process if you are left-handed.

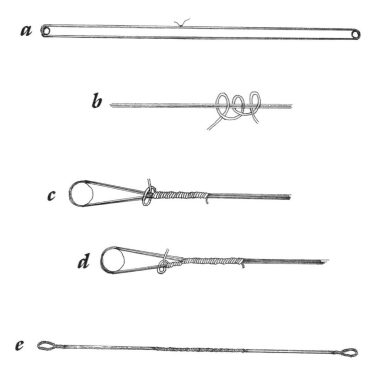

Making a bowstring from dental floss: (a) putting floss on the jig; (b) tying half hitches to form the serving of the string; (c) serving the string together to start end loop; (d) serving around jig peg to make end loop; (e) completed string.

A stronger string can be made from the dental floss in the survival kit. Measure the bow tip to tip as the string would run. Now subtract about three inches and in a piece of wood insert two pegs that distance apart. Hold the end of the floss midway between the pegs. Take the dental floss around the pegs five times, coming back to the free end. Cut the floss off with a few inches to spare. Pull the ends toward each other to tighten the floss evenly and tie the ends together, cutting off the excess floss. You will now have two sets of strings held apart by the pegs.

Loops will need to be put into the ends by "serving" the string. About an inch and a half below one peg, take another piece of floss about two feet long, and tie the two sets of string *together*. Start tying a series of half hitches (see diagram), working up toward the peg. When about three-quarters of an inch is covered, quit tying half hitches around both sets, and split off, tying them around *one set only*. You will need to continue on around the peg doing this, and may find the needle from the kit to be helpful. Continue on around until you get to the part where you tied the sets together. Continue on for a little ways and then tie off the floss securely. Do the same for the other end, forming another loop to go onto the bow. The center of the string is served about three inches each side from the center point, also using a series of half hitches. This will keep the string from wearing at the point of contact with the arrow. Place one loop over one tip and, bracing the bow as described above, slip the free loop over the other end. This is an extremely strong string. Now sit down and make another one anyway.

The bow is one of the easier to learn of the primitive weapons. The nondominant hand grasps the bow midway. With the dominant hand, nock an arrow on the string's midpoint. Most people place the arrow on the same side of the bow as the hand holding it, but some put it on the other side with equal success. The arrow is laid across the hand holding the bow—I like to lay it on my extended index finger and point at the target with it. My favorite grip on the string is to grasp it with the pads of the index, middle, and ring fingers, holding the arrow between the index and middle fingers. The string is drawn back toward the cheek, and released. It is usually best to sight along the arrow and a little above the desired point of impact. After a while it is instinctive. You may want to protect the inside of the bow arm, as the string can bruise or burn it easily. A glove on the bow hand will help discourage slivers coming off the arrow into your hand.

In survival situations, tools may be much handier than weapons. If I gave more time to weapons, it is because the instructions for their construction and use require more details. One of the benefits of making such items is that it keeps away boredom, which can often make a survivor attempt to leave when staying is the best option. Weapons also provide a sense of security and control over the situation and have psychological value. Just do not let your weapons give you a false sense of power and get you into trouble.

12 Weather Hazards

Visitor, mopping brow: "Whew! What do youse think the temperature is?"
Me: "I dunno. I don't pay attention to these cold snaps. They never last."
—Conversation on 85°F day in April 1985.

Deserts are defined by the amount of precipitation they receive, or, more realistically, don't receive. In most definitions, the evaporation rate will well exceed the precipitation. Most people consider deserts to be scorching hot, and, in fact, some of their biggest hazards derive from extreme heat. The greatest danger, however, is the extremes they can go through. Hot days can be followed by shivering cold nights. You can be dying for water in one moment and drowning the next. Part of weathering the desert is to be philosophical. I tell people to remember that when the thermometer reads 116°F, the wind chill is actually lowering it to 107°F! Actually, I rarely look at a thermometer. We use them in search and rescues because they help us calculate life expectancies for victims. Other times I consider them a measurement of misery. Nobody looks at a thermometer when they are comfortable, but let it be hot or cold and people refer to them to know which expletive to use to describe the current temperature.

It is hard to prepare for a land that fluctuates so wildly in climate. For instance, the wintertime high in Big Bend National Park is 86°F, and the wintertime low is -3°F. That is quite a gap, but when you consider that both readings were taken in January of 1949, you can see what a roll of the dice desert weather can be! In rocky terrain, the stone readily absorbs heat during the day, creating ground temperatures far above the ambient air temperature. With little humidity to act as insulation, however, this heat quickly radiates back into the atmosphere as the sun goes down. That is why desert nights can be so cool. This is not a firm rule. Some desert nights can also be hot, depending on things such as atmospheric pressure, prevailing winds, and your particular location. If you are in Death Valley, you can expect nighttime temperatures of over 100°F.

HEAT

I have already discussed heat and how to beat it by trying to keep skin temperatures below 92°F. You can receive excess heat through several means. Direct exposure to sunlight is a major factor in desert fatalities, caused by improper clothing or lack of shelter. Reflected heat can come from light soils or rock, and is almost as damaging as direct sunlight. Radiated heat is what is being released from the ground or rocks that have been heated by the sun. This is why it is so important to not sit directly on unshaded ground or hot rocks. Ambient temperature is also a major factor. This is the heat that envelops you from the surrounding air that has been heated by direct sunlight and contact with the ground. You may find some relief in the shade, but for the most part, you are stuck with the surrounding air temperature.

People are always proclaiming relief from desert climates by saying, "It's a dry heat!" There's not much humidity in my oven, either, but stick your hand in when it's on and you will get burned. In terms of human comfort, it is true that dry heat is more tolerable than a combination of high temperature and high humidity. Remember, however, that while you seem to be perspiring less than in places with higher humidity, you are still rapidly losing precious water. Always keep your wits about you and remember to conserve your sweat by limiting exercise, having proper dress, and utilizing shelter.

COLD

While cold is proportionately less of a problem than heat in most deserts, when it is happening to you, statistics matter little.

Cold saps your body warmth in the reverse of heat. Without direct or reflected sunlight, you depend more on your internal body temperature, clothing, fire, and shelter for warmth. Sitting on cold rocks or cold ground will cause heat to radiate out of your body. The surrounding cool air will also draw out body heat. Other factors, such as rain and wind, will further cool the surrounding environment, and in turn yourself, if you are unprepared.

Cold is a consideration in the winter months, in freak storms, and at night. If you thought you would not need a well-built fire

Only Fools and Newcomers Predict the Weather

People constantly want me to predict the weather, sometimes for specific dates months in advance. Caller in December: "Hi! We're going to be down there March 7. What kind of clothes should we bring?" The answer is, "Enough to dress in layers. It can be cold, beautiful, or borderline hot." Unpredictable weather killed a man in 1986 in Big Bend National Park. I was managing the horse operation in the Chisos Mountains and woke up to an unusually warm February morning. Not having much business, we started painting the corrals. By 10:00 you could feel the temperature dropping by five degree increments. By 10:30 we could not see through the snowflakes as big as quarters.

Three thousand feet below us in the Sierra Quemadas a man was solo camping. Also inspired by the springlike weather, he set out for a day hike from his camp dressed in a pair of shorts and a light windbreaker. Later, his camp was found empty and a search was started. What actually happened is not known, but this is the most likely scenario. He had camped near a side drainage of a larger dry creek. He was following the dry creek when the storm hit. He either miscounted the number of side drainages he had passed, or in the blizzard mistook the one he entered for the one where he was camped. Whatever the reason, he wound up one drainage short of his goal. As the snow melted two days later, he was found frozen to death, huddled up on the lee side of a boulder. Had he carried extra clothes to dress in layers he may have survived. A fire would also have helped. While rare, extremes like this are why I refuse to play weatherman.

with stone heat bins and reflectors because the day was so warm, you may spend a teeth-chattering night. Even on summer searches, I carry two rescue blankets, one for me and one for John Doe, the "I don't need a jacket" person.

RAIN, FLASH FLOODS, LIGHTNING, AND HAIL

Rain may be a blessing to the stranded desert traveler. It may be a source of water for those without, or it may cool the desert for a while. It may also soak the unprepared and leave them freezing without a fire, or send torrents of water down in flash floods. Many desert areas have brief afternoon thundershowers, which make the nights cooler and the following days steamy. It pays to always watch the horizon for incoming clouds, especially the formation of looming thunderheads, which can bring rain, lightning, and hail. The clouds appear to be towering cauliflower shapes called cumulonimbus clouds. A 10,000-foot thunderhead may take only thirty minutes to form. Such storms are caused by factors lifting clouds upward, cooling them and causing precipitation. The uplifting can be caused by four processes: thermal lifting, orographic lifting, frontal lifting, and lifting by convergence.

Air heated near the ground rises and may take moisture with it as it is thermally lifted. As it cools at higher altitudes, precipitation may occur. Days where the ground is shimmering with rising heat may end in a thunderstorm. Terrain features, such as mountains, cause orographic lifting, which pushes clouds up to the saturation point. Watch for these developments over mountains. A cold front moving in may push its way under and lift a warmer air mass, causing frontal lifting. A temperature drop may precede this type of storm. Convergence lifting may be a process of all three of the above, or independent of them. It occurs when a low-pressure system draws air into an area horizontally, displacing air upward.

It is imperative to remember that you do not need to be directly involved in rain to be caught in a flash flood. Some desert drainages cover thousands of square miles, and a storm upstream can send floods your way. It is important to watch clouds far from you as well as close. People often talk about a "wall of water" when describing flash floods. That has not been my experience. I find that they are a flow of water starting shallow, but rapidly rising. There

Get Thee to a High Mountain

A tragedy occurred in 1974 in a canyon on Big Bend Ranch, where I work, before it became a state park. A group of young adults enrolled in a very well known outdoor program camped in a canyon called Arroyo Segundo, which enters an even larger drainage, Fresno Creek. Arroyo Segundo is the location for Mexicano Falls, the third highest waterfall in Texas, which the campers were downstream from. After a tiring day the group selected a campsite on low-lying ground, even though a large storm was threatening. The instructor had been working back-to-back groups and was suffering from fatigue and burnout. To have some time to himself he camped away from the students further up the canyon.

The storm gathered over the canyon and deposited heavy rains in Arroyo Segundo, causing the creek to flash. The students had been told some scare stories about a previous flash flood, and panicked as the water started rising. Without supervision, some of the students climbed a nearby cottonwood tree instead of seeking high ground. Stories vary on what happened next. Some said the young woman lost her balance, some said a branch broke, one blamed someone else for stepping on her fingers. No matter the cause, the woman fell into the flood. She was found the next day dead, a couple of miles down Fresno Creek.

People analyzing this point out all sorts of errors. The group should have given more attention to the weather. The instructor should have been there. Cottonwood trees are often seen falling in flash floods and are not a safe perch. Others said they should have had better instruction, such as to go to high ground. The simple fact is, if they had selected a safe campsite, the young woman would not have died.

are ways to keep from becoming a flash flood's victim. Dry creek beds supply some of the easiest walking, and at times may be the only sensible route. If water starts to flow where there was none before, start looking for a place to exit. It does not hurt when walking in creek beds to constantly look for escape routes. If there was a light flow in the creek bed that is becoming stronger and muddier, it is time to bail out. I know of no reason to camp in a drainage.

Such storms may also bring in hail, which is harder to prepare for. If you see an approaching thunderhead and get into the plastic bags from your survival kit and hunker down in the open, you may be beat to a pulp. Large hail would also make short work of many expedient shelters, including my favored *kowa*. Again, it pays to always observe your surroundings. Are there rock shelters nearby? This would be a good time to consider an automobile a shelter, although extremely large hail can shatter the windows. If caught in the open, try to crawl under any sturdy-looking bush, get in a depression, and put yourself in a ball, covering your head by any means possible. When I was a horse wrangler in the Chisos Mountains, we were told that anytime hail started on the South Rim, we were to get our people off the horses, strip the blankets and saddles off, and cover our clients with them. It would be a bad day to be a horse.

Lightning can accompany these storms and presents a very real danger. In many desert environments, you may be the tallest thing around. You are at much more danger from lightning in a storm than you are from snakebite anytime. If you are in a group caught in the open, scatter out, at least thirty feet apart. Try to stay on dry ground; rubberized materials, such as a poncho or sleeping mat, will help if dry. Crouch down with your feet together to minimize a path for electrical ground currents. This is why you should not lie down flat. Shallow rock shelters are not a good idea in lightning

Noah Only Had Two with His Flood

There is another flash flood hazard I experienced when I was about twelve years old. One summer night my father and I were hunting with our 'coon dogs in a floodplain along the Rio Grande. A rain in the high country above us started filling the low area with water and we evacuated ourselves and our pack of dogs to a knoll, which quickly became an island. We found we were not the only desert dwellers with the same idea. We soon found our haven to have several rattlesnake refugees, which drove the dogs nuts and seemed like some kind of Freudian snake dream. If you are forced to seek higher ground in a flood, be alert for other animals also seeking sanctuary.

storms, as a bolt can jump across the opening. Deep caves are better, but stay away from the walls and assume the crouch position. The same applies for any exposed shelters. I would not stay in a shelter made with a metalized rescue blanket. Do not get under solitary trees.

So, I have told you to try to find a rock shelter in the event of rain or hail, and to leave it in case of lightning. But in the desert you can have all three! Whether to stay or leave is largely a judgment call, but you can estimate how close lightning is if you can see it or the flashbulb effect it creates. The sound of thunder travels at different speeds depending on terrain, air temperature, elevation, and humidity, but as a rule of thumb, sound travels about a mile every five seconds. By counting off the seconds between the time you see the flash and hear the thunder, you can divide by five and get a rough estimate of how far away the thunderstorm is and if it is getting closer.

WIND AND DUST STORMS

High winds and the dust they can carry present other problems in the desert. Such winds can inhibit firestarting, make starting a fire dangerous, also make flare signals a hazard, and impede shelter construction. Long steady dust storms can impede travel and blind the survivor for the duration. If you are caught in a dust storm, try to find shelter, even if it is only the lee side of a boulder. If none, sit with your back to the wind, close your eyes, and try to cover your mouth and nose. Unfortunately, some dust storms can last for days. Do not worry about being buried alive; you can easily stand up and sit down again before that happens.

Most desert places are free of tornados, but they do happen rarely, usually in places where people say they are impossible. Seeking shelter in low areas, sturdy rock shelters, or lying flat on the ground is about the only defense for those caught in the open. Do not stay in an automobile, mobile home, or travel trailer, as these are often overturned in tornados. A much smaller version is the dust devil, a whirlwind that dances across hot flats, and is only a minor nuisance. These may temporarily blind you if they overtake you, but by merely sitting down, closing your eyes, and covering the mouth and nose, you can wait until it quickly passes. Dust devils occur when broad expanses cause heat to rise uniformly until its continuity is disturbed, perhaps by something as trivial as a bounding jackrabbit. I once instantly became engulfed in a dust devil I caused by firing a .357 magnum pistol.

Desert winds may also come in short but strong gusts. These can take you by surprise and blow you off your feet. There are several instances where people were blown off precipices by unexpected gusts of wind and killed. If you are journeying along a bluff or cliff, this can be prevented by keeping back from the edge at least the same distance as you are tall. Traveling with a walking stick will also help you keep your footing.

PREDICTING DESERT WEATHER

Since this is not meant to be a work of fiction, I will not try to do what scores of weather forecasters and several government agencies attempt. It is a well-known fact that meteorologists were invented to make economists look good. Forecasts made in a survival situation without scientific training and satellite imagery are bound to be even less reliable. However, there are still some good indicators that may foretell coming weather.

Cloud formations will be the most accurate predictor for the stranded person. Clouds forming turrets, often in line, may converge to form thunderheads later in the day. High wispy clouds may precede a warm front, and possibly rain in a day or two. Gray clouds in a single uniform layer may turn dark and produce drizzling rain. They indicate stable air and may stay for a long time.

Air stability can be determined by several factors, such as wind, clouds, and even how the smoke rises from your fire. Stable air is indicated by clouds in layers with no vertical motion, or even fog, which occasionally occurs even in desert areas. Steady winds also indicate stable air. Smoke rising evenly and dissipating slowly also is a sign of stable weather.

Unstable air is indicated by smoke rapidly rising to great heights, upward or downward currents, clouds growing vertically, gusty winds, and sometimes dust devils. If you do have a working radio, listen for forecasts. With satellite observation, long-term forecasts are becoming more accurate. Unfortunately, the forecasts are often given only for well-populated areas and neglect other places. Try to be prepared for anything.

MICROCLIMATES

Desert climates are a combination of altitude, terrain, vegetation, latitude, and position between mountain ranges. Not only will different deserts have different climates, but locales within each desert may show wide variations. Even very localized areas can have microclimates, to the benefit or detriment of the survivor.

Long, broad playas may not have much difference in temperature from one spot to the other, but in more broken terrain there may be some noticeably cooler or warmer spots. Air convection, caused by rising and falling air of different temperatures, is largely responsible for microclimates. Topography, such as mountains or canyons, may amplify the effect of convection currents. The mouths of some canyons will blow cooler air than others. Some mountain slopes will be warmer at night than spots a few hundred feet away. I have noticed rock shelters that were once heavily occupied that are cooler than others nearby with less archeological evidence.

It pays to take note of the temperature differences between one place and another. If you are moving about and enter an area that is more comfortable, do not be tempted to consider it a sudden change in the weather. It could be a consistent condition peculiar to that spot. Microclimates should be considered in shelter location or in selecting an overnight camp. Vegetation can also be an indicator of microclimate. Long, broad creosote flats are not as likely to lead to cooler refuges as areas with greener and more diverse plants.

Desert Hazards, First Aid, and Sanitation

13

*There are no such things as poisonous snakes
—you can eat any of them.*

—Bob Cooper, *1996*

The concept of the desert being a hostile place inhabited by venomous creatures has been around since Mosaic literature. Actually, there is less to fear from desert denizens than creatures in the woodlands, tropics, and mountains. Yet, every place has its rules of survival. You don't cross the street without looking both ways. In some cities you don't buy a hotdog from a street vendor without looking around to see if someone is watching where you keep your money. I'll take the snakes and scorpions any day.

VENOMOUS ARACHNIDS AND INSECTS

What fierce reputations scorpions have. Scorpion researchers hunt them at night with black lights, causing the little critters to glow in the dark. If you do this some time, you will be amazed at how many there are that you never see otherwise! If scorpions were aggressive, we would be in real trouble. With the exception of the bark scorpion (*Centruroides exilicauda*), found in parts of Arizona, New Mexico, and Mexico, most North American scorpion stings are merely painful, unless one has an allergic reaction. Prevention is the best medicine. Be careful in turning over rocks, picking up firewood, and putting your hands in places you cannot see. Do not

DESERT HAZARDS, FIRST AID, AND SANITATION 197

merely shake your boots before putting them on. Give them several good thumps, as scorpions hang on tenaciously. I have been stung about half a dozen times, once for not clearing out my boots.

Treatment of scorpion envenomation (which is a sting, and not a bite) is controversial, with some calling for cold packs to slow the spread of the venom, while others recommend hot compresses. If heat has a palliative effect, it is not because it breaks down scorpion venom. Experiments by Dr. Dean Watt of the Creighton University College of Medicine show that bark scorpion neurotoxins do not break down from heat until they reach 92°C (197°F) and are kept at that temperature for upward of *eighty* minutes. You could not stand to hold something that hot on your skin. Suctioning with an Extractor may remove some of the venom if done quickly. Scorpions do not leave their stingers. Wash the stung area with soap and water if available. In this and all cases, keep your tetanus vaccinations current.

Spiders are also present in much greater numbers than we perceive. Tarantulas are quite adept at scaring the pants off desert visitors, but are gentle and shy. They can inflict a painful but not especially dangerous bite. This usually comes from being handled. They can rub their legs over their hairy abdomen, scattering fine chemical-laden hairs that irritate the eyes and nose. Most spiders are venomous to some degree, but many only mildly so. Black widows and the brown or violin spiders do inflict bites that are very toxic, but there are no viable first-aid procedures for the field. Neither is normally fatal, but help should be sought as soon as possible. Washing the bitten area and applying a cool compress are recommended procedures.

Most people are aware of bees and wasps. Both can be serious to allergy-sensitive people, but usually stings are only painful. Bees leave their stingers in the skin, which should be scraped out. Removing the stinger with tweezers can compress the attached venom sac, and inject even more. Wasps retain their stingers and can sting repeatedly. Suctioning may remove some of the venom. For bee stings and other bites or stings, making a paste from the Benadryl in the survival kit may help. Taking Benadryl or prescription medication internally may be necessary for sensitive people.

Ants are also familiar to everyone. Some pack quite a painful sting, while some bite with their mandibles and squirt formic acid into the wound. Even the ones that don't bite or sting are annoying.

Some get up into trees or high bushes and can get down your collar if you brush against the plant. Treat ant stings like any other insect sting.

The velvet ant is an insect many people will not recognize. These are beautiful fuzzy insects, often in bright colors such as red, orange, or yellow, with white and black also found. Sometimes they are more than one color. Should you pick up one of these small creatures for a closer look, you will quickly find that it is actually not an ant, but a wingless wasp with one of the most painful stings in North America! Treat as a wasp sting, and don't do it again.

Another real pest that many people may not know is the conenose bug. These vile little blood suckers have saliva that helps keep your blood from clotting and at the same time anesthetizes the bite so you are unaware you are soup du jour. The saliva is also toxic to humans and causes severe itching for up to a week afterward. If you scratch the bite, it can become very inflamed, growing from a welt to a large open sore. Allergic reactions can cause swelling of the mouth and throat, necessitating an antihistamine such as Benadryl. In parts of Mexico the bugs carry a protozoan causing trypanoso-miasis. Conenose bugs especially like pack rats. Before using any cave or rock shelter for a refuge, check carefully for pack rat nests. These mini-vampires attack in your sleep, so choose your bed care-fully. Washing the bite with soap and water and not scratching is the only field treatment.

Although millipedes and centipedes are neither arachnids nor insects, they crawl, can be problems, and will be included in this section. They are actually myriopods ("many-footed"), and look far more fierce than they are. Centipedes have their legs out to the side, while millipede legs are shorter and under the creature's body. Centipedes inject their venom through modified front legs called *gnathopods*. Centipede stings are mildly toxic but painful. Allow the wound to bleed, wash with soap and water, and apply an antiseptic.

Millipedes do not inject venom, but they do have toxin glands that produce irritants to deter enemies. This can cause blistering if it comes in contact with the skin, and real problems if you rub it into your eyes. Wash skin with soap and water, and irrigate the eyes thoroughly until the pain subsides. Unless one walked across you in your sleep, handling them would be about the only way to come into contact with their toxin.

DANGEROUS REPTILES

Thanks to Hollywood, deserts are perceived to abound with venomous reptiles. Actually, woodland areas can outdo most deserts in the number of venomous snakes. In addition, the number of fatalities from snakebite in the United States is extremely low. An average of 7,000 people a year are envenomated, and only about fifteen die. In some years more people are killed by their own dogs than from snakebite! Bites from venomous snakes and lizards are a possibility, however, and would have serious consequences for a person unable to reach help. Once again, prevention is the best remedy.

As in dealing with insects and arachnids, do not put your hands in places you cannot see. This is especially true when climbing up rocky hills. Do not step over rocks, logs, or off ledges without looking first. Always watch carefully. If you see a snake, do not mess with it. Do not panic, either. I have no statistics, but I would be willing to bet that more people hurt themselves running from snakes than are actually bitten. Instead, use the Alloway Twelve-Step Program for Snake Avoidance. It is really easy. Take four steps to the side, four steps forward, and four steps back to your direction of travel. You will stay healthy and the snake can keep its venom for its intended meal.

Still, envenomation happens. There are two types of reptile venom—hemotoxic and neurotoxic. Hemotoxic venom, which is common to pit vipers (rattlesnakes, copperheads, and water moccasins), breaks down the victim's blood and muscle tissue. Its purpose is not only to kill small prey, but to also start predigesting the animal. Neurotoxins, on the other hand, kill prey by attacking the central nervous system, causing paralysis, asphyxiation, and cardiac arrest. Neurotoxins are considered more deadly venoms than hemotoxins, but fewer desert reptiles have them. They are found largely in coral snakes and the world's only venomous lizards, the Gila monster of the Mojave and Sonoran Deserts, and its close relative, the beaded lizard of Mexico. The most dangerous pit viper in the United States is the Mojave rattlesnake (also found in the Sonoran and Chihuahuan Deserts), with potentially fatal neurotoxic venom and a pretty short temper. The *Audubon Society Nature Guide to*

Deserts says, "Its venom is extremely toxic and causes more respiratory distress than that of any other North American pit viper." In other words—you ain't breathin'.

There is no consensus on the treatment of venomous snakebite. Tourniquets, incising the fang marks, and ice packs are not generally recognized as proper treatment anymore. Some improvised treatments are bizarre, such as taking a "stun gun" and placing the electrodes on each side of the bite and shocking the area with several thousand volts, rotating the gun, and repeating the process several times. The theory is that the electrical current breaks down the enzymes in the venom. This treatment has not found much favor in the medical community for pit viper bites.

As an emergency medical technician, I am allowed by local protocol only to suction the bite, apply a restrictive band above the area tight enough to limit venal flow returning to the heart, but not arterial circulation, and transport the person to medical care. It is now believed that incising the fang punctures only serves to spread the venom to surrounding tissue by opening more blood vessels. Ice on hemotoxic bites may further damage the already weakened tissue. Tourniquets stop circulation and can result in the loss of a limb.

At one of my classes, Bob Cooper demonstrated a treatment that is very successful in Australia. Using elastic bandages, one is applied a few inches above the bite, and rolled on, not too tight, down past the bite and to the end of the extremity. Another, overlapping the first bandage, is applied at the bite area, and rolled up the limb. This has met skepticism in the United States, however. The venom of Australian snakes is largely neurotoxic, and it appears that limiting the venom's distribution helps to keep the central nervous system in control of the vital organs. Some physicians here fear that this application to a hemotoxic pit viper bite would concentrate the venom and increase damage in the particular area. There is a real need for comprehensive research into treatment of venomous snakebite in backcountry conditions.

If you are bitten, the best advice I can give is the following. Get away from the snake. Stay as calm as possible, and sit or lie down. If you have a suction device, such as an Extractor, try to use it on the bite within five minutes. Do not incise the bite. Wrap a flat band at least three-quarters of an inch wide two to four inches above the bite, loose enough that you can still put a finger under. As swelling occurs, check the band and loosen as needed. Remove tight jewelry such as rings that can be a problem should swelling occur. Clean the wound with soap, water, and an antiseptic if available, but do not rub vigorously. If on an extremity, keep bitten area at a level below the heart. Try not to move, which accelerates the spread. Do not drink alcohol. Some advise not to suction a coral snakebite. Above all, do not panic.

Because of panic reactions, some physicians are now recommending not to treat snakebite in the field at all. They feel that if the person remains calm and does not become agitated trying to treat the bite with questionable methods, he or she is better off. There is a lot of merit to this. I suggest that if field treatment is going to cause more excitement (such as shocking yourself with a stun gun), forego it. To stay calm, try to remember that snakebites in the United States are rarely fatal, and that many snakebites involve no venom injection at all.

DANGEROUS ANIMALS

There are few animals to fear in North American deserts. In fact, you are the most dangerous thing alive in these environments. You

can get into trouble, however, by intruding into an animal's turf. I
have already mentioned that javelinas are aggressive when angered.
They have another problem of having very poor eyesight and will
come closer to investigate if they cannot smell you. If they start
coming close, yell at them and make human-type noises. They usually will dart away. If a javelina starts popping its teeth at you, it is
issuing a warning and sharpening its tushes at the same time. Back
off slowly.

Almost any animal with young will try to protect them. No matter how cute something is, you have no right to disturb it, and the
mother will tell you this right off. Coyotes are normally very timid,
but messing with their pups in a den will get you a face full of fur
and teeth. Even young animals will put up a good fight if you
molest them.

There have been some incidents of mountain lion attacks in
recent years. Mountain lions are normally very secretive and want
little to do with people, but they do get used to folks sometimes
and can be problems. Do not scream and run from a lion.
Everything they eat dies this way. Face the animal and make yourself as tall as possible. Hold your arms out and try to look bigger. If
you are in a group, get together. Yell, make lots of noise, and throw
things at the animal if within reach. Do not bend over in front of
the cat to pick up something to throw. Mountain lions are not
accustomed to having aggressive behavior directed at them, and
usually will flee. Mountain lions love to eat domestic dogs. Keep
dogs restrained, or they may bring a big kitty back to you. The best

thing to do is to leave pets at home. They can give and receive diseases by coming in contact with wild animals and are considered enemies by most wildlife. I know of no unprovoked bobcat attacks, but treat them the same as mountain lions.

Black bears may be encountered in some mountainous areas surrounded by deserts, but they are handled the same as other places. Make noise on trails so as not to surprise them. Secure your food away from yourself at night, and don't annoy them. Black bear attacks are extremely rare, and most occur only when provoked or from very old animals who no longer have the speed to catch wild prey.

What I look for most are the previously discussed insects and reptiles. Watching where you are going and carefully inspecting camp areas will help keep you safe from them. Forget all the movies in which all of the desert, from rattlers to buzzards, are conspiring to make you the entree. You are much safer from attack in a desert than in most American cities.

POISONOUS AND DANGEROUS PLANTS

There are surprisingly few extremely poisonous plants in North American deserts. Poison ivy and poison oak may be found in some perennial springs, but contact poisons are very rare. Ingesting unknown plants is hazardous, but most desert plant poisonings are not fatal if treated, and many cause only stomach upset or diarrhea. Of course, if you are already distressed, plant poisoning will not help. There are several plants you should especially watch for, however, and not take internally.

All members of the genus *Datura* are especially toxic and should not be consumed for any reason. There have been sporadic cases of ingestion since the 1960s to exploit their hallucinogenic properties, usually resulting in a good session with the stomach pump at the hospital. They have lush foliage, large and beautiful trumpet-shaped white flowers, and thorny seed pods the size of a golf ball or smaller. One popular television program in the late 1980s showed the seeds being used as an anaesthetic for a gunshot victim, which would be extremely dangerous. Please leave it alone.

Mexican buckeye (*Ungnadia speciosa*) was discussed as a possible fish poison. I sometimes encounter people who claim it is edible, but I have serious doubts. It seems that the seeds may be safe in certain stages of growth, but I also know of one person who was

Datura, *Datura spp.*

Mexican buckeye seeds, *Ungnadia speciosa*

hospitalized for eating a few. Another friend reported eating one, waiting, and experiencing the biggest singular episode of flatulence he had ever had. There are a few people who have recommended eating one buckeye for a feeling of altered states. I do not consider cyanide compounds to have recreational uses and advise that this is a very dangerous practice.

All portions of the Texas mountain laurel, or mescal bean (*Sophora secundiflora*), are extremely toxic. The seeds were used by Archaic Desert people as hallucinogens, but the dosage is critical

Texas mountain laurel, *Sophora secundiflora*

Tree tobacco, *Nicotiana glauca*

Baileya, *Baileya multiradiata*

and death is extremely possible. It is reported that even keeping a bouquet of the beautiful purple flowers, which smell like grape bubble gum, in a room while sleeping will cause extreme headaches and nausea. There is no application for mescal bean in a survival situation.

The black ripe berries of silverleaf nightshade (*Solanum elaegnifolium*) look quite edible, but they are not. Ingestion may cause vomiting, nausea, diarrhea, and abdominal pain. The berries are used to curdle a delicious Mexican goat milk cheese called *asadero*, but the amount is critical. The blue-violet flowers have yellow centers. Enjoy them by sight only.

Tree tobacco (*Nicotiana glauca*) with its large green leaves looks like it would make a good pot herb, but it is not to be taken internally. An introduced species, it grows prolifically along many desert waterways. It can cause severe diarrhea, dizziness, and disturbed vision and hearing. For you smokers who think you can harvest the leaves and have some smokes while you are waiting, the uncured dried leaves will make you feel like the top of your head is going to blow off, and it also produces auditory hallucinations of explosions to complement the feeling. Its medicinal applications are external only.

Baileya, a pretty yellow flower, is sometimes called desert marigold because of its similar appearance to the domestic flower. It does not appear to be particularly edible, which is fortunate, because *Baileya multiradiata* is one of the most poisonous desert plants. Drymary, or inkweed (*Drymaria pachyphylla*), is an unobtrusive plant that is easily overlooked, but it is also one of the more poisonous of desert plants.

While contact poisons are rare in desert plants, that is not to say that all plants are safe to handle. Desert plants are often extremely thorny, with some like catclaw acacia perfectly able to rip you to shreds if you get tangled up in it. The *Opuntia* genus of cacti are well known for their tiny *glochids* that are much more annoying than larger cactus thorns. Remember, in a survival situation, any wound, no matter how small, can be a serious problem if it becomes infected. Examine plants carefully before walking through them or handling them. Some cacti, like tasajillo, prefer to grow in the shade of nonthorny shrubs such as creosote bush. Walking through without looking can earn you a leg full of spines and glochids.

SPECIAL FIRST-AID CONSIDERATIONS

Wilderness emergencies have their own problems in that they occur in remote areas with no quick access and generally far from a hospital. People in my area taking their emergency medical courses are often confounded by textbooks that are written on the assumption that we are in an area that has a seven-minute ambulance response time. I have had people die in my hands while we waited along a paved highway for an hour and a half for an ambulance. It was no fault of the medics, just the realities of living in a remote area. I cannot overemphasize the need for caution and prudence in desert areas. Second chances are seldom given.

HEAT-RELATED INJURIES

The most common desert emergencies are hyperthermia and dehydration. These two maladies are often accelerated by each other and cause severe metabolic instability that is often fatal. Dehydration can be prevented by sufficient water intake, limiting activity, and minimizing perspiration. Hyperthermia, in which the body temperature is usually elevated by hot weather, can be prevented by water and salt intake, proper clothing and shelter, and restricting physical activity. Heatstroke, heat exhaustion, and heat cramps are the main heat-related injuries.

HEAT CRAMPS

Heat cramps are the least severe of the three heat-related disorders. These are muscular spasms that are brought on by loss of salts in the body from profuse perspiration. This is becoming more common with desert visitors who are on low-sodium diets. Such diets are probably good advice for people with sedentary occupations in climate-controlled surroundings, but take a hike in the desert and you may find yourself fatigued, profusely sweating, and with severe muscular cramps in the limbs, extremities, and abdomen. Faintness and dizziness along with nausea and vomiting are also symptoms. The patient will usually display normal body temperature and mental status.

Extremely hot weather is not a prerequisite for heat cramps. A person exercising strenuously and drinking water, but not replacing salt lost to perspiration and urine, may suffer. If heat cramps occur, the patient should be removed to a cooler environment, and moist towels (or the disposable diaper in the large survival kit) should be placed on the forehead and over the cramping muscles. Some medics do not recommend administering salt water until help arrives, but our situation is different. If salt is carried in the kit (and it should be), dissolve one teaspoon in a quart of water and have the patient sip it at the rate of a half pint every fifteen minutes. Do not give salt tablets directly. Crush them and dissolve if necessary. Unlike with some heat-related injuries, the victim of heat cramps may be able to treat themselves. Always have plenty of water to drink when replacing salt.

HEAT EXHAUSTION

This is the most common heat-related injury overall, but not in deserts. It usually occurs in hot humid climates where people are involved in physical exertion. It can also happen under some circumstances in the desert. It may be brought on by drinking insufficient water for the environmental temperature or by drinking enough water but not replacing salts. To regulate rising body core temperatures, the blood vessels dilate to take blood closer to the skin. This causes a rapid drop in blood pressure, putting the victim in shock. The patient may exhibit rapid pulse, pale color, headache, vomiting, nausea, diarrhea, fatigue, dilated pupils, and thirst. Profuse sweating and a normal to below normal body temperature are classic symptoms. To confuse the issue, some people may show a slightly high body temperature. It may also be accompanied by heat cramps. The patient may lose consciousness.

Remove the patient to a cooler place, preferably in the shade. If the person is conscious, have him or her start drinking water, slowly at first. Do not try to give water to an unconscious person. Have the person lie down on their back and remove clothing (unless in direct sunlight), and loosen what cannot be removed. Sponge with cool water and fan the victim. Elevate the feet about twelve inches. If the patient is unconscious, be prepared to roll them over in the event of vomiting, to prevent aspiration. Get help if possible. Field treatment may include intravenous fluids, which require advanced training. After symptoms pass, replace salts as described above.

HEATSTROKE

Also called sunstroke, heatstroke is far more common in desert environments and is the most dangerous heat-related injury. This is a true emergency, with up to a seventy percent mortality rate. The elderly and children are especially prone to heatstroke. The classic form is when people lose the ability to sweat, but in exertional heatstroke, caused by exercise, sweating is observed with muscle stress. Heatstroke represents a total breakdown in the body's thermal regulation abilities. The body core temperature zooms to 105°F and above. The patient will have hot reddish skin, wet or dry, but often dry in deserts, and a rapid, strong pulse of 160 or more, but weakening as damage occurs. The pupils will be constricted, but dilating as the injury progresses. Decreased blood pressure will occur, possibly accompanied by convulsions. Heatstroke victims will become mentally unstable as the brain is subjected to the high heat. The person may be difficult to treat due to confusion, anxiety, aggression, or even psychotic or hysterical behavior. Loss of consciousness is very likely.

As with all heat-related injuries, remove the patient to a cooler, shady spot. Remove as much clothing as possible and immediately start wetting down the body. The need for cooling is so immediate that urinating on the patient is justified. Wrapping in a wet blanket or sheet and fanning is a good treatment. If cold packs are unavailable (almost a certainty in desert survival situations), place cool wet compresses at the person's armpits, groin, each side of the neck, behind the knees and around the ankles. These are areas that the blood flows close to the skin and can be cooled. Use wet clothing, yours and the victims, if nothing else is available. If near a body of water, immerse the victim, keeping the airway clear. As the body temperature drops to 104°F, be prepared for convulsions. Do not allow the patient to aspirate vomitus. Heatstroke victims are in severe danger of brain damage or death. Lowering the body temperature is critical.

DEHYDRATION

The remedy for dehydration is obvious—water. Water must be replaced in quantities commensurate to environmental temperature and physical exertion. It may be necessary to force yourself to drink, even if you are not thirsty. People suffering dehydration may go through mental instability. Crankiness to outright aggression may signal the onset of dehydration. Irrational decisions brought on by the brain's inability to think clearly have caused many deaths. Desert newcomers in recreational activities often confuse cold beer for water. The beverage actually is a diuretic and speeds dehydration. It is no fun to tend to someone who has mental instability from both dehydration and alcohol. It is important not to sip water, but to take a good drink. Sipping does not allow the water to get to the brain and vital organs. Drinking too much quickly may cause vomiting, and loss of valuable water, but a good slow drink will cure dehydration.

DIARRHEA

In situations with limited water, diarrhea must be stopped quickly. Using medications from the survival kit, or one of the remedies discussed in Chapter 9, the body must be forced to conserve water. Near a good water source, however, diarrhea may not be so critical. In some cases, such as poisonings or some intestinal infections, it may be best to let it flush out the body. Many viral diarrheas run their course in twenty-four hours. In normal cases the person with diarrhea needs to replace water equal to the stool lost *plus* two quarts. In desert settings expect the extra water needs to be higher. Accompanying the dehydrating effect of diarrhea is the loss of salts and electrolytes. These may be replaced with powdered sports drinks dissolved in the drinking water. Sanitation, purified water, proper cooking, and not eating unfamiliar foods are the best preventions.

SANITATION

The settling of the American frontier in the nineteenth century saw plagues of cholera along the immigrant routes resulting from poor sanitation. In our modern environments we take sanitation for granted. Human waste and garbage are disposed of quickly and toilet paper is easy to find. We can wash our hands at leisure, and our clothes are well taken care of. While we don't give sanitation much thought, it is critical in survival settings. All persons involved must work to protect the water supply, keep camp clean, and keep insects and parasites away.

Urination and defecation should be kept well away from camp and water sources. Distances vary, but the park I work in requires at least one hundred yards. Unless several people are urinating in the same spot, it is not much of a problem in the desert's accelerated evaporation rate. Many desert plants would gladly accept the moisture. In one ranch I worked on we did not use the toilets for urine. It makes no sense, especially in the desert, to use good water to carry away waste water. I selected a creosote bush and devoted my morning micturition to it. The bush thrived. Just do not urinate near your camp or shelter.

Defecation is another matter. It not only can cause foul odors and draw flies, but it can attract larger animals. It may not be energy efficient to dig a community latrine, but the cathole method works well. Walking well away from camp and water sources, dig a small hole, eight to ten inches is sufficient, and defecate in it. If you are using toilet paper, burn it in the hole, and bury the ashes and feces. Some people disagree with burning paper for various reasons, but in my area javelinas tend to dig up these catholes, eat the feces, and leave the toilet paper scattered. Burning helps. Some people prefer the "smear" technique, in which the feces are smeared on a flat surface to dry quickly, avoiding holes being dug and animals excavating the cathole. In Mexico some people hunting javelinas defecate in their trails to draw them in. Consider excrement also as a source of trap bait. However, you do not want javelinas in camp, so take a walk.

Refer to Chapter 9 for plant alternatives to toilet paper and menstrual pads. You may not find suitable vegetation to replace toilet paper where you are at. As a matter of fact, just looking at most desert plants can convince you to wait a while. Smooth rocks may be found in creek beds that can be employed. Old timers give the advice, often taken for a joke, to select a smooth round rock and turn it over and brush the sand off the bottom and use that side—which is cooler. Try the technique on a sunny day and you will find it is no joke. Much of the world uses the "water wipe" where the bottom is merely scrubbed with the hand and water. This is viable only if you have an abundant water supply and carry it along with you to the latrine site. Carefully wash the hands afterward.

Bathing may actually be more harmful than good in desert situations. Regular bathing can remove protective body oils and dry the skin faster than going natural. In addition, bathing may waste valuable water, or pollute a water source. Sanitation, such as washing hands, feet, body crevices, and perhaps the hair, may be called for. The disposable diaper from the big kit can be moistened and used like a sponge bath. Whether using natural soaps derived from plants or the soap brought with you, it must not be used near a water source. Even biodegradable soaps sold in camping stores can damage a desert water pool. Remove water from the source and carry it away, dumping it on the ground when done. Leeching pits are not necessary in arid areas unless a large volume of waste water is produced. Scrubbing with sand is better than nothing if water is not plentiful enough for washing.

Clothes usually do not require much care for purposes of sanitation, but socks and underwear should be kept clean. The underwear could usually be discarded, but clean socks will help keep the feet free from blisters and athlete's foot. Even rinsing out socks will help, but natural soaps, such as guayacan root, will keep them clean and your feet healthy.

Try to keep the fingernails clean and short. The scissors found on some Swiss Army knives are excellent for this. Long dirty fingernails can harbor germs and parasite eggs, which can be transferred to food, water, or sores on the body. Do not bite your nails or pick at sores or scabs. Toenails should also be kept trim and clean.

Brush the teeth, even if only using a finger and water. Ground charcoal from the campfire will also help clean the mouth. Leatherstem is an excellent dental hygiene plant, if available. Comb the hair regularly to help keep out parasites.

If you are taking fish or game, they must be cleaned far from camp. Like feces, game offal will also bring in flies and unwanted animals. It is advisable to hang small animals on a limb for a little while to give external parasites a chance to abandon the carcass without selecting you as the next host. Game should be cooked or smoked as soon as possible. Smoked fish, fowl, and mammals will last for a long time in dry conditions, but raw meat should not be kept raw long. It will become flyblown, spoil, or attract other animals. Leftovers, such as bone, gristle, and unwanted skins, should be discarded well away from camp, or used as bait. While skinning, keep exposed cuts and sores covered, and always wash the hands thoroughly afterward, with soap, if possible.

Besides keeping you healthy and strong, sanitation and hygiene have great psychological benefits. You will feel better if you are not plagued with flies, smelling rotting garbage, or stepping in someone's stools. Feeling clean may not be completely possible to those accustomed to daily bathing, but grooming will help you feel more comfortable. When you need a lift, and if you can spare the water, a good yucca root shampoo will not only leave your hair squeaky clean but brighten the spirits.

Traveling and Wayfinding

14

A desert extended around them, and stretched to the southwest as far as the eye could reach, rivalling the deserts of Asia and Africa in sterility. There was neither tree, nor herbage, nor spring, nor pool, nor running stream— nothing but parched wastes of sand, where horse and rider were in danger of perishing. Their sufferings, at length, became so great that they abandoned their intended course, and made toward a range of snowy mountains brightening in the north, where they hoped to find water.

—Washington Irving, *Adventures of Captain Bonneville, 1843*

Considering that a stationary person conserves water and calories and is easier to find, the best advice is usually to stay where you are. There may be circumstances, however, that make travel necessary. Dwindling water supplies may cause relocation. Physical safety may cause a move. The truly unfortunate will need to extricate themselves because no help will be forthcoming. It must be said again that if you are in a location with ample water, it is safest to stay put until rescue. If you are forced to walk out, you must establish a route, reduce your exposure to heat, and negotiate terrain.

FINDING DIRECTIONS

The subject of orienteering by map and compass is complex and worthy of a separate text. Every wilderness traveler should have orienteering skills, but more and more people are leaving the road without this knowledge. Many people think a compass always points to true north. Quite a few people cannot look at a map and orient it to landmarks in their view. I believe this is because we have been raised with television and movies, projected on a flat screen in only two dimensions. In teaching orienteering classes I find many

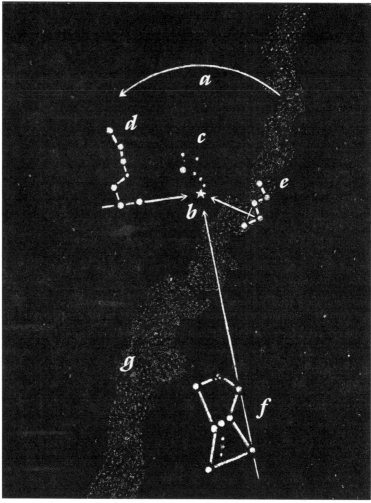

Finding north with constellations: *(a)* rotation of constellations around Polaris; *(b)* Polaris; *(c)* Little Dipper; *(d)* Big Dipper; *(e)* Cassiopeia; *(f)* Orion; *(g)* Milky Way.

people, especially the young, have a hard time visualizing in three dimensions. Studying well-written books or attending classes on the subject are a must. Even for the person comfortable with orienteering, circumstances may arise where map and compass are lost, making navigating by other means necessary.

Navigating by the sun and stars is the most accurate natural way of determining north. Finding Polaris, the North Star, is a nighttime means in the Northern Hemisphere. The easiest way to

Some Misconceptions about Celestial Navigation

Polaris is not the brightest star in the sky. To the contrary, it is rather dim and takes some practice to learn how to find. Once you learn its position, lying between the Big Dipper and Cassiopeia, finding it becomes almost instinctive. Some stories tell of lost people waiting for Polaris to "rise." Because Polaris is positioned almost directly over the North Pole, it does not rise. It merely becomes visible as darkness falls, if nothing is obscuring it. It is in a fixed position and neither rises or sets.

When facing Polaris, the other stars appear to rotate counterclockwise around it. This is the exact opposite of what most people would expect. One book even gave diagrams on the Big Dipper rotating clockwise around the Pole Star, claiming the handle of the Dipper served as an hour hand, and that that is how cowboys riding night herd knew when their shift was over! It is simple to figure this out. The sun and stars do not actually move around Earth. It is Earth's rotation that gives the appearance of movement. If the sun rises in the east and sets in the west, so do the moon and stars not close to Polaris. Stars close to Polaris neither rise nor set, but appear to circle it. These are called circumpolar stars.

At lower latitudes the Dipper may actually disappear beneath the horizon, which is why it is important to know how to use Cassiopeia to find Polaris. Conversely, at the same latitudes Cassiopeia will dip below the horizon, but the Big Dipper will be up.

If celestial navigation by Polaris seems difficult, try finding south in the Southern Hemisphere by the Southern Cross. This constellation points you to a relatively void spot in the night sky, from which you must drop a straight line to the horizon to find south. Do this for a while and you will love to have a Pole Star with pointer constellations on each side!

locate Polaris is to find the Big Dipper, a large constellation made up of bright stars that is easy to find. The Dipper appears to rotate counterclockwise around Polaris, and depending on the time of the year, the handle may be pointed in any direction. The end of the Dipper opposite the handle has two bright stars called Merak and Dubhe, making up the forward portion of the dipper. Using them as pointers, draw a line going from the bottom of the Dipper (Merak) to the top (Dubhe). Proceeding in a straight line about four times the distance between these two stars, you will come to Polaris, which is the last star in the handle of the Little Dipper. Many people expect the Pole Star to be very bright, but it is sometimes difficult to spot until you get accustomed to locating it.

At times clouds will obscure the Big Dipper, or at lower latitudes it may be below the horizon at certain times of the night. Fortunately, the constellation Cassiopeia is opposite Polaris from the Big Dipper at roughly the same distance, and can be seen if the Dipper is below the horizon. Cassiopeia is roughly shaped like a **W**, with the center star pointing almost directly at Polaris.

If the northern portion of the night sky is obscured by clouds, it is still possible to get a fairly accurate reading of north by using the constellation Orion. Drawing a line through the two bright stars to your right in the constellation will give a northerly direction.

If you are camped for the night, it is not a bad idea to put a forked stick in the ground and lay another stick in the fork pointing to Polaris. That way the next day you will have an accurate reading to north.

Daytime also produces accurate ways of finding north, but the sun must be shining. If you have a watch, you can find north by using the sun. If you are on daylight savings time, set your watch

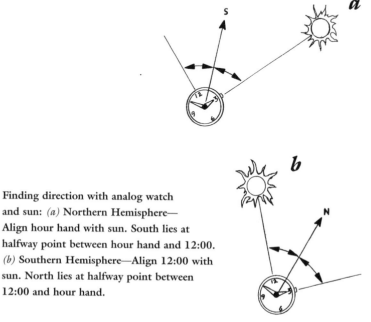

Finding direction with analog watch and sun: (*a*) Northern Hemisphere— Align hour hand with sun. South lies at halfway point between hour hand and 12:00. (*b*) Southern Hemisphere—Align 12:00 with sun. North lies at halfway point between 12:00 and hour hand.

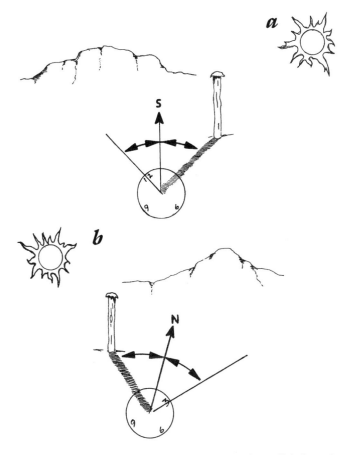

Finding direction using the sun, if time is known (e.g., digital watch or radio broadcasting): *(a)* Northern Hemisphere—Clock face is drawn in dirt at the end of shadow. Shadow becomes hour hand. Locate 12:00. South lies halfway between shadow and 12:00. *(b)* Southern Hemisphere—Clock face is drawn in dirt at the end of shadow. Shadow becomes 12:00. Locate position of hour hand. North lies halfway between shadow and hour hand.

back an hour to unlegislated time. In the Northern Hemisphere hold the watch horizontally and point the hour hand at the sun. South will lie halfway between the hour hand and 12:00. What about at 6:00, when the hour hand is directly opposite 12:00? Remember, the sun rises in the east, so at 6:00 A.M. facing east, south will be to your right. At 6:00 P.M., the sun will be in the west, so south will be on the left. At noon when the hour hand is at the 12:00 position, the hour hand will be pointing roughly south, but this method is more accurate earlier or later in the day.

In the Southern Hemisphere, point the 12:00 position toward the sun, and north will be halfway between the hour hand and 12:00. If you are having problems aligning with the sun, put a twig or straw in the ground and lay the watch next to it. In the Northern Hemisphere, align the shadow of the twig with the hour hand. In the Southern Hemisphere align the shadow with the 12:00 position and the central pivot of the hands.

This is not completely accurate. It will vary depending on your location in a time zone. It is also less accurate south of the Tropic of Cancer and north of the Tropic of Capricorn.

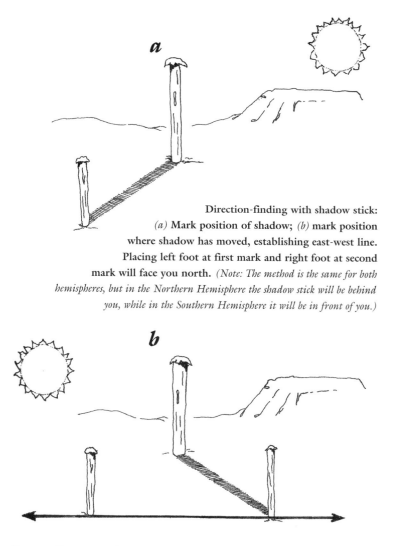

Direction-finding with shadow stick:
(a) **Mark position of shadow;** *(b)* **mark position where shadow has moved, establishing east-west line. Placing left foot at first mark and right foot at second mark will face you north.** *(Note: The method is the same for both hemispheres, but in the Northern Hemisphere the shadow stick will be behind you, while in the Southern Hemisphere it will be in front of you.)*

This method can also be used with a digital watch by using the top edge as 12:00 and estimating where the hour hand would be. Even if you don't have a watch, but hear the time on a radio or some other way, you can still find directions. Put a stick in the ground. Draw a clock face in the dirt or on a piece of paper and arrange it so the stick's shadow bisects it. In the Northern Hemisphere, use the shadow for the hour hand and draw a line where the 12:00 position would be. South is halfway between the shadow and 12:00. In the Southern Hemisphere, assume the shadow is at 12:00 o'clock and draw a line where the hour hand should be. North lies between the shadow and the line.

The shadow stick method is another way to find north using the sun. A quick way to find north is to drive a stick, about three feet long, into the ground. Mark the tip of the stick's shadow, and wait about fifteen minutes. Mark the spot where the shadow's tip has moved to. In the Northern or Southern Hemisphere, put your left foot at the first marker and your right foot at the second, and you are facing north. This method can also be done with moonlight and is even a bit more accurate.

A variation of this method is even more accurate if you have more time and a piece of string or bootlace. In the morning, set the stick in the ground, but this time take the string, two or three feet long, and tie it loosely to the shadow stick. Pull the string taut and out to the tip of the shadow. With a stick at this point, use the string

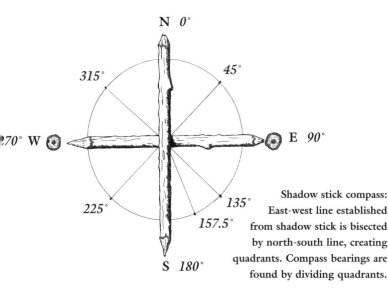

Shadow stick compass: East-west line established from shadow stick is bisected by north-south line, creating quadrants. Compass bearings are found by dividing quadrants.

to draw an arc in the dirt. Mark the spot on the arc where the shadow's tip is located. Watch the shadow in the afternoon and see where it intersects the arc. Mark that spot. Again, putting the left foot at the first mark and the right foot at the second will face you north.

These two methods can also help you determine compass bearings. Draw a line or lay a straight stick between the two markers. Taking another straight stick, align it halfway between the two markers at a ninety-degree angle. Most people are quite good at doing this. You have now divided your field of view into quadrants. North is directly in front of you at zero degrees. Directly to your right is east, or 90 degrees. Directly behind you is south at 180 degrees. West is directly to your left at 270 degrees. If you divide these quadrants in half, you add 45 degrees, so if you wanted to determine where southeast is, or 135 degrees, you would draw a line exactly halfway between the right and rear points of the sticks— 90 plus 45 is 135 degrees. By further dividing and adding (half of 45 degrees is 22.5) you can keep adding in a clockwise manner to come close to any compass bearing you want. In this way you can align a map to landmarks without a compass.

Even if it were true that moss grows on the north side of trees (this is not always true), the desert is short on both. Some barrel cacti point towards the sun, and therefore in a very general southern direction in the United States. Learning the stars and how to use the sun are the best ways, outside of having a compass, to find directions.

Things Are Not Always as They Seem

Almost all survival manuals recommend walking at night in the desert. This is good advice in general, but it does pose problems. One geologist in the Chihuahuan Desert had his vehicle break down one afternoon. He decided to wait until dark to walk for help. There was plenty of moonlight and he could see the road well as he walked. He was curious at passing some cow manure, as he had seen no cattle. Suddenly one of the "cow pies" uncoiled and crawled off.

TRAVELING

Walking out will require you to use some sense, negotiate terrain, and keep on course. Traveling at night will preserve your water reserves and cause less dehydration. However, walking cross-country can lead you into dangerous vegetation and animals, or into terrain hazards such as canyons or bluffs. Lechuguilla is an indicator plant found almost exclusively in the Chihuahuan Desert. Early Spanish explorers wrote very unappreciative accounts of the crippling plant, saying it often prohibited moving at night through hostile territory when the cover of darkness was desirable. Clear desert nights with a good moon make reading possible, and it may be possible to travel safely. I recommend staying on roads for night travel, which avoid most terrain obstacles, are clear of dangerous plants, and make it easier to see snakes and other animals.

If you do have a compass and are navigating by it, take the bearings you need using landmarks during the day. For example, if you see a patch of green vegetation in the distance you believe to indicate a spring, take a bearing on it. At night you can walk toward it, even though you cannot see the trees, by taking occasional compass readings. You can also plot a course by using a map in this way, taking bearings during the day on landmarks you may not be able to see at night. Bear in mind that night travel will reduce your chances of dehydration and heat-related injuries, but it also has its risks.

A common problem with people not familiar with deserts is judging distances. Most people estimate desert distances at about a third of what they actually are. This is because without intermediate vertical objects, such as trees, the uninitiated have no familiar references. Heat can also cause a magnifying effect in still air, and make mountains seem much closer. Fortunately the openness of desert terrain usually supplies distinctive landmarks, unlike in woodlands or plains.

Broad desert expanses can cause confusion for the traveler. This can be avoided by keeping landmarks in sight, and looking behind you to familiarize yourself with how the features look should you get turned around. You may get in low spots where you temporarily lose sight of landmarks. To keep from getting turned around or walking in circles, check where your shadow is and keep it in the same position as you walk. This will change throughout the day, so keep checking where it falls in relation to your landmarks.

Mirages are another Hollywood staple to scare people off the desert. They can look like water and lure people toward broad dry flats. This is especially true in dehydration victims with impaired judgment. However, most people can tell the difference between mirages and lakes. Mirages can be confusing because they make it harder to determine distances, either pulling objects closer or setting them further away in optical illusions. Sometimes mirages will occlude the bases of mountains, making them look like they are floating in the air and making distance estimates very inaccurate. They sometimes can reverse images. I have seen mountains appear to have been bisected and have their bases balanced on their peaks. Mirages can also distort natural features to look like human-made structures, and vice versa.

LEAVING SIGNS

As you travel you should leave signs, so anyone following you will not miss your trail. Leaving detailed notes tied to brush with pieces of cloth are the best. Be sure to put the time and date on these if possible. If you have a walking stick, drag it occasionally in sand or gravel. If you change course suddenly, drag the stick in that direction. Forked sticks can be set in the ground with another stick placed in the crook to indicate direction of travel. Making rock cairns occasionally will help. If you change directions, indicate so by making three cairns in the direction of travel. Try to leave footprints by walking in open areas in softer soils. While my profession requires me to teach low-impact camping, such as keeping fires in firepans and hauling out the ashes, this is a different problem. Douse your campfires but leave them in place (along with notes if possible), to indicate to rescuers that you are able to start and maintain fires and that they should continue the search. Whatever you do, try to make it easy to follow you. It is not to your advantage to test their tracking skills.

Debriefing

15

"I have heard you have a saying," Paul said,
"that polish comes from the cities, wisdom from the desert."

—Frank Herbert, *Dune*, 1965

You have been rescued. There is nothing you would like more than to get in some air-conditioning and take in a large iced tea. But there are some things that must be done first. Before you leave the area, take up any traps you have set. You may be required to come back and remove your vehicle, dismantle shelters, clean up campfires, and do some restorative work. What you owe search and rescue personnel is a good and honest debriefing. SAR is a science of statistics. Using debriefings, SAR personnel create a database to determine probability of success. They take into consideration the person's age, experience, sex, health, education, and other factors to determine how an individual is likely to behave in certain situations. These are combined into Search Probability Theory, which considers the probability of the person being in the search area, probability of detection, and the probability of success. Such information will be used in future searches, and with a bigger database, more lives will be saved.

Statistics seem to count fatalities over success. Through preparation, you may never get into trouble and be unknown all of your life. By surviving you will not be put into the fatality figures. Your experience is needed, however, and debriefing with the SAR unit is a small debt to pay. They want to learn from you, and you have things to share. Tell of your successes and failures. Tell them about the time they were so close, but missed your signal. Tell them about your mental status and how you coped with fear and controlled panic. Not only do these go into profile data, but they are used for future instruction in SAR, survival, and wilderness safety classes. You need not prepare for a debriefing. They will take you through it and get you on your way.

We—I and you, my readers—need to debrief about the desert. I hope you come to the desert and find all the special things that have made it such a big part of my life. Not all people view the desert as a providing and fragile ecosystem. Desert rivers are pumped dry and the water replaced with sewage. Some consider it a place for low-level nuclear waste, which they tell us is safe. Safe for a barren wasteland, but not for the region where it was produced. Others see it as a place no one cares for or owns, and believe dirt-bike races and cross-country driving are acceptable. The desert is not inhospitable, but it does require special survival strategies. The desert also requires some special care for it and its inhabitants to survive. The very word desert evokes the word *deserted*, but it is far from unpopulated. Special plants, animals, and people take refuge in the desert, and they deserve the same respect as forests, woodlands, or mountain ecosystems. Because some people living outside of deserts consider them useless, abuse comes from every corner. Rivers are dammed, golf course architects attempt to make deserts imitate Scotland, and everything from sewage to toxic wastes is dumped in desert "wastelands." We must fight such gross abuses.

Martha Gellhorn put it quite well when she wrote, "People who foul landscapes do not take their sustenance from the natural world." We need to protect the desert through considerate use, economic alternatives, and using our vote. For those who see what the desert truly is, its use as a dumping ground is not only unwarranted, but an attack on the very environment that nurtured humankind in its infancy. Please use this book wisely and practice its contents with respect to the desert. We need not fear the desert. We should fear for it.

APPENDIX A
Wilderness
Survival Schools

*The addresses and phone numbers in Appendixes
A and B are correct as of June 1999.*

Arizona Outdoor Institute
4733 Gloria Drive
Prescott, AZ 86301
520-445-9617
Dave Ganci, *Director*

Big Bend Ranch State Park
P.O. Box 2319
Presidio, TX 79852
915-229-3416
FAX: 915-229-3506
E-mail: *bigbendranchsp@brooksdata.net*
David Alloway, *Lead Instructor*

**Bob Cooper Outdoor
Education Pty. Ltd.**
P.O. Box 8486
Perth Business Centre
Perth 6849
W.A., AUSTRALIA
011-61-8-9377-1767
Bob Cooper, *Director*

**Boulder Outdoor
Survival School**
P.O. Box 1590
Boulder, CO 80306
800-335-7404
FAX: 303-442-7425
Josh Bernstein, *President*
www.boss-inc.com

**David Alloway's Skills
of Survival**
P.O. Box 583
Terlingua, TX 79852
877-371-2634
David Alloway, *Director*
www.skillsofsurvival.com

**National Outdoor
Leadership School**
288 Main
Lander, WY 82520
307-332-6973
www.nols.edu

Outward Bound
100 Mystery Point Rd.
Garrison, NY 10524-9757
800-243-8520

School of Self Reliance
Box 41834
Los Angeles, CA 90041
323-255-9502
Christopher Nyerges, *Director*
self-reliance.net

Tracker Inc.
P.O. Box 173
Asbury, NJ 08802-0173
908-479-4681
Tom Brown, *Director*
http://members.aol.com/trackerinc.

World Survival Institute
Box 394
Tok, AK 99780
907-883-4243
Chris Janowsky, *Director*
www.wildernesssurvival.com

Equipment Sources
APPENDIX B

**David Alloway's Skills
of Survival**
P.O. Box 583
Terlingua, TX 79852
877-371-2634
www.skillsofsurvival.com
—*Kits, knives, books, videos.*

**Bob Cooper Outdoor
Education Pty. Ltd.**
P.O. Box 8486
Perth Business Centre
Perth 6849
W.A., Australia
011-61-8-9377-1767
—*Bob Cooper Outback Survival
Kits (very well done personal kits)
and MK III knives.*

Major Surplus and Survival
435 W. Alondra Blvd.
Gardena, CA 90248
310-324-8855
—*Survival gear
and military surplus.*

Nitro-Pak Preparedness Center
475 W. 910 South
Heber City, UT 84032
435-654-0099
—*Survival kits, gear, and
dehydrated/freeze-dried foods.*

The Survival Center
P.O. Box 234
McKenna, WA 98558
360-458-6778
—*Gear, water purification,
preserved food.*

SamAndy
P.O. Box 141741
Irving, Texas 75014
972-887-9336
—*Expanded survival kits, advanced
gear, preserved food.*

Campmor
P.O. Box 700-C
Saddle River, NJ 07458-0700
www.campmor.com
—*Outdoor clothing, first-aid kits,
survival supplies.*

Cutlery Shoppe
390 East Corporate Drive
P.O. Box 610
Meridian, ID 83680-0610
208-884-8500
—*Wide selection of knives
and survival supplies.*

Glossary

AGAVACAE: Plant family that includes yuccas, lechuguilla, century plants, sotol, and beargrass.

AMOLE: *(Ah-MO-leh)* Spanish for soaps derived from plants.

ARROYO: *(ah-ROY-oh)* Spanish for creek or creek bed.

ATLATL: *(at-LAT-ul)* Aztec for spearthrower.

BELLOTAS: *(beh-YO-tahs)* Spanish for acorn, specifically, milder ones that are readily edible.

CHIRRUPES: *(chee-ROO-pehs)* Spanish for the seed pods of mesquite (*Prosopis spp.*).

COPROLITE: Preserved or fossilized dung. Valuable for determining past diets of animals and people.

CUTBANK: Places along arroyos where water has cut vertical banks, often tall. Can collapse and be dangerous.

ETHNOBOTANY: The science that studies how humans have and still use plants.

GLOCHIDS: *(GLOW-kids)* Small spines found on the *Opuntia* genus of cacti; hard to remove and very annoying.

IXTLE: *(EEST-leh)* Colloquial Spanish for fiber extracted from plants belonging to the family Agavacae.

JACAL: *(ha-CALL)* Spanish for hut or crude dwelling.

KOWA: Apache for a brush hut or wickiup.

NOPALITOS: *(no-pa-LEE-toes)* Spanish for the young pads of prickly pear cacti when used as foods.

PLAYA: *(PLY-uh)* Spanish for beach. Often used to describe broad desert flats.

QUIOTE: *(kee-OH-tay)* The bloom stalk of plants belonging to Agavacae. Useful green as food, or dried for construction, tools, and weapons.

ROCK SHELTER: Shallow cave big enough for shelter or occupation. Some are merely overhangs of rock along cliff faces.

SAR: Search and Rescue. Applies to operations, equipment, and personnel.

TINAJA: *(tee-NAH-ha)* Spanish for a waterhole, usually caused by erosion in rock creek beds and filled by rainfall.

WADI: *(WAH-dee)* Arabic for dry creek bed.

WARP: In weaving, the stationary element.

WEFT: The element in weaving that moves. It is woven around the warp, or stationary part of the work.

XITE: *(SHEE-teh)* Colloquial Spanish for the pulp of lechuguilla leaves used as amole or soap. A by-product of lechuguilla fiber extraction. Pronounce carefully.

Selected References

EMERGENCIES AND FIRST AID

Adolph, E.F. and Associates. *Physiology of Man in the Desert.* 1947.

Darvill, Fred T., Jr., M.D. *Mountaineering Medicine: A Wilderness Medical Guide.* Berkeley, Calif.: Wilderness Press, 1983.

Forgey, William W., M.D. *Wilderness Medicine.* Pittsboro, Ind.: Indiana Camp Supply Co., 1979.

Kennedy, Barbara, M.D. *Caring for Children in the Outdoors.* Oakland, Calif.: Adventure Medical Kits, 1987.

Reifsnyder, William E. *Weathering the Wilderness: The Sierra Club Guide to Practical Meteorology.* San Francisco: Sierra Club Books, 1980.

Werner, David, Carol Thuman, and Jane Maxwell. *Where There Is No Doctor: A Village Health Care Handbook.* Palo Alto, Calif.: The Hesperian Foundation, 1992.

PLANTS AND ANIMALS

Bell, Willis H., and Edward F. Castetter. "The Utilization of Yucca, Sotol, and Beargrass by the Aborigines in the American Southwest." In *Ethnobiological Studies in the American Southwest.* Albuquerque: University of New Mexico Press, 1941.

Benson, Lyman. *The Cacti of the United States and Canada.* Stanford, Calif.: Stanford University Press, 1982.

Ford, Karen Cowan. *Las Yerbas de la Gente: A Study of Hispano-American Medicinal Plants.* Ann Arbor: University of Michigan Press, 1975.

Foster, Steven, and Roger Cara. *A Field Guide to Venomous Animals and Poisonous Plants.* New York: Houghton Mifflin, 1994.

Harrington, H.D. *Western Edible Wild Plants.* Albuquerque: University of New Mexico Press, 1967.

Hiles, Harold T. *Guide to the Protein and Nutritional Values of Plants Used by Native Americans of the Southwest.* Fairacres, N.Mex: Southwest Research Native, 1993.

Johnston, Marshall C. "Medicinal Plants of the Southwestern United States." In *Arid Land Plant Resources.* Lubbock: International Center for Arid and Semi-arid Land Studies, Texas Tech University, 1979.

Mares Trías, Albino. *Ralámuli Nu'tugala Go'ame (Comida de los Tarahumaras).* Chihuahua City, Mexico: Don Burgess McGuire, 1982. (Text in Spanish and Ralámuli.)

Moerman, Daniel. *Medicinal Plants of Native America.* Vols. I and II. Ann Arbor: University of Michigan, 1986.

Moore, Michael. *Medicinal Plants of the Mountain West.* Albuquerque: Museum of New Mexico, 1979.

———. *Medicinal Plants of the Deserts & Canyons West.* Albuquerque: Museum of New Mexico, 1989.

Niethammer, Carolyn J. *American Indian Food and Lore,* New York: Macmillan, 1974.

———. *The Tumbleweed Gourmet.* Tucson: University of Arizona Press, 1987.

Powell, A. Michael. *Trees and Shrubs of Trans-Pecos Texas.* Big Bend National Park, Tex.: Big Bend Natural History Association, 1984.

Stoops, Eric D., and Jeffrey L. Martin. *Scorpions and Venomous Insects of the Southwest.* Phoenix, Ariz.: Golden West Publishers, 1995.

Tull, Delena. *A Practical Guide to Useful Plants.* Austin: Texas Monthly Press, 1987.

Tweit, Susan J. *The Great Southwest Nature Fact Book.* Anchorage: Alaska Northwest Books, 1992.

Viesca, Carlos T. *Medicina Prehispánica de México.* Mexico City: Panorama Editorial, S.A., 1986. (Text in Spanish.)

Villacis R., Luis. *Plantas Medicinales de México*. Mexico City: Editorial Epocha, S.A., 1978. (Text in Spanish.)

Vogel, Virgil. *American Indian Medicine*. Norman: University of Oklahoma Press, 1970.

Warnock, Barton H. *Wildflowers of the Big Bend Country, Texas*. Alpine, Tex.: Sul Ross State University, 1970.

————. *Wildflowers of the Davis Mountains and Marathon Basin Texas*. Alpine, Tex.: Sul Ross State University, 1977.

Watt, Dean D. "Neurotoxic Proteins in Scorpion Venom." *Journal of Toxicology Toxin Reviews* 3 (1984): 2, 73.

Weniger, Del. *Cacti of Texas and Neighboring States*. Austin: University of Texas Press, 1988.

Werner, Floyd, and Carl Olson. *Learning About and Living with Insects of the Southwest*. Tucson, Ariz.: Fisher Books, 1994.

Whiting, Alfred F. *Ethnobotany of the Hopi*. Flagstaff, Ariz.: Northland Press, 1966.

SURVIVAL

Alloway, David. "Saddlebag Survival Kit." *The Western Horseman,* March 1985.

————. "Repairing Windmills and Pumps." *American Survival Guide,* April 1986.

————. Desert Survival Workshop course notes. Presidio, Tex.: Texas Parks & Wildlife Dept., Big Bend Ranch State Park, 1994.

————. Youth Wilderness Safety course notes. Presidio, Tex.: Texas Parks & Wildlife Dept., Big Bend Ranch State Park, 1996.

————. 1997. "Desert Survival Myths." *Wilderness Way* 3, no. 2 (1997).

Alloway, David, and Cathy Fulton. Women's Survival Workshop course notes. Presidio, Tex.: Texas Parks & Wildlife Dept., Big Bend Ranch State Park, 1996.

Angier, Bradford. *Survival with Style*. New York: Vintage Books, 1974.

Asher, David B., SFC, Bradley Guile, SFC, and Guy W. Thompson, SFC. *Desert Survival: A Guide to the Chihuahuan Desert*. El Paso, Tex.: Department of the Army, Fort Bliss, 1990.

Brown, Tom. *Tom Brown's Field Guide to Wilderness Survival*. New York: Berkley Books, 1983.

Cooper, Donald C., Patrick Lavalla, and Robert Stifle. *Search and Rescue Fundamentals.* Olympia, Wash.: Emergency Response Institute, 1990.

Dalrymple, Byron. *Survival in the Outdoors.* New York: Outdoor Life Books, 1972.

D.A.R.E.S. *Desert Awareness.* Phoenix: Desert Alpine Reserve Emergency Services, 1989.

Dunlevey, Maurice. *Stay Alive: A Handbook on Survival.* Canberra: Australian Government Publishing Service, 1991.

Ganci, Dave. *The Basics of Desert Survival.* Merrillville, Ind.: ICS Books, 1991.

⸻. *Desert Hiking.* Berkeley, Calif.: Wilderness Press, 1993.

Goodchild, Peter. *Survival Skills of the North American Indians.* Chicago: Chicago Review Press, 1984.

Irwin, Stephen R., M.D. *The Providers: Hunting and Fishing Skills of the North American Natives.* Blain, Wash.: Hancock House, 1984.

Lehman, Charles A. *Emergency Survival.* Los Angeles: Medical and Technical Books, 1979.

⸻. *Desert Survival Handbook.* Phoenix: Primer, 1993.

Nelson, Dick, and Sharon Nelson. *Desert Survival.* Glenwood, N.Mex.: Tecalote Press, 1977.

Olsen, Larry Dean. *Outdoor Survival Skills.* Chicago: Chicago Review Press, 1990.

Sisley, F.C., Col. USMC. *U.S. Marine Corps Desert Handbook.* Boulder, Colo.: Paladin Press, n.d.

U.S. Department of the Air Force. *Air Crew Survival.* AF Pamphlet 64-5. Washington, D.C., 1985.

U.S. Department of the Army. *Survival Kit, Individual, Vest Type.* SC 8465-90-CL-PO2. Washington, D.C., 1985.

⸻. *Army Aircraft Survival Kits.* TM 55-1680-317-23&P. Washington, D.C., 1987.

⸻. *Survival.* FM 21-76. Washington, D.C. El Paso, Tex.: Department of the Army, Fort Bliss, 1992.

Wheat, Margaret. *Survival Arts of the Primitive Paiutes.* Reno: University of Nevada Press, 1967.

Wiseman, John. *The SAS Survival Handbook.* London: Harvill, 1994.

TOOLS AND WEAPONS

Alloway, David. "Using the Atlatl as an Educational Tool." In *The Cache: Selected Papers on Texas Archeology*. Austin: Office of the State Archeologist, Texas Historical Commission, 1996.

Dickson, D. Bruce. "The Atlatl Assessed: A Review of Recent Anthropological Approaches to Prehistoric North American Weaponry." *Bulletin of the Texas Archeological Society* 56 (1985).

Laubin, Reginald and Gladys. *American Indian Archery*. Norman: University of Oklahoma Press, 1980.

Oakley, Kenneth P. *Man the Tool-maker*. Chicago: University of Chicago Press, 1959.

Peckham, Stuart. *Prehistoric Weapons in the Southwest*. Santa Fe: Museum of New Mexico Press, 1982.

Savage, Cliff. *The Sling for Sport & Survival*. Port Townsend, Wash.: Loompanics Unlimited, 1989.

Tappan, Mel. *Survival Guns*. Rogue River, Oreg.: The Janus Press, 1980.

Tate, Bill. *Survival with the Atlatl*. Aurora, Colo.: Tate Enterprises Unlimited, 1987.

Waldorf, D.C. *The Art of Flint Knapping*. Branson, Mo.: Mound Builder Arts and Trading Company, 1984.

———. *The Art of Making Primitive Bows and Arrows*. D.C. Waldorf and Valerie Waldorf, 1985.

Whittaker, John C. *Flintknapping: Making and Understanding Stone Tools*. Austin: University of Texas Press, 1994.

WAYFINDING

Mooers, Robert L., Jr. *Finding Your Way in the Outdoors*. New York: Outdoor Life Books, 1972.

Newman, Bob. *Wilderness Wayfinding: How to Survive in the Wilderness as You Travel*. Boulder, Colo.: Paladin Press, 1994.

Randall, Glenn. *The Outward Bound Map and Compass Handbook*. New York: Lyons & Burford, 1989.

Index

ash (tree): for construction and weapons, 151, 180, 183; as fuel, 79; for primitive firestarting, 84; as water indicator, 68

aspirin: preference for in survival kits, 23; salicin as natural substitute, 148–149. *See also* analgesics

atlatl: darts for, 151, *179,* 180–182; throwing techniques for, *181,* 182–183; types of, *181,* 182–183

Atriplex canescens. See fourwing saltbush

Australia: navigating by Southern Cross, 217; snakebite treatment in, 202; survival knives used in, 41; training in, 14, 39, 165

Australian Aborigines: boomerangs of, *176;* and fires, 78, 91; knives used by, 41; and making stone tools, 171

Baccharis spp. See seepwillow

Baileya multiradiata, 206; toxicity of, 207

barrel cactus: damage of for water, 10; as food, 143; precautions as water sources, 69; seeds as bait, 143

bastard search, unnecessary search, 113

beaded lizard, venom of, 200

beargrass: precautions in harvesting, 153; for primitive firestarting, 87; in shelter construction, 108; for weaving, 153

bears, attacks and precautions, 204

bees, treatment of stings, 198

Benadryl: for allergic reactions, 23, 199; for insect stings, 23, 198; as sleep aid, 23

Berberis spp. See algerita

bicolor mustard, as food, 143

Big Bend National Park: deaths in, xix, 2, 190; temperature extremes in, 188

Big Bend Ranch State Park, search and rescue in, 16

bipedalism, advantages of, xv, xvi

birth control, cessation of and unexpected menstruation, 23–24

boomerangs, types and techniques, *159, 176,* 176–177

boots, suitable for desert, 102–103

bow drill, for firestarting, 82–87, *84, 86*

Bridger, Jim, in the abandonment of Hugh Glass, 5

broomweed, in bedding, 110

Cabeza de Vaca, Alvar Nuñez, ordeal of, 5

cactus fruit, as food, 143–144

cactus pulp: as food, 144; hallucinogenic properties of some, 144

cane: for arrows, 184; for atlatl darts, 180; as food, 144; for shelter, weapons and fishing poles, 151

Cassia spp. See senna

catch basins, as water sources, 75–76

cattails: for arrows, 184; for food, 144

Celtis spp. See hackberry

cenizo: as beverage tea, 144; as medicine, 148

centipedes, treatment of stings, 199

century plants: cooking of, 94–95, 145; as cordage, 174; as fish

lechuguilla, *139;* for atlatl darts, 151; for bowstrings, 185; cooking of, 94–95; cordage of, *141,* 173, 174; for fiber, 152–153; for fire making, 83, 87; as fish poison, 154; as food, 146; as indicator plant of Chihuahuan Desert, 223; sandals of, 175; in traps, *163, 164*
Leucophyllum spp. See cenizo lightning. *See* weather
Lomotil, antidiarrheal drug, 23
Long, David, ranger at Big Bend Ranch State Park, 9
long mamma cactus, hallucinogenic properties of, 144
Lophophora williamsii. See peyote
lotebush: as food, 146; as medicine, 149

magnesium bar, for firestarting, 20, 80, 91
maidenhair fern, as medicine, 150
Mammilaria macromeris. See long mamma cactus
Marrubium vulgare. See horehound
meclazine, in survival kits and limitations of, 23
medications: Benadryl, 23, 198, 199; birth control pills, 23; in survival kits, 23
menstruation: expedient menstrual pads, 154; resulting from cessation of birth control, 24; treating menstrual cramps, 151
mescal bean, toxicity of, 205, *206,* 207
mesquite: as food, 146; as fuel, 79; limitations as water indicator, 68; as medicine, 150
Mexican buckeye: *139,* as fish

poison, 154; toxicity of, 204–205, *205*
Mexican walnut, as food, 147
millipedes, treating contact irritation of, 199
mirages, and landmark distortion, 224
mirrors, for signaling, 21, 34, 45, 110, 115–117, *116*
misinformation: on celestial navigation, 217; on edibility of all cacti, 143–144; on fungi as survival food, 143; on survival knives, 41, 157; survival related, 7; on transpiration bags, 68
Mojave Desert, location of, xvii, *xviii*
Mormon tea: as beverage, 147; as medicine, 150
mountain lions: and domestic dogs, 203; precautions for, 203–204
mullein: for firestarting, 87; for hygiene, 154; as medicine, 150

nausea. *See* vomiting and nausea
navigation: and finding compass bearings with shadow stick, *221, 222*; misconceptions on celestial navigation, 217; by stars *216,* 216–218; by sun and shadow stick, *220,* 221–222; by sun and time, *218,* 218–221, *219*
Nerysyrenia camporum. See bicolor mustard
Nicotiana spp. See tobacco
Nolina spp. See beargrass
Norman, Geoffrey, writing on survival kits, 18

oak, *139;* acorns as food and
medicine, 143
ocotillo, *140;* as food and beverage, 147; as medicine, 150; in
traps, *163,* 163–164,
Olson, Larry Dean, author of
Outdoor Survival Skills, 183, 184
Opuntia spp. See cholla; prickly
pear cactus; tasajillo
Outside Magazine, on survival, 18

panic, control of, 3, 4
peyote, hallucinogenic properties
of, 144
Phragmites australis. See cane
Pilbara (Western Australia),
training in, 39, 122, 165
pipelines, as water sources, 61–62
pita: cordage from yucca leaf, 107,
141, 153, 174; in shelter
construction, 107–108
pitahaya: as food, 144; and gastric
reactions, 144
plants: for construction, 151–152;
and doctrine of signatures, 135;
edibility test of and precautions, 141–143; ethics of
harvesting, 10, 135–136; for
fiber and cordage, 152–153,
173–176; as fish poisons, 154;
for food and beverages,
141–147; identification of,
135; for medicines, 148–151;
as obstacles to travel, 223;
poisonous and dangerous, 204;
precautions concerning, 135;
preparation of, 135; for sandals,
141, 174–176; as water indicators, 68, 223; as water sources,
69; for weapons, 180
plastic bags: for carrying water, 21,
67; for collecting water from

pumps and auto air conditioners,
67; for shelter, 34; for transpiration bags, 65–66
plastic sheet, in survival kit, 25
playa lakes, as water sources, 75
Populus spp. See cottonwood
potassium permanganate (Condy's
crystals): as firestarter, 81; as
water purifier, 52
predators, in Chihuahuan Desert,
42
preparation: for emergencies, 1–3,
112–113; psychological, 3–6;
of vehicles, 127
prickly pear cactus, *140;* to clarify
water, 71; as food, 144, 147;
as medicine, 150, 151
prickly poppy, 138, *140;* as medicine, 151
Prosopis spp. See mesquite
psychological factors of survival:
aberrations resulting from
dehydration, 47, 49, 211;
allure of tools and weapons, 19,
35, 126; and benefits from
hygiene and sanitation, 214;
and controlling panic, 3–4;
fantasies of living off the land,
155; food preferences and,
155; and heatstroke, 210; and
mirages, 224; preparation, 3–6
pumps and pumpjacks: expedient
repairs, 60–61; parts of, *60;*
as water sources

Quercus spp. See oaks
quiotes (bloomstalks from
Agavacae species): for atlatl
darts, 180; in baking pits, 95,
107; for construction, 151; for
firestarting, 83, 85, 87; as food,
144; for kindling, 79; in shelter

construction, 107–108; for sun goggles. 10, *100;* in traps, 162

rabbit sticks. *See* boomerangs
radar, factors and limitations in search and rescue, 117
rain. *See* weather
reptiles: as food, 164; medicinal uses of, 167; precautions of, 164; venomous lizards, 164
rescue blankets. *See* space blankets
retama, as water indicator, 68
Rio Grande: contamination of, 53; floating, 8; rivers as water sources, 70–71
roadrunners, medicinal uses of, 167
rock shelter: dangers of building fires in, 92–93; as emergency shelter against weather, and precautions in use of, 193–194
rule of three (concerning oxygen, warmth, water, and food), 11
Ryan, Nolan, Texas Parks & Wildlife Commissioner, 167

saguaro cactus: as represents the Sonoran Desert, xviii; unsuitability as water source, 69
salicin, natural aspirin substitute, 148–149
Salix spp. See willows
salt: and electrolytes 50, 211; and heat cramps, 208–209; in survival kits, 23
salt cedar: damage to springs, 69; as water indicator, 68
sandals: from native plants, *141*, 174, 176; types and construction, 175
sanitation. *See* hygiene and sanitation
SAR. *See* search and rescue

Savage, Cliff, author of *The Sling for Sport and Survival,* 177
scorpions: bark scorpion (*Centuroides exilicauda*), 197; prevention and treatment of stings of, 197–198
search and rescue (SAR): and bastard searches, 113; and children, 113–114; clothes for, 101; debriefing of, 11, 15, 225–226; equipment for, 18, 37; and Forward Looking Infra-Red (FLIR), 121; and passive search, 114, 123; personnel, 11; and psychics, 114; and Search Probability Theory, 225; and statistics, 225; techniques of, 49, 112–113, 124; and victim profile, 15
seepwillow: for arrows, 152, 184; for firestarting, 84, 87; in shelter construction, 107, 152; as water indicator, 68
senna, as laxative, 151
shampoo, from plants, 149, 153
shelter: artificial, 103–105, *105,* 132; clothes as, 98–103, *99, 100;* from natural materials, 105–111, *108, 109, 111;* needs in desert, 103; as priority, 12
signals: audible signals, 114, 123–124; body signals for aircraft, 117–118, *119;* confusion in air-to-ground signals, 125; confusion in ground-to-air signals, 120; ground-to-air signals, 117, *118;* with mirrors, 21, 34, 45, 110, 115, *116,* 117; smoke as, 118–119, 121; vehicles used as, 132, 133; visual, 115–122

Tappen, Mel, survival gun writer,
43
Tarahumara Indians: and meaning
of Chihuahua, xvii; weaving,
152
tasajillo: *140;* glochids on, 207;
hallucinogenic properties of,
143-144
Texas mountain laurel, toxicity and
hallucinogenic properties of,
205, *206,* 207
Texas persimmon, as food, 148
Thelesperma spp., as beverage and
medicine, 151
throwing sticks. *See* boomerangs
tinajas: dangers of, 76; expedient
water purification in, 96; as
water sources, 76
tinder: agave and yucca fiber,
78-79; cottonwood bark, 78;
flammable liquids, 79, 81;
herbivore droppings, 81;
juniper bark, 78
tobacco: and auditory hallucinations, 207; as medicine and
precautions, 151; toxicity of,
207; tree tobacco as water
indicator, 68, *206*
Tom Miner Basin, Montana,
relating to saddlebag survival
kits, 27
tools and weapons: animal skewers,
159, *160;* atlatl, *179,* 180-182,
181; from bone, 167; boomerangs, rabbit sticks, and throwing
sticks, *159, 176,* 176-177;
bows and arrows, *182,*
183-187; cordage, 172-174;
expedient traps, 160-164,
161, 162, 163; slings, 177-179;
stick snare, 161-162, *162;* from

stone, 15, 168-171, *169, 171;*
as survival priority, 14-15; of
wood, 172
topography, and locating water,
74-75
trapping. *See* hunting and trapping
traps and snares: illegal uses of,
164; leghold snare, 161; lift
snare, 161-162; ocotillo quail
trap, 161, *163,* 163-164;
Ojibwa bird snare, 161, *162,*
162-163; stick snare, *161,* 162
traveling: and landmarks, 223; and
leaving signs, 224; and locating
water, 223; and mirages, 224;
and using shadow to keep on
course, 223
troughs (livestock): dangers of
diseases, 61; as water sources,
61-62
Tylenol and Tylenol No. 3, uses
and limitations in survival kits,
23. *See also* analgesics
Typhus spp. See cattails

ultraviolet (UV) rays: and eyes,
100; protection against, 103;
and skin, xvi, 6
Ungnadia speciosa. See Mexican
buckeye
urine: distilling for water, 63; in
emergency cooling, 210; moni-
toring for dehydration, 50; and
sanitation, 212
U.S. Air Force: M6 survival gun,
43; survival kits, 32; survival
knife, 32; training, 134
U.S. Army: aircraft survival kits,
32; issue handgun for survival,
32; SERE (Survival, Evasion,
Resistance, Escape) knife, 35